SPECTATOR SOCIETY

SPECTATOR SOCIETY

The Philippines Under Martial Rule

by

Benjamin N. Muego

Ohio University Center for International Studies
Monographs in International Studies

Southeast Asia Series Number 77
Athens, Ohio 1988

Library of Congress Cataloging-in-Publication Data

Muego, Benjamin N.
   Spectator society.

   (Monographs in international studies. Southeast
Asia series ; no. 77)
   Bibliography: p.
   1. Philippines--Politics and government--1946-1986.
2. Martial law--Philippines. I. Title. II. Series.
DS686.5.M84 1988   959.9'046   88-25304
ISBN 0-89680-138-1

ISBN 0-89680-138-1

To Justin

for his roots are in the Philippines

BENJAMIN N. MUEGO is an Associate Professor of Political Science at Firelands College (a branch campus of Bowling Green State University), 901 Rye Beach Road, Huron, Ohio 44829.

CONTENTS

viii

ACKNOWLEDGEMENTS

There are several people and institutions that I would like to thank for helping me complete this book. At the top of the list is the Institute of Southeast Asian Studies in Singapore for the post-doctoral grant that enabled me to gain access to some primary materials and periodicals that were not readily available in the United States. The institute's librarian, Mrs. Pat Lim, was particularly helpful. So was Professor Kernial Singh Sandhu, the institute's director who provided me with office space and very able secretarial help.

I am also indebted beyond words to a former mentor, colleague and friend, Professor Consuelo Valdez-Fonacier, late of the University of the Philippines, who so graciously sent me government publications, newspaper clippings, and a wealth of sundry informaton about the martial law regime (all at a time when such materials were difficult to obtain), at her own expense, over a period of several months.

I owe the title of this book, Spectator Society, to that great Filipino civil libertarian, humanist and intellectual, Salvador P. Lopez. Ambassador Lopez or "SP" (as he prefers to be addressed by his friends and admirers), the Aquino government's permanent representative to the United Nations, first used the phrase in a Dillingham Lecture at the East-West Center of the University of Hawaii in 1974, when he urged Marcos to abolish martial law and restore civil liberties to the Philippines. He did so at great risk to his life and limb and to his career as the tenth president of the University of the Philippines. Lopez subsequently stepped down from the UP presidency to go into full-time teaching with the academic rank of University Professor. In retrospect, Lopez' courage served as an inspiration to his colleagues and students who battled Marcos and his authoritarian regime until the triumph of "people power" in February 1986.

James L. Cobban, general editor, Monographs in International Studies at Ohio University was instrumental in helping to literally retrieve this study from the dustbin. His persistent phone calls and gentle prodding led to a physical search that culminated in the recovery of the rest of this manuscript which I had all but given up for lost. Hopefully, Jim's meticulous reading of the manuscript, including the endnotes and bibliography has made this study more readable and accurate. Mark O. Van Cauwenbergh a former student and good friend, did a yeoman job of typing the manuscript from a rather messy copy, and under somewhat harried circumstances. I am deeply grateful to both.

As is usually the case in studies of this kind, however, factual errors as well as mistakes in judgment and interpretation, if any, are mine alone. My hope is that this work contributes, even if only modestly, to an understanding of a clouded chapter in Philippine contemporary history.

Chapter 1

PROLOGUE

I

The Philippines has come full circle since the completion of the first draft of this manuscript in 1982. At the time, Ferdinand E. Marcos had just announced yet another change in the official designation of his regime. Shedding previous labels such as "new society," and "command society," which had presumably outlived their usefulness, Marcos started referring to his regime as the "new republic." Apparently he thought that calling his faltering regime by another name, in the wake of his earlier "lifting" of martial rule was a clever public relations ploy.

The lifting of martial law--at least in form--on 17 January 1981, four days before a friendly administration was to take over in Washington, D.C., was in retrospect, calculated to win the support of Ronald W. Reagan and his conservative government. And win it, he did! In September of the following year, the Marcoses with an entourage of hundreds of government officials, cronies, and sycophants, descended on Washington, D.C., by the plane-loads for an official state visit. In the lavish and gala receptions that followed, Marcos and Reagan feted each other, praising the other for his commitment to democracy and the "democratic way of life."

Those heady days of 1982 are long gone. Today the Marcoses are pathetic figures in exile--Ferdinand, shorn of his once dictatorial powers and ill-gotten wealth and Imelda, given to crying spells. Both have been forsaken by all except the most dedicated and loyal of their former cronies and ubiquitous sycophants. Ferdinand now openly begs Corazon C. Aquino, the woman he used to deride as incompetent, to allow him to return to the Philippines supposedly to pay his last respects first, to a departed sister and later to his mother,

1

who too had passed on. Imelda has been reduced to
what must be a fate worse than death, shopping for
used military clothing and footwear (she of the
3,000 pairs of shoes!) at Honolulu Army and Navy
stores, still holding on to the hope of one day
returning (or being allowed to return) to the
Philippines, where she was once social and cultural
queen and the belle of the ball. Fate worse than
death, indeed, since this is the same prima donna
who used to comandeer Philippine Air Lines' BAC-111
jets (at taxpayer expense) on shopping sprees to
Neiman-Marcus and Bloomingdale's, where legend has
it that Neiman (or was it Marcus?) personally waited
on her, adjusting a hem here and there or compli-
menting her for impeccable taste in finery and
jewels.

There is more than a touch of irony here.
After all, it was Marcos' refusal (reportedly at
Imelda's instigation) to allow the late Benigno
"Ninoy" S. Aquino, Jr., to return to the Philippines
in 1983 that marked the beginning of the end for the
Marcos dictatorship. "Ninoy" Aquino's brutal
assassination at the Manila International Airport by
still unknown military assailants and the national
and international outrage that it touched off,
caused the Marcos grip on the military and civilian
bureaucracy to gradually loosen, and catapulted an
obscure and self-effacing housewife to the
presidency of the Philippines. The humiliating
election defeat Aquino, a political novice, dealt
Marcos and his handpicked running mate Arturo M.
Tolentino, in spite of massive cheating and fraud,
in February 1986 was the ultimate in poetic justice;
the paradigm of "good" prevailing over "evil."
Aquino, the grieving and virtuous widow returning
home from exile to bury her slain husband, triumphs
over the crime's suspected mastermind in the
ritualized combat of politics.

The Philippines as a nation has come full
circle as well. Politically, it has returned to the
American-style presidential system that Marcos had
scuttled and replaced with a bastardized parliamentary system, by the stroke of a pen, on on 17
January 1973. Even the status quo ante political
parties, the Nacionalista (NP) and the Liberal
(LP) are back, albeit encumbered with contending
factions (the "Salonga wing" and "Kalaw wing" for
the LP and the "Ople wing" and "Cayetano wing" for
the NP). The old politicians former political
dynasties have returned as well, once again
lording it over old fiefdoms. And where some

2

dynasties, like the Laurels' of Batangas, have been swept out, new dynasties have emerged to replace them. The most visible and best known of these nascent dynasties is without a doubt, the Aquino-Cojuangco dynasty, with no less than six members of the Aquino, Cojuangco, Oreta, Sumulong, and Tanjuatco families, all first-degree presidential relatives holding elective public office in the legislative and executive branches of the government. Other Aquino and Cojuangco relatives are reputed to wield political clout from behind the scenes as well.

Graft and corruption, the bane of all previous administrations from Roxas' to Marcos', have also returned with a vengeance. And as it did before press freedoms were curtailed during the martial law years, the Philippine media feasts on sensationalized stories of "corrupt" public officials, cronies and presidential relatives. Through innuendo and gossip, the metropolitan press has linked presidential brother Jose "Peping" Cojuangco, Jr. and his wife Margarita "Ting Ting" de los Reyes-Cojuangco to graft and corruption in the <u>arrastre</u> (portside stevedoring) and barter trade industries, respectively. Another presidential relative tarred with the corruption brush is Francisco "Komong" Sumulong, the president's maternal uncle and in 1988, Majority Floor Leader of the House of Representatives. It is significant that Aquino herself has not been implicated directly or indirectly in any corrupt or questionable act; she remains clean and virtuous in the eyes of the general public and is still extremely popular.

Even the campaign style and gimmickry employed by Aquino as she took to the hustings in January 1987 urging ratification of the new Constitution, and later during the May 1987 legislative elections, were uncannily similar to the Marcoses' when they were still the dominant personalities in Philippine presidential politics. Aquino travelled throughout the country on well publicized campaign rallies, during which she usually announced pork barrel outlays (usually waving a ubiquitous check) for whatever region she happened to be visiting at the time. During her visit to Santiago, Isabela, hometown of former Agrarian Reform Minister Heherson T. Alvarez, in January 1987, for instance, she even distributed Certificates of Land Title (CLTs) to landless peasants. Some certificates reportedly still bore the signature of her predecessor, although this had been crossed out. Where Marcos'

3

campaign sorties were not complete until Imelda had belted out her plaintive version of Dahil Sa Iyo or some other romantic ballad, so did Aquino's, with her daughter Kris, singing Whitney Houston's much-abused Greatest Love of All or some other pop song of more recent or contemporary vintage. Intended or not, the similarities in verbal and political legerdemain, were uncanny indeed; it also made Aquino's persistent "Marcos-bashing" appear just a bit sanctimonious.

None of these apparent contradictions derogate Aquino's accomplishments in the relatively short span of two years. Almost single-handedly, she has restored the central government's legitimacy, first, by causing the drafting and ratification of a democratic and progressive Constitution in record time, and and second, by reconstituting the legislative and judicial branches of government. The credibility of both branches was severely damaged by Marcos in his haste to transform the Philippines into his vision of a "new society." The nationwide constitutional plebiscite on 3 February 1987, the legislative elections in May three months later, and finally, the provincial and local elections in January 1988, were all marked by high voter turnout. By Philippine standards, these elections were remarkably peaceful and free of the usual electoral irregularities, a fact that was as much a tribute to Aquino's leadership as it is to the Filipino people's commitment to democratic processes.

The economy was in a moribund state when Aquino took over the reins of government on 25 February 1986. While the economy has since registered some real gains, topped by a dramatic 5.1 percent growth rate in 1987, it is still a long way to full recovery. Notwithstanding the fact that the GDP registered positive growth rates between 1986 and 1988 (in contrast to the zero or negative growth rates during the last three years of the Marcos regime), seventy percent of Filipinos still live below the poverty line set by the government at P1,400.00 or US$120.00 a year.

Another major problem that has its roots in the country's economic woes, and which appears to have deteriorated even further, are the Philippines' twin insurgencies: the Muslim secessionist movement in Mindanao and Sulu and the communist insurgency throughout the country. In spite of her early success in convincing the leaders of both insurgencies to explore the possibility of a peaceful resolution to the seventeen-year conflict (for which incidentally, Aquino risked the collective ire of the military establishment), culminating in an aborted sixty-day truce (November 1986 through February 1987), things have gone downhill ever since. Far from suffering a diminution in its mass appeal, the New People's Army, the military arm of the Communist Party of the Philippines (CPP) Philippines, appears instead to have gained in the number of its armed cadres from an estimated 22,000 regulars in 1986 to some 24,000-26,000 in 1988.

Generous offers of amnesty from the Aquino government have been largely spurned by the rebels, even as Aquino's inner braintrust quibbles about how to best deal with the insurgents. Perhaps even more vexing to the Aquino government is what all this implies--that the insurgents do not trust Aquino any more than they trusted Marcos. Even the earlier hope of Aquino's advisers that a number of soft-core guerrillas, driven to the hills by Marcos' repression and corruption, would lay down their arms and "rejoin society" the moment the Marcos dictatorship was overthrown, has been all but dashed. In recent months, the National Democratic Front, the left-wing umbrella organization with whom Aquino attempted to negotiate, has stepped up its verbal attacks on Aquino and her government. The New People's Army has likewise intensified its military operations.

In response to these developments, and at the urging of ideological hard-liners in the civilian and military establishments, Aquino has, as she once threatened to do, "unsheath[ed] the sword of war," by directing her armed forces chief of staff and field commanders to fight the insurgents with every weapon and every tactic they have at their command. In a corollary move, Aquino endorsed the activities of vigilante groups such as Alsa Masa in Davao, whose brutality and tactics are reminiscent of the Marcos regime's dreaded Civilian Home Defense Forces (CHDFs). This controversial policy shift drew immediate denunciations from Philippine and other international human rights organizations. And in what must be the most galling condemnation of all, Amnesty International in April 1988, cited the Aquino regime for various "human rights violations" especially involving suspected dissidents. On human rights issues as well, the Philippines has come full circle!

The sky-rocketing population of the Philippines is another serious problem that bedevils the Aquino presidency. A nation with an aggregate land area of only 115,000 square miles (roughly the size of the

5

state of Arizona), the Philippines had an estimated population of fifty-seven million in 1988 (compared to Arizona's less than three million). The population growth rate is an alarming 2.7 percent (lower than the all-time high of 3.2 percent in 1968, but still quite high by United Nations Fund for Population Activities [UNFPA] standards). At the current growth rate, the Philippines could come close to exceeding, if not actually exceed its estimated carrying capacity of eighty million people by the year 2,000.

Under Aquino--perhaps because of pressure from the Catholic Church (the Philippines is eighty-four percent Catholic) and more specifically from Jaime Cardinal Sin, one of the president's staunchest supporters--the Philippines has been reluctant to pursue an aggressive birth control program. On the contrary, rudimentary population control measures instituted by the previous regime have been indefinitely deferred or totally eliminated. The magnitude of the problem is such that the private and public sectors must generate approximately 700,000 new jobs annually just to cope with increments to the work force.

The archaic and feudal land tenure system in the Philippines is another issue that is both complex and potentially explosive. The "Mendiola Massacre" of 11 January 1987 underscored the volatility of the agrarian problem. On that date, twenty-three demonstrators were shot and killed by Philippine marines who were brought in to reinforce security at Malacanang Palace after a militant peasant group, the <u>Kapisanan ng mga Magbubukid ng Pilipinas</u> (League of Filipino Peasants) staged a protest sit-in in front of Malacanang demanding an audience with Aquino to discuss their grievances against the Ministry of Agrarian Reform. Since then, Aquino has announced total support for the Comprehensive Agrarian Reform Program (CARP) recently approved by the Philippine Congress.

Under this program, all lands classified as "in agricultural use" are subject to land reform. The new law sets out to accomplish its declared goal--that of redistributing all [agricultural] lands to landless farmers and "regular farmworkers irrespective of tenurial arrangement"--in three stages. During the first stage (the first four years), lands currently planted to rice and corn, "crony lands" under sequestration as well as other lands "voluntarily offered" will be redistributed. Public and private agricultural lands in excess of

6

fifty hectares will be redistributed during the second stage, also programmed to occur during the first four years. The third stage (from the fourth through the seventh year) calls for the redistribution of landholdings from twenty-four to fifty hectares. Even public lands leased to foreign multi-national corporations are, in the language of the law, "programmed for acquisition and redistribution immediately." It will be noted that in past land reform laws (enacted during both Macapagal's and Marcos' terms as president), foreign agribusiness operations were placed beyond the scope of land reform. Current exemptions such as "commercial farms" devoted to the production of livestock, poultry, or fish and prawn culture was tacked on to CARP as a concession to legislators with ties to the landed gentry, led by the president's younger brother Jose "Peping" Cojuangco, who threatened to amend the bill to death.

With Aquino fully committed to the enactment of a comprehensive land reform measure, and given the prevailing mood in the country, there was very little doubt that Congress would eventually enact CARP. What is in doubt is whether the executive branch has the political will to fully and even-handedly implement the program. Another nagging question is whether land reform is really the social panacea that it has been touted to be given the Philippines' runaway population growth and the scarcity of land that may be parcelled out to landless peasants who want them. Indeed, it may well be that land reform is at best only a stop-gap solution; a palliative that may appear to cure the problem of agrarian unrest but in reality exacerbates the issue or merely postpones the inevitable. Eventually, the Philippine government will have to explore alternative models and find other methods of dealing with this divisive and incendiary issue. As this book goes to press, Aquino is under tremendous pressure both from peasant groups and progressive organizations on the one hand, and the landed gentry and their representatives in the media and Congress on the other, to make "meaningful land reform" a reality.

II

I had an opportunity to return to the Philippines in 1986-87 after an absence of over seventeen years. Like most Americans--but even more

7

so as a Filipino-American who likes to think that he was somehow modestly involved in the struggle to restore democracy to the Philippines--I had great expectations about the new government and Aquino, as the country's new leader. I expected to see a radical restructuring of Philippine government and politics. I thought the opportunity to do so had never been better. Not only was Aquino exceedingly popular; she was also vested by the interim charter (aptly called "Freedom Constitution") with plenary powers.

Had she chosen to institute drastic reforms (including land reform), to throw all the rascals out, and dealt decisively with the country's other chronic political and social problems before her plenary powers ran out (with the investiture of a new Congress in July 1987), the Filipino people, as they did at EDSA a year earlier, would have come out by the millions in an unprecedented show of support. In retrospect, however, it seems that Aquino was indecisive, and allowed herself wittingly or unwittingly to be manipulated by a very protective cordon sanitaire whose members had their own hidden agendas to pursue and scores to settle against real or imagined enemies. Consequently, she missed some golden opportunities to institute genuine and meaningful reforms.

I sensed an aura of liberation all over the country, although it was an aura of liberation gone berserk. In a sense this was understandable. The Marcos regime's repressive policies of the previous fourteen years vitiated virtually all independent political expression. Through his control of the mass media, Marcos successfully blocked out all potential challengers or critics from the public eye, leaving himself, his wife and an anointed few a monopoly of publicity and media exposure. Predictably, therefore, "all hell broke loose," after the dreaded regime was finally overthrown, and the halters to free expression finally removed. As with the lifting of the proverbial floodgates in the face of a swollen river, the force unleashed was torrential and early on, was out of control. It was obvious even to a cursory observer that those who felt excluded and persecuted during the lifetime of martial rule believed it was their turn to get even; to retaliate against their tormentors.

This tendency was most apparent in the disposition of so called "crony assets". A super-body, the Philippine Commission on Good Government (PCGG), was vested with quasi-judicial powers soon after

8

Aquino was sworn into office and charged with the responsibility of recovering billions of dollars in government funds and property plundered by the Marcoses and their cronies. The principal weapon used by the PCGG in carrying out its mandate was "sequestration." As a legal concept, sequestration puts a piece of property "on hold" while its legal status, including ownership, is determined through appropriate judicial proceedings.

A sequestered property, therefore, could not be disposed off or alienated while its status remained unresolved. Several sequestered properties, however, were auctioned off even before the judicial proceedings could commence. The Philippine metropolitan press reported, almost on a daily basis, accounts of how some PCGG operatives or their close associates and relatives wound up as owners of sequestered properties. In some cases, PCGG-designated trustees reportedly helped themselves freely to the assets of properties they were charged to temporarily oversee.

Even at the street-level, it was apparent that the indiscipline and freewheeling tendencies of the status quo ante had quickly reasserted themselves. For instance, a fenced-off government property in Lahug, Cebu City, (not far from where I lived) was quickly overrun by squatters and land speculators who set up businesses and makeshift homes overnight even as huge painted signs posted on the property declared that trespassing was unlawful and that violators "will be prosecuted to the full extent of the law." All of this was going on in plain view of law enforcement authorities. A new and sturdier concrete fence that the Lahug Airport Authority attempted to build around the property was vandalized and torn down just as soon as it was erected. I suggest that this was not an isolated event; that this was endemic throughout the Philippines and symptomatic of a mindset that if something was out there to begin with, it must be there for the taking.

At the Cebu Country Club where the wealthy people of Cebu City played golf, tennis or the popular game of mahjong (with uniformed servants and nursemaids in tow) the conversation often turned to politics. Almost everyone especially the menfolk, had a theory about why the political system was "not working." It does not work, one wealthy Filipino-Chinese businessman posited, because no one wants to pay taxes and the public treasury is chronically empty. He himself pays "only a little" on a multimillion peso annual income because the kawatans (thieves) in public office frequently appropriated government funds and property for their own use, and he did not want them to get rich at his expense. Nothing much had changed except perhaps the names and faces of the corrupt and corruptible.

I left the Philippines one academic year later, rather disappointed and disillusioned. Except for the restoration of governmental legitimacy, the reconstitution of the three branches of government, some economic gains, Aquino's own personal triumphs, and massive role reversals (the former "outs" are now the "ins," and vice versa) I saw nothing new in the Philippines. The other changes that have occurred, if any, have been largely superficial or cosmetic. In the meantime, class cleavages continued to widen as the rich became even richer and the poor even poorer.

"Marcos bashing," the practice of blaming Marcos and his regime for most of the country's problems was beginning to wear thin when I left the Philippines in April 1987. Indeed, if it were not for the zany antics of the so called "loyalists," Marcos might have long ago receded into obscurity. What made "Marcos bashing" appear hollower in recent months is the fact that the Aquino government had been in power now for over two years. Yet she still has to show results especially where it makes a major difference--in the lives of the common people. There is also something terribly hypocritical when Aquino herself, her close associates, or both, engage in some of the activities for which the Marcoses are lampooned harshly ridiculed. This growing public perception was undoubtedly reinforced when Aquino's own Lakas ng Bayan (People Power) coalition, entered into an alliance with known Marcos henchmen in the former president's home province (Ilocos Norte) in provincial and local elections held in January 1988 in an obvious attempt to undercut Marcos' residual influence in the Ilocos region as a whole.

Sooner or later, the people are going to tire of scapegoatism and facile rationalizations, as some of the most influential opinion makers in the mass media apparently already have, and to begin demanding concrete achievements and results. A recent national poll showed that the percentage of Filipinos who continue to harbor "strong negative feelings" about the Marcoses has sharply declined, from over seventy percent in 1986 to only slightly over thirty-nine percent in May 1988. Furthermore,

10

more Filipinos today agree than disagree with Vice-President Salvador H. Laurel's assessment that the Aquino government's adamant refusal to allow Marcos to return home for his mother's funeral was both "cruel and unFilipino."

It is possible, of course, that I left the Philippines disillusioned because I expected too much, too soon. Or that I was looking at Philippine society and politics through western prisms. Whatever it was, it was an uncanny feeling returning to an old familiar place seventeen years later, only to see the same things, listen to the same platitudes and shibboleths, see the same old political personalities in the evening news saying the same things they were saying seventeen years earlier. The only difference was that while many of them used to unabashedly praise Marcos, now they are damning him to the high heavens. And while seventeen years before, they wore Nacionalista, Liberal, or Grand Alliance colors, now they were draped in the finery of <u>Laban</u>, <u>Lakas ng Bansa</u>, <u>Pilipino Democratic Party</u> or a reconstituted wing of this or that old party. And to think that Philippine society and politics was supposed to have undergone radical transformation from 1972 through 1986.

Perhaps I was just being maudlin or hopelessly naive in believing that "EDSA" was a revolution in the true sense of the word; that "EDSA" was just the first salvo in a profound social and political movement. What I witnessed during my Fulbright year at the University of the Philippines in Cebu City (the country's second largest city) and in my travels throughout the country were extremely troubling. I saw poverty the likes of which I had never seen before. I saw environmental degradation that was mind-boggling in its senselessness--coral reefs blasted off the ocean floor by dynamite-fishing, shorelines littered with raw and untreated sewage, fresh water depositaries like Laguna de Bay heavily silted, criss-crossed with commercial fish traps owned by wealthy and influential people and clogged with islands of water hyacinth. Other tell-tale signs of environmental abuse were legion.

In downtown Manila, in the heart of the university belt, the decrepit buildings and student "dormitories" that crowded the narrow streets in 1969 still stand, except that the wear and tear of the past seventeen years had begun to take their toll. At the Fuente Osmena in Cebu City, meanwhile, there were scantily-clad, visibly malnourished children everywhere, begging for a few centavos and

11

handouts. Destitute children of all ages and their parents also plied their trade at Roxas Boulevard in the heart of Manila's tourist belt, annoying passersby and scavenging for bits and pieces of food discarded by wasteful tourists.

At the university where I taught, a small but vocal group of student activists insisted on blaming America and "American imperialism" for every major Philippine economic or social problem. They often talked about revolution and spouted nationalistic and revolutionary rhetoric; slogans I have all heard before, seventeen years earlier, in the halcyon days of the University of the Philippines at Diliman, Quezon City, when I was chairman of the University Student Council, long before "new society," "people power," and "EDSA," were part of the Philippines' political lexicon.

Chapter 2

PATTERNS OF CHANGE

On 23 September 1972, President Ferdinand E. Marcos announced the contents of a document he had signed two days before: a Proclamation placing the Philippines under absolute martial law and suspending the privilege of the writ of habeas corpus.[1] Almost simultaneously, leaders of the Nacionalista and Liberal parties critical of his administration, and a motley group of student militants, newspapermen, workers, peasants, and those who were simply referred to as "oligarchs," were rounded up by elements of the Philippine Constabulary and placed in hastily established military detention camps.[2]

All newspapers, including The Manila Times, the Daily Mirror, The Philippines Herald, The Philippines Free Press, The Weekly Graphic, and the five radio-television networks were either closed or taken over by the military authorities. Strict government censorship was imposed on all incoming as well as outgoing information. There were also coordinated raids on some academic institutions such as the state-owned University of the Philippines and the Philippine College of Commerce in which dissident professors and students were arrested. President Marcos justified all these acts as necessary to "save the Republic and reform [our] society."[3]

In the ensuing weeks and months, Marcos issued presidential decrees, proclamations, and general orders which prohibited the "ostentatious display of wealth and extravagance;"[4] proclaimed "the entire country as a land reform area;"[5] declared the "emancipation of the tenant from the bondage of the soil;"[6] and announced the takeover of the properties of some of the so-called "oligarchs."[7] He further announced that henceforth he alone would "govern the nation and direct the operation of the entire government;"[8] and he banned all public assembly "including strikes and picketing in vital industries."[9] Still later, Marcos declared that the 1935

13

Constitution under whose authority, ironically, he had proclaimed martial law, had been superseded by the new Constitution framed by a Constitutional Convention which was assembled in 1971.[10]

To meet the requirement of ratification, President Marcos issued Proclamation No. 1102 declaring that the new Constitution had been duly ratified.[11] The "ratification" referred to was not achieved through a nationwide plebiscite as required by law but by so-called barangays or "citizens assemblies" voting publicly under the supervision of military authorities.[12] For the first time in the nation's history, fifteen-year olds were allowed to vote supposedly in order to broaden the base of citizen participation in the democratic process and to afford ample opportunity for the citizenry to express their views on important national issues.[13]

While the declaration of martial law and the suspension of the privilege of the writ of habeas corpus were not exactly unforeseen by observers of the contemporary Philippine political scene, the swiftness and comprehensiveness of Marcos' moves took many by surprise. Questions such as: How could a polity with a long and viable democratic tradition metamorphose overnight into a one-man rule? What really motivated Marcos--to "save the republic and reform society" or to perpetuate himself and his family in power? How long can Marcos as the Philippines' virtual dictator maintain himself in power? How long will the military subordinate itself to civilian authority before it is tempted to take over power itself? What is going to be the role, if any, of the Roman Catholic Church in either supporting martial rule or bringing about its downfall? What is the nature of the present governing coalition in the Philippines, and from where does each group derive its strength? These were only a few of the many questions raised by the radical political change in the Philippines. This study will systematically examine the various factors and forces that brought about the "New Society,"[14] as well as those that seemed to sustain it, at least for nine years.

In Search of a Workable Paradigm

In any study of this type it is essential to formulate a workable conceptual framework through which the subject-polity may be systematically analyzed. As a consequence of the renewed interest in comparative political research especially on third-world countries from the mid-1950's onward, there are several general works dealing with methodology and model building, mostly under the rubric of change, development, and modernization.[15] From these works, a number of paradigms have emerged, for example, traditional, transitional, and prismatic systems, modernizing regimes, mobilization systems, and the movement regime.

The Paradigm of the Movement Regime

The transformation of the Philippines from an American-style presidential democracy into what one Filipino political scientist called "constitutional authoritarianism"[16] offers an interesting case study of a "movement regime," that is, a revolutionary mass-movement regime under single-party auspices.[17] The paradigm of the "movement regime" as an analytical tool in comparative politics was introduced by Robert C. Tucker in 1961 to fill in the gap left by extant models such as the "transitional society"[18] or the "prismatic society," (a variant of the transitional model developed by Fred W. Riggs in his research on public administration in developing bureaucracies).[19] As explained by Tucker, movement regimes are:

> born in revolutionary struggle, and once in being they strive to maintain revolutionary momentum. The movement to displace the preexisting system of order then becomes a revolutionary movement for national renovation, or a movement to carry the revolution beyond the national borders, or both.[20]

More comprehensive than other models, "a comparative politics of movement regimes is not a regional affair, and defies the classifications of political systems according to geographic zones."[21] Writing about the genesis of the movement regime, Tucker points out that there is a "correlation between the movement-regime and the conditions of economic and cultural backwardness, feudalism, stagnation, etc., that lend a special cogency to revolutionary calls for the renovation of the nation."[22]

Movement regimes tend to be headed by a "dominating individual personality," who may not

15

necessarily be an absolute autocrat. The "broad tendency is oligarchical rule by the top leadership of the ruling party under the overall direction of the dominant personality . . ."[23] In terms of objectives, the "revolutionary movement" is:

> aimed at the modernization of the state, and this typically involves many elements of an internal social revolution. Old class relations in society, old patterns of land tenure, old customs, old traditions of thought and generally old ways of conducting the business of life are assailed in an internal revolution of national renewal.[24] [Emphasis mine.]

On the life expectancy of movement regimes, Tucker suggests that they may undergo "extinction" when the revolutionary dynamism subsides or "metamorphosizes" when the dynamism alters. Another possible outcome is "'metamorphosis' as a result of the alteration of the dynamism."[25] In the event of a metamorphosis "a movement regime of one species turns into one of another species as a consequence of a qualitative change in the motivation of revolutionary politics. Such a change is determined in its turn by a change or changes in the leadership situation within the regime."[26]

Another writer, Alfred Diamant has summarized the common features of what he called "developmental movement regimes" as follows:

1. The movement regime is headed by what one observer has called a 'Presidential monarch--a kind of chief';
2. Developmental movement regimes do not attempt to distinguish sharply between a vanguard or elite party and the mass movement or mass base;
3. The mass party is constructed on the now familiar cellular principle, with the structure reaching down into the grass-roots society;
4. Associated with the party are usually a host of specialized organizations--or rather the regime in its pursuit of total mobilization, attempts to create a network that will cover the entire society;
5. The commitment to development has meant that developmental movement regimes engage

16

in intensive programs of industrialization and of extending trade both domestically and internally; and

6. The need of the movement regime to monopolize not only political power but also the means of physical coercion--the police and army--is a direct result of the highly unstable and fragmented character of the society and the political system itself.[27]

In addition to the preceding features that movement regimes share, they also face the common dilemma that "if the regime does indeed have full control over mass media and tries to use them to displace traditional and anti-modernizing values, it risks raising the expectations of the people without being able to fulfill them, and also fostering a condition of general normlessness by destroying old symbols abruptly before they can be effectively replaced by modernizing ones."[28]

Diamant added to Tucker's discussion of leadership in a movement regime by introducing the concept of charisma. He writes that:

It is not difficult to understand the great utility of charismatic leaders for independence movements because a mass movement which calls on its followers for bravery, sacrifice, and rigid obedience can do so more effectively if the leader's claim to make such demands rests on devotion to his specific and exceptional sanctity, heroism or exemplary character, and on the other normative pattern of order revealed or ordained by him.[29]

Charismatic leadership, however, carries with it the grave problem of accomplishing an orderly succession "to insure the continued functioning of a new state whose institutional, behavioral and value patterns are essentially unstable--in part at least because of the essentially unstable quality of charisma."[30]

Because of the sweeping nature of change in the movement regime, it is almost inevitable for organized resistance or dissidence to arise. Consequently, the movement and its leaders attempt to make the ideology of development prevail throughout the entire society. This politicizing of all social life has two consequences: it makes all political opposition tantamount to treason and it requires

17

that the critic of the movement be silenced as a traitor.[31] When confronted by the threat of mass opposition, the leadership of the movement regime reacts as any minority determined to remain in power. The leaders are likely to begin by eliminating the opposition by means of arrest, exile, or execution until they discover that the opposition is more broadly based, that new leaders take the place of those who have been eliminated and that underground organizations replace outlawed legal ones. When the potential opposition consists of a large part of the population and it becomes impossible to arrest, banish, or shoot all its members, the leaders then resort to mass terror or foreign adventures in order to intimidate those who might otherwise engage in oppositional behavior.[32]

The Transitional Political System

The term "transitional" suggest a polity emerging from the traditional into the modern stage. The transitional polity is characterized by dynamism while the traditional polity is characterized by stasis. Viewed from another angle, the term transitional "applies to any political system in which the structural changes and demands set loose by the uncontrolled forces of transformation exceed the will or capacity of political authority to cope with them."[33] Transition does not presuppose a judgement on the direction being taken by such a polity. A transitional political system may be engaged in "selective modernization without coming any closer to achieving a capacity for . . . systematic transformation . . . [or] it may transform some of its institutions in a manner that is likely to inhibit further transformation."[34]

This sociopolitical dualism appeared to be characteristic of the Philippines, at least before the advent of the New Society. Some definitive works on the Philippines classify the country as a type of "transitional society," an "actively modernizing oligarchy."[35] Two other writers suggest that the Philippines belongs to a group of nations that may be regarded as among the most advanced of the underdeveloped societies where there may still be considerable numbers of traditionally oriented people but where the main focus is on maintaining and operating modern institutions.[36] O. D. Corpuz, a former Minister of Education, Culture, and Sports, explained why the Philippines was a "transitional society" by drawing a clear dichotomy between what he called the "suprastructure" of attitudes and values and the "infrastructure" of traditions and ethics, both of which exerted an influence over the collective behavior of the people and the political system as a whole. Corpuz wrote:

> In the Philippines, it may be said that there is a suprastructure of attitudes and values that is of Western origin and that is characteristic of modernized and technologically advanced societies. On the other hand, there is an infrastructure of traditions and mores (ethos, social customs) that is indigenous. In the suprastructure the dominant attitudes and values are: a confidence in the potency of the individual to solve his own problems; a high respect for individual achievement; stress on technical expertise and impersonal rationality in the social management of public affairs; and a technique of enforcing social responsibility through impersonal legal rules. The infrastructure, on the other hand, has among its components a reliance upon primary groups, especially kinship groups, in the solution of the individual's problems; a high respect for social status rather than individual achievement or merit; an emphasis on primary-group interests as against the interests of the individual or of the vague national community; and a style of social morality based on personal, traditional, or ethical (nonlegal) norms.[37]

These apparently contradictory, but in fact complementary, sets of attitudes and beliefs both continue to have a deep impact on the polity for "what is old has not been abandoned, what is new has not been quite established, [and] both exist, often competitively, side by side."[38]

Because the political culture of the transitional polity is a mixture of diverse elements, there is a tendency for various subcultures to clash.[39] We see this in the Muslim secessionist movement in Mindanao, and in the long-simmering conflict between the old-line politicians and the technocrats. Indeed while traditional and modern societies are marked by integration, transitional states are marked by various stages of disintegration. In the transitional society the "homogeneity of the traditional and the modern society are replaced by discontinuity and heterogeneity."[40] The resulting political and social climate may culminate in what one writer called "a charismatic culture-- one dominated by a leader whose aura of infallibility enables him to proclaim goals and values giving life some significance once again."[41]

The Prismatic Society: A Variant of the Transitional Model

Riggs' "prismatic society" is a complex and elaborately constructed paradigm of the transitional political system.[42] The term prismatic is based upon Riggs' notion that political development is a movement from functional diffuseness (few structures performing numerous poorly defined functions) to functional specificity (many structures performing specialized functions). Modernity is equated with specialization and division of labor. Comparing the prismatic society to the traditional system, Riggs referred to the latter system as "fused" in that functions were concentrated on only a few structures; modern political systems, on the other hand, were diffracted because functions were distributed among specialized structures.

Using the analogy of a beam of light, Riggs compared catalysts for modernization to prisms which diffract light beams. Hence the term prismatic, to refer to a polity that is neither traditional nor modern. Riggs' preference for the neologism prismatic reflected his belief that movement from the traditional stage to modernity is not an ineluctible or inevitable process. As a paradigm the prismatic society is intended to represent:

> that class of political systems that has taken on many of the attributes of modernity while retaining many attributes of traditionalism. Such a system is characterized by institutions that do not precisely resemble either the corresponding institutions in modern societies or the corresponding institutions in traditional societies.[43]

An aspect of the transitional society where Riggs was quite emphatic is that of leadership. There is no blurring of lines between traditional and transitional societies in this regard:

> A transitional society, . . . is one whose leaders have an image of themselves as molders of a new destiny for their people, as promoters of modernization, and therefore as builders of effective governmental machines and national 'power,' as creators, indeed, of 'progress.' They may or may not be successful in this endeavor. Their perceptions of their own roles may or may not be accurate. But it is this sense of self-propelled change which gives a distinctive quality to transitional societies. The elites of <u>traditional</u> societies lack this sense of progress.[44]

The transitional model or Riggs' prismatic society is adequate in some respects, such as the identification of characteristics and features common to all polities at a certain stage of political and economic growth, but it does not seem rigorous enough to serve as the main conceptual framework in the analysis of the New Society. The transitional model would have been adequate had the Philippines remained as it was before 21 September 1972. As it stood from 1972 through 1981, however the Philippines may well have been sui generis. As of 17 January 1973, the Philippines was officially and theoretically a "parliamentary democracy;" in reality however, it was a one-man dictatorship headed by a leader who kept his title from the old regime and whose legal term of office expired on 31 December 1973. Marcos insisted that his New Society was a "revolution"; yet the new regime came into being without any large-scale uprising or bloodshed between revolutionaries and the de jure government.

Revolution as A Method of Change

The concept of "revolution"--its causes, characteristics. dynamics and effects--is often variously understood and misunderstood. Marcos, for instance, proudly referred to his virtually absolute power in the New Society as a revolution, a "liberal

21

revolution," which he carefully differentiated from the type of revolution "which liquidates an entire ruling class as a precondition for the establishment of a new social order . . . the jacobin type."[45] Marcos suggested that his "liberal type revolution" was "non-violent" and was one "carried out by the assimilation of the revolutionary classes into the existing order, resulting just the same in a different social order."[46]

Even a cursory examination of the numerous articles on "revolution" in the Philippine student and metropolitan presses prior to 21 September 1972, revealed that the term tended to be used interchangeably with "coup d'etat," "protracted anarchy," "subversion," and "rebellion," and even when mention was made of wars of national independence such as the Philippine Revolution against Spain.[47] Was Marcos' New Society really a revolutionary regime, and if so, did this regime result from a "revolution"? If the New Society was not a revolutionary regime in the accurate and technical sense of the term, then what was it?

Perhaps the most widely used definition of revolution is one provided by Samuel P. Huntington:

> A revolution is a rapid, fundamental, and violent domestic change in the dominant values and myths of a society, in its political institutions, social structure, leadership, and government activity and politics.[48]

A revolution is "most likely to occur in societies which have experienced some societal and economic development and where the processes of political modernization and political development have lagged behind the processes of social and economic change."[49] Clarifying the scope of revolutions, Huntington posited that "a full scale revolution . . . involve[d] the rapid and violent destruction of existing political institutions, the mobilization of new groups into politics, and the creation of new political institutions."[50] Historical examples cited by Huntington fall into two essential categories: (1) Western revolutions, such as the French, Russian, Mexican, and Chinese (in its first phase) revolutions and (2) Eastern revolutions such as the later phases of the Chinese revolution and the Vietnamese revolution.

Another writer, Chalmers Johnson, offers a more extensive typology of revolutions.[51] According to Johnson, there are six "phyla," or types, of revolution: the jacquerie, millenarian rebellion, anarchistic rebellion, Jacobin communist revolution, conspiratorial coup d'etat, and militarized mass insurrection.[52]

The term jacquerie refers to a "mass rebellion of peasants with strictly limited aims--the restoration of lost rights or the removal of specific grievances."[53] The aborted Sakdalista uprising in the Philippines in 1935 is an example of this type of revolution. The millenarian rebellion, is one directed toward "complete and radical change in the world which will be reflected in the millenium, a world shorn of its present deficiencies."[54] The target of the revolutionary millenarian movement in terms of its formal ideology is the entire community; its overriding goal is the establishment of an earthly paradise.

Anarchistic rebellions or "nostalgic revolutions" occur in response to changes (either nonviolent or revolutionary) in the social system which were made previously in response to the dominant part of the population's perceptions of dysfunctions. Advocates of anarchistic revolutions do not support the primary changes already made but instead consider the system's dysfunctions a result of previously made changes.[55]

The most analyzed type of revolution is the Jacobin communist revolution. The Jacobin revolution is "made by the masses under elite guidance, although the pattern of cooperation is often ad hoc and confused."[56] The ideology of the Jacobin communist revolution "envisages the replacement of the old society with one imagined to be 'enlightened'--typically one that transforms serf, subject, or communicant into a citizen of a national community."[57]

Conspiratorial coup d'etats are "attempts at revolutionary change made by small, secret associations of individuals united by a common sense of grievance that may or may not correspond to the objective condition of the social system."[58] These revolutions are always calculated and they do not include the masses;the ideology is elitist or "tutelary".[59] The coup d'etat has been one of the most common instruments of change in the developing countries of Asia, Latin America, and Africa during the last twenty or so years.

The last of Johnson's six "phyla" is the so-called militarized mass insurrection. While this type of revolution is carried out by the masses, it is guided and directed by a "conspiratorial, revolutionary general staff," and has for its main objective "the replacement of a regime by means of waging a revolutionary war against it."[60] The mainstay of this type of revolution is protracted guerrilla warfare similar to that waged by the Huks in the 1950's and what is being carried out today by the Communist Party's New People's Army (NPA).[61]

In a later and more definitive work,[62] Johnson provided a framework of "endogenous" factors by which one may conceptualize the process through which systems go into a state of disequilibrium, the condition which invariably precede[d] revolutions.[63] Some of the exogenous factors are: "global communications, the rise of external 'reference groups' (for example, the effects of the French and Russian revolutions on neighboring populations everywhere); internal mobilizations and refugee migrations caused by wars; and the work of groups such as Christian missionaries, communist parties, the Peace Corps, and UNESCO--all of which have led to culture contact and the individual comparisons this generate[d]."[64] According to Johnson, endogenous factors are more difficult to conceptualize and "consist primarily of internal 'innovations' which affect the value structure as much as technological innovations . . . affect adaptation to the environment."[65]

Peter Calvert asserts that a conceptual framework of revolution should include any one or all of the following:

1. A process in which the political direction of a state becomes increasingly discredited in the eyes of either the population as a whole or certain key sections of it.
2. A change of government (transition) at a clearly defined point in time by the use of armed force, or the credible threat of its use; namely an event.
3. A program of change in either political or social institutions, or both, induced by the political leadership after the transition of power has occurred.
4. A political myth that gives the new political leadership short-term status as the legitimate government of the state.[66]

If one applied the Huntington, Johnson, and Calvert typologies strictly, it is readily apparent that the transformation of the Philippines from a presidential democracy to one-man rule, or as Marcos preferred to call it, the New Society, was not a revolution, whether of the jacquerie, millenarian, anarchistic, Jacobin, conspiratorial coup d'etat, or militarized mass insurrection variety. Instead of the masses rising against the government, the president himself initiated the "revolution" and the revolutionary changes both in the politico-legal processes and in the collective lifestyle of the people.

The strategy used to institute the radical policies of the New Society was the imposition of so-called "transfer-culture goals," and this strategy seemed to correspond more to post-revolutionary strategies of totalitarian systems. Because these transfer-culture goals required sacrifices from the population and "entail[ed] means that [were] not popularly supported," thus involving the anticipation of popular resistance, the transfer-culture goals were imposed by a "revolution from above," with profound consequences for the potentials of the total social system.[67] Marcos' abolition of the legislative branch, suspension of civil liberties, suppression of open opposition to his regime, assumption of plenary powers over all aspects of public and private life, and threat to abolish private property altogether, undoubtedly had profound implications for the political system as a whole.[68]

Martial Law and the Philippine Political System

The legal device used by Marcos to launch his New Society was martial law. What is the scope and various dimensions of martial law? Is martial law indigenous to Philippine law and politics, or is it a concept borrowed from elsewhere? There is a great deal of ambiguity and vagueness in extant definitions of martial law. There is also a tendency to use the term loosely and to equate it with "military law." Perhaps the classic definition of martial law, at least in American jurisprudence, was expressed by Chief Justice Samuel Chase in a dissent in Ex parte Milligan:

> There are under the constitution three kinds of military jurisdiction: one to be exercised both in peace and war; another to be exercised in time of

25

foreign war without the boundaries of the United States, or in time of rebellion and civil war within states or districts occupied by rebels treated as belligerents; and a third to be exercised in time of invasion or insurrection within the limits of states maintaining adhesion to the National Government, when the public danger requires its exercise. The first of these may be called jurisdiction under MILITARY LAW, and is found in acts of Congress prescribing rules and articles of war, or otherwise providing for the government of the national forces; the second may be distinguished as MILITARY GOVERNMENT, superseding as far as may be deemed expedient, the local law, and exercised by the military commander under the direction of the President, with the express or the implied sanction of Congress; while the third may be denominated MARTIAL LAW PROPER, and is called into action by Congress, or temporarily, when the action of the Congress cannot be invited, and in the case of justifying or excusing peril, by the president, in times of insurrection or invasion, or of civil or foreign war, within districts or localities where ordinary law no longer adequately secures public safety and private rights.[69] [Emphasis mine.]

Martial law as interpreted by the courts and legal scholars, then, is a temporary measure to which the authorities (either the congress or the president, or both) resort in times of emergency, for the purpose of restoring order and stability.

During the period of martial law, the civilian governmental structure, including the courts, is superseded by the military structure and military law. The military serves as a mere agent or instrument of the civil government for the specific purposes of restoring order and quelling lawlessness. One might view martial law as an act of self-defense on the part of the state based on extreme necessity or, as put more eloquently by the United States Supreme Court in Moyer v. Peabody, martial law is "founded on necessity and inherent in government [for] . . . unless the right and power

26

exist, peace and good order, security . . . government itself . . . may be destroyed and obliterated . . . when the domination of the mob becomes so powerful that it cannot be stayed by the civil authorities."[70]

Martial law may either be absolute or qualified in scope. It is absolute "when the military displaces the civil government and governs a particular territory according to the dictates of military necessity and the laws of war."[71] In a situation of absolute martial law, the military may exercise all of the executive, legislative, and judicial powers of the government. Limited martial law, on the other hand, exists when the military is "limited to exercising some functions of the civil government in the area or scene of disorder or conflict, particularly restoration and maintenance of the peace, [and] regulation of activities affecting the peace and order situation."[72] Under limited martial law, the military and civilian authorities share certain powers and prerogatives. Martial law may be said to exist in a domestic community "when the military rises superior to the civil power in the exercise of some or all of the functions of government."[73]

As a corollary to martial law, certain procedural and substantive guarantees of due process such as the privilege of the writ of habeas corpus are also temporarily set aside. The privilege of the writ of habeas corpus is described by the eminent American constitutionalist, Joseph Story as:

> "the great bulwark of personal liberty; since it is the appropriate remedy to ascertain whether any person is rightfully in confinement or not, and the cause of his confinement; and if no sufficient ground of detention appears, the party is entitled to his immediate discharge."[74]

Habeas corpus has its origins in common law and is:

> "most beneficially construed; and . . . applied to every case of illegal restraint, whatever it may be; for every restraint upon a man's liberty is, in the eyes of the law, an imprisonment, wherever may be the place, or whatever may be the manner, in which the restraint is effected."[75]

27

Story held that the right to suspend habeas corpus should be confined strictly to cases of rebellion and invasion which threaten public safety, and he called this restriction "a very just and wholesome restraint which cuts down at a blow a fruitful means of oppression, capable of being abused in bad times for the worst of purposes."[76]

The Constitutional Basis of Martial Law

The Philippine president's martial law powers, unlike those of his American counterpart derived from an express constitutional provision. Article VII, Section 10, paragraph 2 of the 1935 Constitution provided:

> The President shall be commander-in-chief of all armed forces of the Philippines and, whenever it becomes necessary, he may call out such armed forces to prevent or suppress lawless violence, invasion, insurrection, or rebellion, or <u>imminent danger thereof</u>; when the public safety requires it, he may suspend the privilege of the writ of habeas corpus, or place the Philippines or any part thereof under martial law.[77]
> [Emphasis mine.]

Martial law was unknown to Philippine law prior to 1916 when the United States Congress enacted P.L. 240 (Organic Act for the Philippine Islands) otherwise known as the Jones Law. Although the Spaniards apparently knew of martial law, (the rough equivalent was <u>estado de sitio</u> or "state of siege") they never resorted to it during their 355-year control of the Philippines,[78] nor did the Constitution of the short-lived First Philippine Republic (12 June 1898 to 30 December 1898) contain any provision on the subject.[79]

The martial law provision of the Jones Law (Section 21) was part of the definition of the powers of the "Governor-General of the Philippine Islands." The pertinent portion reads:

> He [the Governor-General] shall be responsible for the faithful execution of the laws of the Philippine Islands and of the United States operative within the Philippine Islands, and

28

whenever it becomes necessary he may call upon the commanders of the military and naval forces of the United States in the islands, or summon the posse comitatus or call out the militia or other locally created armed forces, to prevent or suppress lawless violence, invasion, insurrection, or rebellion; and he may, <u>in case of rebellion or invasion, or imminent danger thereof, when the public safety requires it, suspend the privilege of the writ of habeas corpus; or place</u> the islands, or any part thereof, under martial law.[80]

Explaining the meaning of Section 21, Maximo M. Kalaw wrote "The Governor-General is the representative of American sovereignty in the Philippines, and sovereignty implies force, hence, he must have under his control and direction the agents of force."[81]

An examination of Article VII, Section 10, paragraph 2 of the 1935 Constitution and Section 21 of the Jones Law will show that the two are identical. In his book <u>The Framing of the Philippine Constitution</u>,[82] Jose M. Aruego, who was a delegate to the 1935 Constitutional Convention, recalled that "there was unanimous support in the Convention in favor of making the president the constitutional commander-in-chief of all the armed forces to prevent or suppress lawless violence, invasion, insurrection, or rebellion."[83] There was a serious disagreement among the delegates on whether the executive or legislative branch of government would have the authority to suspend the privilege of the writ of habeas corpus.

<u>The Amendment That Never Was:</u>
<u>Araneta's Prophetic Analysis</u>

One camp headed by delegate Salvador Araneta (who was in self-exile in Canada throughout the martial law period) was in favor of giving the authority to the National Assembly, while another camp (which eventually prevailed) favored vesting the authority with the president.[84] In the light of Marcos' proclamation of absolute martial law on 21 September 1972, it is instructive to review Araneta's arguments in defense of the position that only the National Assembly should have the authority to suspend the writ of habeas corpus.

Delegate Araneta's proposed amendment read:

In case of rebellion, insurrection or invasion, when the public safety requires it, the National Assembly may suspend the privilege of the writ of habeas corpus. In case the National Assembly is not in session, the President may suspend the privilege of the writ of habeas corpus with the consent of the majority of the members of the Supreme Court, but this suspension of the privilege of the writ of habeas corpus will be considered revoked if the President does not call a special session of the National Assembly within 15 days from the decree suspending the writ of habeas corpus or if the National Assembly fails to confirm the action of the President within 30 days.[85] [Emphasis mine.]

Defending his proposed amendment, Delegate Araneta argued that the draft provision lifted almost verbatim from the Jones Law (the version which prevailed and became Article VII, Section 10, paragraph 2 of the 1935 Constitution) would give the chief executive the sole authority to determine the existence of the reasons for the suspension of the writ of habeas corpus.

Because of existing precedents in Philippine jurisprudence at that time, it was highly unlikely the Supreme Court would have reviewed the findings of the executive; consequently, hypothesized Delegate Araneta, arrests would be effected by military men who tended to act arbitrarily. The net result would be that many people might be detained who in fact had no connection with the disturbances.[86] To grant the power to suspend the privilege of the writ of habeas corpus to the National Assembly--or as indicated in Araneta's proposed amendment even to the president provided he had the consent of the majority of the members of the Supreme Court--would, Araneta contended, reduce if not remove the possibility of abuse and, accordingly, protect the life and liberty of individuals.[87]

A Reticent Supreme Court: The President's Power is Absolute

Before 21 September 1972, Philippine courts had not had many opportunities to deal with the question of martial law. Before President Marcos' limited suspension of the privilege of the writ of habeas corpus (Proclamation No. 889) on 21 August 1971, "the privilege of the writ of habeas corpus had been suspended [only] twice in Philippine history."[88] In 1905, the American governor-general suspended the writ under the authority granted him by the Philippine Bill of 1902 and again in 1950, President Elpidio Quirino suspended the writ of habeas corpus ostensibly to cope with the Huk threat.[89] In both instances the Philippine Supreme Court upheld the presidential action, stating basically in Barcelon v. Baker [5 Phil. 87 (1905)], and in Montenegro v. Castaneda [L-4331, 30 Aug. 1952], "the findings of the executive upon which he bases his order suspending the privilege of the writ of habeas corpus are conclusive and final upon the Courts."[90]

On 11 December 1971, the Philippine Supreme Court upheld the constitutionality of President Marcos' Proclamation No. 889 temporarily suspending the privilege of the writ of habeas corpus. Echoing the doctrine enunciated in the Barcelon and Montenegro cases, the high court said "the function of the court is merely to check, not to supplant, the Chief Executive or to ascertain whether he has gone beyond the constitutional limits of his jurisdiction and not to exercise the power vested in him or to determine the wisdom of his act."[91]

In what was apparently a continuation of its conservative posture vis-a-vis the chief executive, the Philipine Supreme Court also avoided ruling on the constitutionality of some of the more recent acts of the Marcos martial law regime, such as the cancellation by edict of a scheduled plebiscite on the new constitution and its subsequent ratification, also by presidential decree, in what an editorial in the St. Louis Post Dispatch called a "rigged-up referendum by a show of hands" in 32,000 "Citizen's Assemblies."[92] In dismissing ten identical petitions by legislators, newspapermen and other concerned citizens, the Supreme Court said the issue had become "moot and academic"[93]

The lone dissenter, Justice Calixto Zaldivar chastised his colleagues for "indulging in [the] niceties of 'procedural technicalities' and evad[ing] the task of declaring that the proposed Constitution has been validly ratified as announced in Presidential Proclamation No. 1102."[94] Addressing himself to the majority's determination that the case was "moot and academic," Zaldivar wrote as follows:

> I cannot agree with my worthy colleagues who hold the view that the petitions in all these cases have become moot and academic simply because the relief prayed for by the petitioners cannot be granted after Proclamation 1102 (announcing the ratification of the proposed Constitution) was issued by the President of the Philippines.
>
> This Court has decided cases even if no positive relief could be granted, or even if the party has withdrawn his appeal if the case presented to the Court for resolution is a clear violation of the Constitution or of the fundamental personal rights of liberty and property.[95]

From the Barcelon case in 1909 to the present time then, the Philippine Supreme Court has adhered very closely to the letter of Article VII, Section 10, paragraph 2 of the 1935 Constitution that the president's judgement on the existence of an emergency is absolute, final and conclusive.

In turn, this dovetails with the view expressed by Aruego:

> The authority to decide whether the conditions for the suspension of the writ have arisen is the President. His decision is conclusive. The courts have no power to inquire into the question of whether or not his decision on the matter is correct.
>
> Under the same two conditions, the President may place the Philippines or any part thereof under martial law. In other words, the Executive calls upon the military powers to assist him in the maintenance of law and order.[96] [Emphasis mine.]

Enrique M. Fernando, Chief Justice of the Supreme Court at that time, and an authority on

Philippine constitutional law, expressed a similar viewpoint when he wrote:

> Once the President has declared the suspension of the writ of habeas corpus, because in his opinion there is a case of invasion, an insurrection, or rebellion, or imminent danger thereof and the public safety requires it, the exercise of such prerogative cannot be questioned in courts. That is a matter solely with the presidential discretion, this determination being conclusive and binding on all the other departments of the government, including the courts.[97] [Emphasis mine.]

The American and Philippine Founding Fathers Compared

An interesting feature of the Philippine president's martial law powers was that while the grant is virtually absolute, the Constitution also prescribed specific "conditions" under which martial law may be imposed. These conditions were as follows:

1. There is actual invasion, insurrection or rebellion, or;
2. There is imminent danger of invasion, insurrection or rebellion, and;
3. Public safety (necessity) requires the imposition of martial law.[98] [Emphasis mine.]

On closer scrutiny, these conditions were hardly limitations at all, since the power to determine "imminent danger" was vested solely in the president, a power with which the courts have been most reluctant to interfere. The presidential prerogative to declare martial law on the basis of his assessment of "imminent danger" of invasion, insurrection or rebellion was precisely what the United States Supreme Court warned about in Ex parte Milligan:

> Martial law cannot arise from threatened invasion. The necessity must be actual and present; the invasion real, such as effectually closes the courts and

33

deposes the civil administration.[99]
[Emphasis mine.]

It was obvious, therefore, that the framers of
the Philippine Constitution differed fundamentally
from their American counterparts on the subject of
emergency powers. America's founding fathers--in
spite of Alexander Hamilton's rhetoric and
influence--were reluctant to invest the chief
executive with an express and open-ended grant of
authority in martial law situations, but the
Philippine founding fathers thought that such an
express grant was not only advisable but absolutely
necessary. John H. Romani commented as follows:

> If anything, the extent of the Presi-
> dent's authority may be too great,
> rather than insufficient, again empha-
> sizing an underlying difference in
> fundamental beliefs between the framers
> of the Philippine Constitution and those
> who drafted the American document.[100]
> [Emphasis mine.]

Summary

Of the four models of change examined earlier,
the paradigm of the "developmental movement regime"
seems to most closely approximate the New Society of
the Philippines. The model is broad and comprehensive enough to encompass some of the more unique
features of the regime, such as the subordination of
the military to civilian authority even as the Armed
Forces of the Philippines (AFP) acted as the main
enforcer of the regime's edicts and proclamations;
the launching of the "revolution" by the incumbent
president himself not by his political adversaries;
and the large scale cooption of technocrats and
intellectuals, including the president's erstwhile
enemies and detractors.

At the same time, the paradigm of the
developmental movement regime is rigorous enough to
meet the minimum requirements of scholarly research.
Certainly, Marcos qualified as the "presidential
monarch"--the indispensable "charismatic leader"
Diamant described. The citizen's assemblies or
barangays were indeed organizations geared for
"total mobilization" as well as being devices for
citizen feedback, reaching as they did all the way
"down into the grassroots of the village." The New

Society was also committed (at least on paper) to "intensive programs of industrialization or extended trade both domestically and internationally," and like the Tucker-Diamant model had a monopoly "not only [on] political power but also [on] the means of physical coercion--the police and army."

The martial law powers of the American and Philippine chief executives were cut from the same bolt of cloth, supported by the same set of judicial precedents, and intended by the founding fathers of both countries to cope with essentially the same types of emergency situations. But while the American chief executive derived his emergency powers from an extrapolation of his role as commander-in-chief and from a series of specific congressional delegations of authority, the Philippine president's powers, under the 1935 Constitution, were based on express constitutional authorization.

The concept of martial law and its corollaries, such as the suspension of the privilege of the writ of habeas corpus and the "calling out" of the troops to quell disturbances, was introduced into Philippine constitutional law by the United States, and, as had been the case with almost everything else that the Philippines borrowed from the United States, the Filipinos tried to "improve" on it. Thus what the American founding fathers deliberately left vague and ambiguous--to allow for future interpretation and incremental growth--the framers of the Philippine constitution made explicit and rigid. Consequently, Philippine courts have been left with very little room in which to maneuver or perform acts of "social engineering." In a strict comparative sense, the Philippine chief executive under the 1935 Constitution was considerably more powerful than his American counterpart; indeed, the former's martial law powers were virtually absolute.

In the United States, the courts have played a major role in defining and delimiting the extent of the president's martial law powers. While it is basically true, as the late Clinton Rossiter suggested, that the "contours of the presidential war powers have . . . been presidentially, not judicially shaped,"[101] the United States Supreme Court had on various occasions--for example, in the <u>Milligan</u>, <u>Merryman</u>, <u>Duncan</u>, and <u>Youngstown</u>--cases spoken out against actual presidential abuse of emergency powers or warned against potential presidential abuse.

The Philippine Supreme Court, has been most reluctant and timid vis-a-vis presidential war powers. All its determinations on the subject so far--Barcelon, Montenegro, Prudente, and Monteclaro--have been affirmations of presidential absolutism and primacy over the legislative and judicial branches of government. In one sense, however, the supreme courts of the United States and the Philippines share the common tendency to "agree that the case is moot," to seize with relief upon technicalities which prevent them from taking jurisdiction or, if forced to rule, to decide the issue on the "narrowest possible grounds."[102]

Chapter 3

THE MATRIX OF CHANGE

The Philippines is one of nine countries that make up the geographico-political entity known as Southeast Asia. With an estimated population of over fifty-five million, it is the seventeenth most populous country in the world. As a developing nation, the Philippines is in the middle stages of industrialization and technological growth. A country known for its poverty and low standard of living, the Philippines has an estimated annual per capita GNP of $772.00--low compared to Singapore's $6,526.00, but high compared to Indonesia's $556.00.[1] Until 1972, the Philippines, Malaysia, and Singapore were described as "practicing democracies." Thailand, Burma, and Indonesia on the other hand were described as "military regimes." Vietnam and Cambodia were described as being "dominated by one or two strong leaders who head differing structures of government." Laos was simply a "no-party nonstate."[2]

For a long time, the Philippines was also known abroad as the "show window" of American democracy in the Far East. But on 21 September 1972, Marcos, the constitutionally-elected president of the Philippines, proclaimed absolute martial rule, suspended the privilege of the writ of habeas corpus and other civil liberties and established an authoritarian regime, called the New Society, which lasted for nine years.[3]

The Philippines Under Spanish Rule

The Philippines, like all of Southeast Asia with the exception of Thailand, was a former colony, first of Spain and then of America. Spanish rule over the islands lasted approximately 355 years. The Philippines had been discovered in 1521 by Ferdinand Magellan who was searching for a new route to the East Indies in pursuit of the lucrative spice

37

trade. Magellan was slain by a native chieftain, Lapu-Lapu, in a battle some historians call the first Filipino resistance to alien domination.[4] Nevertheless, the Spaniards took possession of the Philippines by the middle of the sixteenth century, and the city of Manila was established in 1572 by Miguel Lopez de Legazpi.

The Nature of Spanish Colonial Rule

Spain's colonial rule over the Philippines, as over the rest of its colonial empire, was from its inception to its end, exploitative and oppressive. The Filipinos were treated by the Spaniards as serfs, or in Jose P. Rizal's phrase "hewers of wood and drawers of water" and contemptuously referred to as indios.[5] Filipinos were also denied participation in the colonial government except at the lowest levels and even then only in token forms, for example, as gobernadorcillos (petty governors) at the village level who only assisted the Spanish authorities in publicizing edicts from the crown and collected taxes. The Philippines was a dependency of the Viceroyalty of New Spain, governed through the Council of the Indies, which was the supreme governing body for all of the Spanish overseas empire.

Throughout the Spanish period the religious authorities played the dominant role in civil affairs. Because of the theocratic nature of the Spanish monarchy, the ecclesiastical authorities exerted a strong influence over the civil authorities. The abuses and overall profligacy of the friars went unchecked since the Archbishop of Manila possessed veto power on the selection of who was to be governor general of the Philippines. The religious authorities were thus able to insure that whoever was assigned to the Philippines tacitly tolerated various friar excesses. Here, as elsewhere, the "royal patronage of the clergy" made the church the most important agency of the crown in subduing and pacifying the Spanish colonial empire.[6]

Be that as it may, there were brief interludes which proved to be beneficial to the Philippines especially in the economic sphere. During the administration of Jose Basco y Vargas (1778-1787) under the enlightened reign of Charles III (1759-1788), a "'general economic plan' for the development of the natural resources of the Philippines" was formulated and put into effect."[7] In connection with the program, Basco improved the schools and promoted the teaching of the Spanish language, a policy which the friars opposed. In the political arena, the granting of Philippine representation to the Spanish Cortes (1810-1813, 1820-1823, and 1834-1837) proved in the long run to mark the beginning of the struggle between liberalism and constitutionalism, and conservatism and absolutism in the Spanish mainland even "if it did not accomplish anything for the Filipinos . . . because the delegates were Spaniards and represented Spanish interests in the Philippines."[8] The Philippines rejected Joseph Bonaparte, and like Spain's other insular possessions, Cuba and Puerto Rico, did not break away from Spain until 1898.

One of the more tangible results of this struggle as far as the Philippines was concerned was the appointment of a liberal governor general, Carlos Maria de la Torre, an outcome of the Spanish revolution of 1868 which temporarily removed the Bourbons from the Spanish throne. Governor General de la Torre's administration, although short-lived (1869-1871) was one of the best liked by the Filipinos, and it later proved instrumental in stimulating nationalism.[9]

Assimilation or Revolution: The Propaganda Movement

Feelings against the "friarocracy" (the neologism was Marcelo H. del Pilar's, one of the most outspoken critics of the role the clergy played in colonial politics), and its attendant evils and inequalities was behind some one hundred revolts taking place in various parts of the country beginning with the Rajah Lakandula and Rajah Sulayman revolts in 1574 and continuing throughout the seventeenth and eighteenth centuries.[10] Among these were the Diego Silang revolt in the Ilocos provinces (1762-1763), and the Cavite Mutiny of 20 January 1872 which resulted in the execution of three Filipino priests, Jose Burgos, Mariano Gomez and Jacinto Zamora.[11] Because of the absence of any central leadership or unifying element in these revolts, as well as the Spaniards' superior weaponry and organization, the authorities were invariably able to quell and subdue these rebellions.

Despite the colonial government's policy of refusing the Filipinos any appreciable measure of education (except during the Basco and de la Torre years) there developed a native _pricipalia_ or ilustrado class whose members were native Filipinos or mestizos who had achieved some degree of economic success. This class included the landed gentry. The children of the principalia or ilustrado class were about the only ones able to acquire college education in the Philippines, or to travel to Europe where they were exposed to liberal ideas, and experienced life in a freer and more enlightened political setting.

These Filipinos launched an organized protest movement in 1889 designed mainly to expose to Spaniards in Spain and to the rest of the world the abuses and defects of Spanish rule in the Philippines. The movement which is known as the Propaganda Movement also took on the task of educating and agitating the Filipinos in the Philippines about their plight and fostering their pride for their race. This was necessary to counteract one of the main effects of Spanish colonialism: the near destruction of the Filipino's spirit and his sense of dignity. Filipinos believed themselves to be inferior, and they passively acquiesced to abuses perpetrated by the Spanish authorities. The Propaganda Movement was not separatist and functioned mainly through its official publication, the La Solidaridad under the editorship of Graciano Lopez Jaena.

Among the notable participants in the movement were the artist Juan Luna who depicted Philippine conditions through such paintings as the much-acclaimed Spolarium, and the polemicist Del Pilar whose main contribution was a strongly worded antifriar volume entitled La Soberania Monacal. Perhaps the best known and most influential of them all was Dr. Jose P. Rizal. Rizal wrote hundreds of essays, letters, scientific tracts, and two major novels, Noli Me Tangere and El Filibusterismo. These were stirring social commentaries which exposed and satirized the abuses of the clergy in the colony as well as the foibles and weaknesses of both Filipino and Spanish society.

A recurrent theme in Rizal's writings was the contention that the Filipino was just as good and able as the Spaniard and, if afforded the proper opportunities, could excel in whatever endeavor he chose. In one of his essays, "The Indolence of the Filipino," Rizal refuted the Spaniards' claim that the Filipino was by nature indolent, and that this indolence was responsible for the Filipino's backwardness. Rizal pointed out that indolence was the effect not the cause of the Filipino's condition, and that this trait was the product of exploitation by the Spaniards, the absence of incentives, and certain predisposing conditions such as the harsh tropical climate, epidemics, and extreme poverty. In his novel El Filibusterismo, Rizal argued through his principal character Simoun against separation from Spain through revolution, pointing out that the majority of the people were not prepared for such a mode of change. In spite of his advocacy of reform and rejection of revolution, Rizal was executed by the Spaniards on 30 December 1896, after a mock trial on trumped-up charges of inciting rebellion and plotting against the Spanish crown.

While the intellectual foundation of the revolution which eventually toppled Spain was laid out by the ilustrado expatriates in Europe, the armed phase of the struggle was initiated by a man of the masses, Andres Bonifacio. He founded and was the first Supremo of the Katipunan[12], a clandestine society which advocated complete separation from Spain. The first open armed clash with the Spaniards took place on 23 August 1896, and from there on the revolution spread to other parts of the country.[13] As a result of a factional dispute within the Katipunan, after Bonifacio's death the leadership of the revolutionary movement fell on Emilio Aguinaldo y Famy. The protracted skirmishing which ensued caused the Spaniards to lose most of the Philippines.

On 18 November 1897, the first part of a truce known as the Pact of Biyak na Bato was signed between the Spanish government and the revolutionary forces led by General Aguinaldo. In accordance with one of the provisions of the truce, Aguinaldo voluntarily exiled himself in Hong Kong where he purchased arms for the revolutionary army. When the truce appeared headed for collapse, Aguinaldo returned to the Philippines, and shortly thereafter, hostilities resumed. On 12 June 1898, after a series of decisive victories against the outnumbered Spaniards, Aguinaldo proclaimed the First Philippine Republic. The Spaniards were driven to their last stronghold, the walled city of Intramuros, awaiting the coup d'grace from the Filipino Revolutionary Army. Low on ammunition and food and cut off from the Spanish mainland by vast oceans, the Spaniards found themselves in an almost hopeless situation. The United States decided to intervene, at first ostensibly in favor of the Filipinos. Eventually the United States annexed the Philippines as her colony in the Far East.

The Philippines Under American Rule

The United States acquired sovereignty over the Philippines from Spain through the Treaty of Paris ratified by the United States Senate on 6 February 1899.[14] The treaty was part of the settlement that followed the abbreviated Spanish-American War. The acquisition of the Philippines came when the United States was emerging as a naval, colonial, and world power during the years of 1891-1918 characterized as one of "extroversion" in the cyclical interpretation of American involvement in world affairs.[15]

The decision to annex the Philippines, while formally made by President William McKinley, was greatly shaped by the machinations of such expansionists as Theodore Roosevelt, Henry Cabot Lodge, Captain Alfred Thayer Mahan, and a cast of lesser but similarly determined actors. In all fairness it should be pointed out that there was considerable opposition to the annexation movement from various sectors of American society.[16] Although McKinley and the expansionst forces prevailed eventually, they barely got the required two-thirds vote in the United States Senate after the leadership of William Jennings Bryan, an erstwhile foe of annexation, induced a last-minute change of heart among Democrats.[17]

When Spain ceded the Philippines to the United States, she no longer had effective political control of her former colony. As mentioned earlier, the Philippine Revolutionary Forces under the command of General Aquinaldo had all but defeated the Spaniards. In fact, the First Philippine Republic was already in existence when the Treaty of Paris was ratified. When the real intentions of the Americans became clear to the Filipinos (who had received the Americans as friends and emancipators), the Filipino-American war broke out.[18] Outgunned but never outfought, the Filipinos resisted the American forces until 1902 when the last Filipino "rebel" general was captured.

Not long afterward, the United States established in the Philippines a civil government and a system of free universal education; it also made efforts to involve the Filipinos in governmental affairs. By preachment and deed the Americans proved that they were not as exploitative and oppressive as their Spanish predecessors.[19] These policies, coming as they did in sharp contrast to the Spaniards' colonial policies, went a long way toward winning the Filipinos' cooperation and good-will. The hostility that was generated by the Filipino-American war was subsequently sufficiently neutralized by the American policy of benevolence and assimilation.

The Thrust of Early American Policy

Early American policy in the Philippines was geared to eventual Filipino self-government. Although the Republican administration had been less receptive to early independence for the Philippines, (in contrast to the Democratic party which had included Philippine independence as an item in its platform for twelve years) both parties actually favored eventual Philippine independence. The difference lay on the duration of the period of tutorship before the grant of full political autonomy.[20]

The first proffer of Philippine political independence--the Jones Law--was formalized during the Democratic administration of Woodrow Wilson in 1916. Although the Jones Law fell short of Filipino expectations, it gave impetus to the Filipinization of the higher echelons of the civil service and the development of Filipino legislative leadership as a foil to the governor general, then the alter ego, of the American president in the Philippines. This aggressive Filipino leadership would later be pitted against an equally trenchant governor general in the person of Leonard Wood who took over from Francis Burton Harrison when the Republicans were returned to power by the American electorate in 1921. The controversy involving Governor General Wood and President Coolidge on the one hand, and Manuel L. Quezon, Sergio Osmena, and Manuel A. Roxas, on the other, served to intensify the Filipino demand for immediate political autonomy.[21]

The Decision to Grant Independence
to the Philippines

Independent of the agitations of Filipino leaders, developments in the United States, especially the worsening economic conditions that

43

led to the Great Depression, were working to hasten
the severance of the Philippines from the United
States. A curious coalition of interest groups
including organized labor, farm lobbies, genuine
anti-imperialists and humanitarians, as well as
jingoist groups which opposed the immigration of
Filipinos to the United States on racial grounds,
combined to pressure the United States Congress to
enact legislation that would ultimately cut the
Philippines loose.[22] It had become abundantly clear
to American leaders including the rabid earlier
supporters of annexation, that the Philippines did
not quite live up to expectations as a source of
wealth, or even as the entrepot of commerce in the
Far East, but had instead become, to borrow George
F. Kennan's classic understatement, a "minor
inconvenience."[23]

In 1932, the Philippine Independence Mission
led by Osmena and Roxas (both of whom would continue
to play major roles in Philippine politics after
independence) succeeded in obtaining the Hare-Hawes-
Cutting Act which set up the timetable for complete
independence after a transitional period of ten
years.[24] As an indication of the United States'
collective state of mind vis-a-vis Philippine
independence, Congress decisively overrode President
Hoover's veto of the measure. The Hare-Hawes-
Cutting Act, however, was aborted by a factional
struggle for power in the Philippines between and
among Osmena, Roxas, and Quezon, with Quezon
ultimately emerging triumphant.

Herbert Hoover was succeeded by Franklin
Delano Roosevelt in 1933. Working on the assumption
that the Democrats might give the Philippines a
"better" independence law, Quezon personally headed
another independence mission to the United States,
only to find an unsympathetic Congress and an indifferent Roosevelt not so much because of opposition
to Philippine independence as such, but because of
the deteriorating economic conditions in the United
States, and executive-legislative preoccupation with
domestic affairs. In 1934, Quezon returned to the
Philippines with practically the same independence
law as the Hare-Hawes-Cutting Act--the Tydings-
McDuffie Independence Act.[25] As provided for in the
Tydings-McDuffie Act, the Philippines held a constitutional convention in February 1935, which drew up
a basic law for the commonwealth (the transitional
form of government) and the subsequent republic.

The Japanese Interregnum

World War II and the Japanese occupation of the Philippines interrupted the Commonwealth period. During that time, "civil liberties were suppressed, the economy was geared to the demands of Japan's war efforts, education was revamped to re-orient Filipino thinking along Japanese lines, and political life was limited to the Japanese-sponsored Republic."[26] The reorganization of the commonwealth government began on 3 January 1943, a day after the occupation of Manila, through a proclamation signed by the commander in chief of the Imperial Japanese Forces, General Masaharu Homma. General Homma announced the end of the American colonization of the country and asserted that the purpose of the Japanese presence was "to emancipate [Filipinos] from the oppressive domination of the U.S.A., [allowing for the establishment of] 'the Philippines for the Filipinos, as a member of a co-prosperity sphere in Greater East Asia, and making [Filipinos] enjoy [their] own prosperity and culture."[27]

The capstone of this policy was the establishment of an "independent" Philippine republic. The Japanese evidently hoped that this would convince Filipinos still loyal to the United States; that it was not Japan's intention to permanently take over the Philippines, but rather to liberate and emancipate it from American colonialism. Preparations for the organization of the wartime republic formally started on 18 June 1943, with the creation of the Preparatory Commission for Philippine Independence headed by Jose P. Laurel, Sr., as president and Benigno S. Aquino, Sr., and Ramon Avancena as vice-presidents. The commission completed preparing a draft of a constitution on 4 September, and this was "ratified in a 'popular' convention two days later."[28] The constitution provided for a unicameral National Assembly. Delegates were chosen on 20 September, and on 25 September the National Assembly elected Laurel president of the new "republic." He was formally inducted into office on 14 October 1943.[29]

The Japanese-sponsored republic failed to get off the ground because the Filipinos in general never accepted the Japanese as emancipators, and because of the Philippines' loyalty and commitment to the American cause. After the fall of Bataan and Corregidor, thousands of Filipino regulars fled to the hills instead of surrendering to the Japanese, and from there waged a relentless guerrilla war against the Japanese authorities. The same guerrillas also provided vital intelligence and logistical support to General MacArthur's troops before and during the entire liberation campaign.

The Postwar Years: From Roxas to Marcos

The Roxas Administration

As a result of the decision in Washington to go ahead with the Philippine independence timetable as set forth in the Tydings-McDuffie Act, President Sergio Osmena reconvened the Commonwealth National Assembly in early 1946. Roxas was elected president of the Senate. Later he became the presidential candidate of a new political party, the Liberal party, a splinter group of the old Nacionalista party.[30] Roxas ran and won against Osmena in the presidential elections of 1946. To qualify as a candidate, Roxas had to be cleared of collaboration charges by General Douglas MacArthur. There is a general agreement among Philippine historians and other students of Philippine affairs that the exoneration and virtual endorsement of Roxas by MacArthur was instrumental in Roxas' victory in the first presidential election held on 23 April 1946.[31]

A year after his election, President Roxas staked his popularity in support of parity rights for American citizens and corporations.[32] In a nationwide plebiscite on the issue, the Filipino people overwhelmingly ratified Roxas' position.[33] The Roxas administration, however, addressed itself primarily to the problems of rehabilitation and reconstruction. Roxas was aided in his rebuilding program by financial assistance from the United States provided through Public Law No. 370 (the Philippine Rehabilitation Act of 1946), as well as the economic benefits that accrued to the Philippines from the Philippine Trade Act of 1946 which accorded Philippine exports preferential treatment in the United States market. Roxas was also responsible for the negotiation of other treaties with the United States, including the PI-US Mutual Defense Treaty and the Military Bases Agreements. He was the United States' greatest advocate and supporter in the Philippines during the early years. It was ironic that he met his untimely death on 15 April 1948 at Clark Air Force Base soon after delivering a speech affirming the loyalty of the

46

Philippines to the United States in the event of
another war.[34]

The Quirino Presidency: Graft, Corruption, and the Huks

After the death of Roxas, Vice-President
Elipidio Quirino was sworn in as president to serve
the remainder of Roxas' term. On top of the
problems of reconstruction and rehabilitation which
had barely begun, Quirino was saddled with the
problem of organized dissidence. At that point, the
Hukbalahap (acronym for Hukbo ng Bayan Laban sa
Hapon or "Army of the People Against the Japanese")
under the leadership of Luis M. Taruc had been
transformed into the military arm of the Communist
Party of the Philippines, committed to the destruction of the fledgling republic.[35]

Most of the Quirino administration's time was
spent in battling the communist-led insurgency.
Thus after the collapse of a short-lived truce with
Taruc and the failure of the Huks to take advantage
of a general amnesty declared several months before
by the late President Roxas, Quirino was the first
president to suspend the writ of habeas corpus. The
suspension, while partial and temporary, was
severely criticized and denounced by civil libertarians and various bar organizations although the
constitutionality of the proclamation itself was
later affirmed by the Philippine Supreme Court.[36]

In 1950, Quirino ran for president against
Laurel, president of the Japanese-sponsored republic. Quirino won although popular consensus held
that the election was one of the most corrupt in the
political history of the Philippines.[37] President
Quirino's term was as corrupt and graft-ridden, a
situation which tended to obscure the successful
liquidation of the Huk problem through a combined
mailed fist-gentle persuasion policy implemented
by Quirino's Secretary of Defense, Ramon F.
Magsaysay.[38] Magsaysay's phenomenal success in
fighting the Huk threat made him an overnight
celebrity. Later, he resigned from the Liberal
party and became the presidential nominee of the
opposition Nacionalista party in the presidential
election of 1953. Magsaysay won over Quirino by the
largest landslide in the nation's brief electoral
history.

The Philippines Under Magsaysay

Magsaysay brought to the presidency a genuine love of the common _tao_ (generic Pilipino meaning "man") and a charismatic brand of leadership that enabled him to rally diverse groups and interests in support of his administration's projects and programs.[39] A major concern of Magsaysay was the "amelioration" of the lot of the people in the rural areas. Toward this end, he launched a three-pronged program, consisting of improvement of the land tenure system along with land resettlement; the extension of easy-term credit to peasants and the building of feeder roads and related infrastructure; and a comprehensive and centrally-directed community development program.

It was during Magsaysay's term, and through his initiative, that the Office of Presidential Assistant on Community Development (PACD) was organized.[40] The PACD was responsible for the recruitment, training, and coordination of community development workers who fanned out into the barrios helping rural folks build roads and bridges under the principle of self-help, and extending necessary technical assistance. As a populist, Magsaysay was difficult to match; he opened the doors of the presidential palace (Malacanang) to the common people and afforded them access to other government offices, something that no president had ever done before. Magsaysay also attempted to stamp out graft and corruption in government by drafting into the civilian establishment young and idealistic military officers as well as newly retired military personnel. His stint as Secretary of National Defense under President Quirino and his excellent rapport with the military made this possible.

Magsaysay's grassroots populism and his charismatic personality would have made him a certain winner had he lived long enough to run for another term. After his tragic death in a plane crash in March 1957, knowledgeable political observers were convinced that Magsaysay could have put together a new and winning coalition outside of the two political parties, and that the people would have followed and supported him completely. It was widely known that Magsaysay was impatient and unhappy about the obstructionism of the "old guard" politicians who controlled Congress.[41] After his death, Magsaysay's closest political lieutenants, Manuel P. Manahan, Raul S. Manglapus, Eleuterio M. Adevoso, Cesar C. Climaco, Frisco T. San Jaun, and

Vicente A. Araneta, established a third party, the Progressive Party of the Philippines, and fared very well in the 1957 presidential elections, especially in the urban areas.

The Presidency of Carlos P. Garcia

The death of Magsaysay thrust another vice-president, Carlos P. Garcia into the presidency. Garcia was a politician of no real national standing from a small province (Bohol) in eastern Visayas. He was included in the national ticket because both political parties believed and practiced "geographical balance" in the presidential candidate selection process. Because he succeeded an immensely popular president and "was an indecisive man who was slow to make decisions and lacking in the dynamic qualities Filipinos require[d] in their leaders,"[42] Garcia's presidency was noticeably mediocre.

Like President Quirino who ascended to the presidency via the death of the incumbent, Garcia sought, and won the presidency in 1957. His victory was unconvincing, however, as he only managed to poll forty-three per centof the votes cast. He could have lost the election to the Liberal party candidate, Jose A. Yulo, had it not been for the candidacy of Manahan and President Quirino's younger brother Antonio, which split the Liberal and independent votes.

Garcia's presidency was primarily dedicated to solving the problem of economic instability. Modest advances were achieved in the area of industrialization. The principal slogan of Garcia's administration was "Filipino First", a throwback to the fierce nationalism of Quezon during the struggle for independence from the United States. Garcia also sought to regulate foreign exchange transactions which had begun to get out of hand. Ironically, the import-export business was one of the areas where graft and corruption involving some of President Garcia's relatives and associates was most rampant. This was largely responsible for his defeat in the election of 1961 by Vice-President Diosdado P. Macapagal, a Liberal. The oddity of a Nacionalista president and a Liberal vice-president sitting side by side was possible since Philippine election law allowed for split-ticket voting in presidential elections.

49

Macapagal, like Magsaysay, was a man descended from the masses.[43] Like Magsaysay, Macapagal was also from central Luzon--Magsaysay was from Zambales and Macapagal from Pampanga, two adjacent provinces in central Luzon, a traditional hotbed of agrarian unrest. Before his election as vice-president, Macapagal served in the House of Representatives and the Philippine Senate. As vice-president, he did practically nothing except to tour the country, strengthening political alliances and establishing new ones. This was possible because President Garcia, departing from the custom of appointing the incumbent vice-president to a key cabinet position, refused to give Macapagal an assignment in his administration.

While Macapagal campaigned on a theme of restoring the people's faith in government by eliminating graft and corruption, his administration emerged badly tainted with scandal. One of Macapagal's lasting contributions, however, was in the area of agrarian reform. It was through Macapagal's leadership that the now-defunct Philippine Congress passed the Land Reform Code of 1963, although in a considerably watered-down version.[44] Amidst great ceremony and fanfare, President Macapagal signed the land reform code in Manila's Rizal Park, declaring that the peasant was thenceforth set free from his age-old bondage. Macapagal's Land Reform Code abolished share tenancy and provided for the expropriation of huge landed estates for resale to tenants but because of loopholes and all sorts of escape clauses in the law itself, the Code was doomed from the beginning.

It was also during Macapagal's presidency that the Philippines nearly became involved in a shooting war with Malaysia over the Sabah dispute. This notwithstanding, President Macapagal was the second president in a row to attempt to reorient the Philippines to her Asian heritage and assume a leadership position vis-a-vis her Southeast Asian neighbors. The establishment of the MAPHILINDO (Malaysia-Philippines-Indonesia) resurrected the idea of a loose pan-Malayan union after the collapse of President Garcia's initiative called Association of Southeast Asia (ASA).

Macapagal lost in his bid for another term in the election of 1965. The man who defeated Macapagal was Ferdinand E. Marcos, who had been president of the now-defunct Philippine Senate and of Macapagal's own Liberal party shortly before being nominated by the opposition Nacionalista party as its standard- bearer in the Fall of 1965. Toward the end of Macapagal's term, Macapagal and Marcos had a parting of ways, and as was common in the Philippines' loose, undisciplined and artificial pre-martial law two-party system, Marcos jumped to the other side and became Macapagal's electoral opponent.[45]

The Marcos Era in Philippine Politics

Marcos' victory came largely as a result of his strong anti-graft and corruption posture. Marcos promised to weed out government corruption in high circles and improve the economy. Before becoming president, he had served several terms in the House of Representatives, two terms in the Philippine Senate, on both occasions garnering the highest number of votes among the senators.[46]

Marcos is a legendary personality.[46] While he was a law student at the University of the Philippines, he was convicted of the murder of his father's political opponent in Ilocos Norte. He reviewed for the bar examinations while in prison and topped the examinations with record-breaking performances in political and constitutional law. After admission to the Philippine bar while in prison, he helped argue his own case on appeal before the Supreme Court, and won a reversal. During the war, he served with the United States Armed Forces in the Far East (USAFFE), fought in Bataan and Corregidor, and emerged from the war as the "Philippines' most decorated war-hero," with twenty-seven various medals.[47]

The first Marcos term was devoted primarily to a massive road building and infrastructure program. Marcos, however, like his predecessors, was plagued by the chronic problems of unemployment, graft, corruption, and runaway inflation. It was not surprising therefore, that during Marcos' adminis- tration, dissent and anti-administration sentiment rose to new and unprecedented heights. Despite these problems, Marcos became the first incumbent president to win a second term.

The 1969 presidential election was notorious for allegations of fraud, terrorism, and other electoral irregularities. The loser to Marcos, Sergio Osmena, Jr., filed a formal protest with the House of Representatives. The subsequent dissolution of the legislative branch under the 1935 Constitution rendered the protest academic and Osmena went into self-exile in the United States where he died several years later.[48]

Summary

The Philippines was colonized by Spain, the United States, and Japan, in that order, for varying periods of time before becoming politically autonomous, first in 1898, and again in 1946. Long before the arrival of the Spaniards, the Philippines had mechanisms for political action, the barangays, and by all historical accounts had a viable legal system and was involved in trade with Cochin-China. The Philippines was the first country in Southeast Asia to revolt against, and prevail, over colonial domination. The Philippines was also the first country in Southeast Asia to gain independence from a former colonial master, the United States, after World War II.

There is little disagreement over the assertion that the Philippines has a long democratic tradition. From the early years of Spanish rule, Filipinos have sought participation in the colonial government, representation in the Spanish Cortes, and, in general, opportunities to have a say in the determination of policies which affected their lives. The writings of Filipino intellectuals in Europe in the mid-1800's were rich in ideas and ideals that derived from such axioms of democratic government as citizen participation in government, rule of law, and the basic freedoms of speech, press, religion, assembly, and association. Even homegrown intellectuals of the revolution such as Apolinario Mabini and Emilio Jacinto, wrote about the same democratic principles and aspirations.[49]

Thus when the First Philippine Republic was proclaimed in 1898, the Malolos Constitution (as the basic law of the First Philippine Republic was popularly known) provided for a government that was both democratic and republican in form. The Malolos Constitution unequivocally stated: "The government of the Republic is popular, representative, alternative, and responsible, and is exercised by three distinct powers, called the legislative, the executive, and the judicial."[50] This early devotion to democratic ideals among Filipinos was further stimulated by the advent of American rule. For unlike their Spanish predecessors, the Americans extended to the Filipinos the institutions of free and universal education and geared the colonial period to tutelage for eventual political autonomy. It was not surprising that when the Filipinos sat down to formulate their basic law in accordance with the mandate of the Tydings-McDuffie Act, the Philippine founding fathers patterned their form of government after that of the United States.

The years following the restoration of Philippine independence by the United States in 1946 were crucial years in the democratic experiment. The transitional nature of Philippine society and the value and belief systems that underlay political and social relationships have served in various ways to impede or stunt the full institutionalization of democratic processes. The manner in which Filipinos conducted their political affairs from the first days of the Second Philippine Republic under Roxas to the beginnings of martial rule in 1972, left much to be desired. Graft and corruption were legion; the people seemed to lose their collective sense of balance and proportion. Then, of course, there were the common and chronic problems that often bedevil the formative years of many developing nations: poverty, inflation, overpopulation, and political instability.

Chapter 4

THE PROCESS OF CHANGE

An analysis of Marcos' public speeches and other official statements from the first time he assumed the presidency in 1965 to the formal declaration of martial law on 21 September 1972, reveals what now, in retrospect, seems to be a coherent body of "revolutionary" ideas. An element that provides thematic oneness to Marcos' numerous speeches and pronouncements is that of radical change, of recasting Philippine society from an "oligarchic society" (this phrase will later fill page after page of Marcos' social analyses and political tracts) into an egalitarian polity where the blessings and resources of the country are equitably shared by all.[1]

The Radicalization of Marcos

The formulation of Marcos' current ideas on "revolutionary change" began as early as 1965, when he said:

> We have come upon a phase of our history when ideals are only a veneer for greed and power in public and private affairs, when devotion to duty and dedication to a public trust are to be weighed at all times against private advantages and personal gain, and when loyalties can be traded in the open market.[2]

Proceeding to describe the plight of the over-whelming majority--the scarcity of jobs, sub-human living conditions, and the worsening state of law and order--Marcos put the blame squarely on the "privileged few" who unabashedly "parade their comforts and advantages before the eyes of an impoverished many."[3] While refreshing in its candor, Marcos' rhetoric did not elicit the overwhelming public response that he must have expected. In a political society like pre-martial law Philippines, one learned to take the politicians' pronouncements with a healthy skepticism, the proverbial grain of salt. For was not Marcos himself one of the privileged few, a creature of the elite?

Indeed, facing a different audience later (a joint session of the Philippine Congress on the occasion of the annual "State of the Nation" address) Marcos overlooked his attack on the "oligarchy" and turned instead to another straw man on whom to blame the nation's ills: communism or the "threat" posed by it. Marcos warned that the Philippines faced:

> a pervasive threat from a military power that has flagrantly resorted to open aggression to attain its ends and has never accepted that general war would be disastrous. Limited but protracted warfare is very much in evidence in areas immediately adjoining our territory. The conflicts in South Vietnam and Malaysia present security problems of the gravest concern. [4]

Marcos' identification of the "privileged few" and the "communists" as early as 1965-1966, as the twin villains behind the Philippines' condition, dovetailed remarkably into his 1972 analysis of the twin evils confronting the Philippines by which he justified the proclamation of martial law.

On the occasion of his second inauguration as President of the Philippines, Marcos continued to hammer at the theme of revolutionary and radical change. At this time of course, the country was in deep economic trouble, and student and worker unrest had escalated to new levels. [5] One prominent Filipino writer described the national scene at that time as follows:

> [in] practically all sectors of Philippine society the traditional instruments of revolution were in wide use: pickets, rallies, boycotts, demonstrations, sit-ins, teach-ins, discussion groups and sporadic clashes with law authorities. The young rebels, unarmed, had learned to produce counterweapons: pillboxes, Molotov cocktails, and assorted

56

explosives. Public gatherings featured
fiery and abrasive oratories, chants and
slogans, incendiary placards and
streamers in flaming red: "Ibagsak ang
imperyalismo, piyudalismo, pasismo!"
(Down with imperialism, feudalism, and
fascism!), "Ibagsak ang pamahalaang
Estados Unidos-Marcos!" (Down with the
United States-Marcos government!). And
the voice of revolution filled not only
the streets in urban centers but reso-
nated in the ancestral villages, for the
rebels had already won access to the
media of mass communication whose
owners, pillars of the oligarchy,
apparently thought the government had
lost its power and its will to govern.[6]

With the foregoing as a backdrop, Marcos called for
dedication, discipline and self-sacrifice, even as
he continued to lash out at the "privileged few":

I hear the strident screams of protest
against self-discipline from the gilded
throats of the powerful, of the privileged, of the opinion makers, of the
wealthy and the cynically articulate--
they who have yet to encounter the
implacable face of poverty. I hear the
well-meaning cries of the uninformed and
the naive. To them I address this plea.
Let them share the burden with the grace
and courage of the poor. Let them find
common cause with the people. Too long
have we blamed on one another the ills
of this nation; too long have we wasted
our opportunities by finding fault with
each other; as if this would cure our
ills and rectify our errors. Let us now
banish recrimination.[7]

If one must read significance into Marcos'
second inaugural, it is that by January 1970, he had
decided to part company with the oligarchy, and cast
his lot with the overwhelming majority of the
country's population--the underprivileged. Again,
Marcos:

The decade of the seventies cannot be
for the faint of heart and men of little
faith. It is not for the whiners, nor

57

for the timid. It is not a decade for
the time-wasters and the fault-finders.
It demands men and women of purpose and
dedication. . . Our society must chas-
tise the profligate rich who waste the
nation's substance--including its
foreign exchange reserves--in personal
comforts and luxuries.[8] [Emphasis mine.]

Marcos' "Fighting Faith": In Search of Revolutionary Theory

The gradual radicalization of Marcos could
very well have reached its zenith in 1971 with the
publication of a book entitled Today's Revolution:
Democracy,[9] described by Isabelo T. Crisostomo as
follows:

> a brilliant study of a revolution.
> Written in a lucid, forceful style in
> the tradition of classic revolutionary
> tracts, the book marks its author as a
> profound political thinker and advocate
> of a type of revolution remarkable for
> its uniqueness. . . President Marcos'
> theory is that democracy is a revolu-
> tionary doctrine, that it is a
> continuing revolution simply because
> democracy has not attained the full
> limits of its potentials.[10]

Crisostomo's generous assessment of Marcos' book was
shared by Richard Critchfield of the Washington Star
who called Today's Revolution a "brilliantly-
reasoned manifesto calling for a government-led,
non-violent revolution to fundamentally remake
Philippine society by redistributing its private
property and wealth."[11]
In his book Marcos suggested that the "democratic revolution [was] constitutional, liberal,
and nationalistic," and argued not only for the
dismantling and replacement of political and
economic institutions which have been proven to be
ineffective, but also for the re-orientation of the
people's values and modes of behavior.[12] According
to Marcos, the democratic revolution was "nationalist" in that "it was faithful to [Filipino]
historical aspirations and exerience, rooted, as it
were, in the historical demands of the people which
gained full expression in the Revolution of 1896."[13]

Drawing from the ideas of Mabini, Marcos underscored the dualist nature of radical change, which consisted of "internal" and "external" components.[14] Paraphrasing Mabini, Marcos wrote:

> in his [Mabini's] view, as in ours, the moral education of the people is a necessity, that should be established on firm foundations, thus purging themselves of their vices. The Revolution of 1896 was not merely a clash of arms leading to physical liberation; it was a cleansing experience, a moral act.[15]

In other words, before any meaningful change could occur, the people must rediscover their faith in themselves, and in their capacity for growth and greatness.

Marcos characterized the "political culture" of the Philippines as populist, personalist, and individualist," and he warned that while this orientation has worked well thus far, "there is no assurance that this will always be the case because of the modernizing--revolutionary--elements in a society which must, as a matter of course, revolutionize itself as an imperative of national development."[16] The political culture must therefore be modified so "the revolutionizing elements can be absorbed within the democratic system, thus achieving not only what is good in itself but also preventing the kind of revolution that is destructive of human freedom.[17]

Marcos posited that the Philippines is an "oligarchic society," where "the economic gap between the rich and the poor provides the wealthy few the opportunity of exercising undue influence on the political authority."[18] Clarifying what he meant by the term "oligarchy," Marcos admitted there were those among the wealthy who were "socially conscious enough to acknowledge the revolutionizing of the social order."[19] Only the "few who would promote their selfish interests through the indirect or irresponsible exercise of public and private power," were the enemies of the people, Marcos concluded.[20] The excesses of the "oligarchy" were further exacerbated by the:

> conservative ethic . . . that so long as one's fortune did not come from outright thievery and graphically illustrated exploitation, it merits, the honor and

respect of men. We confront here a
personal, simplistic ethic that is a
corruption of the individualism which
holds a man solely responsible for his
life. It does not take account of the
fact that no single individual can be
responsible for the social conditions
into which he is thrown by the accident
of birth. Thus this poverty of social
thought popularizes the notion that the
poor are poor because they are not
industrious or lucky.[21]

To redress the inequalities of the "oligarchic
society," Marcos proposed the "democratization" or
regulation of private property and wealth. According to Marcos, democratization simply meant the
'sharing' of private wealth with the entire society,
and this called for the regulation of property for
collective human ends."[22] Further elaborating on
the concept of "regulation," Marcos added as
follows:

In seeking to regulate private wealth
and property, I am mindful of the
oligarchic excesses caused by their
unbridled employment for selfish, not to
say undemocratic, ends. The exercise of
freedom should not, in principle, be
inhibited by economic status, but conditions of mass poverty can so preoccupy
human beings with the struggle for life
that they would compromise their liberties. It is in the search for an
optimum social and economic condition
for the masses that I commit myself to
the regulation of private wealth and
property.[23]

It is significant that Marcos rejected the outright
abolition of private property, suggesting that this
"will stultify private initiative and turn men into
a pure collective being."[24]
    In rejecting the outright abolition of private
property, Marcos took the view that the main concern
of a "progressive society" should not be to "dispos-
sess the rich in order to elevate the poor." For at
this stage, Marcos continued, "the elimination of
inequality does not mean that the dockworker is
going to reside in an expensive villa, dine on
china, ride in an air-conditioned Cadillac, send his

children to private school, and wear imported suits." Instead, the objective should be to secure economic equality for the poor defined in terms of "three square meals, a roof over [their] heads, efficient public transport, schooling for [their] children, and medical care for [their] families."[25]

Justifying the resort to violence to defend the state, Marcos contended that while "violence is never used in a liberal, or constitutional revolution," it may be resorted to in "self-defense," under the threat of the "liquidation of the government which is the immediate purpose of a Jacobin type of revolution."[26] He also maintained that democratic governments were just as susceptible to revolution as autocratic governments, but were more likely to be undisturbed by a revolution, granting a fairly sound economy and a willingness to be ruthless in the suppression of dissent.[27] If violence becomes imperative, the:

> military, although often criticized, is still looked up to by a majority of the people for the protection of their persons and properties. For the military is the strongest organization in such a situation. And since it is still the strongest armed force in such a society it cannot but triumph in this conflict of violence, brought about by the violent revolutionists.[28]

Marcos summarized his dissertation on "constitutional, liberal, and nationalist" democratic revolution by unveiling what he called his "Fighting Faith":

> I believe, therefore, in the necessity of Revolution as an instrument of individual and social change, and that its end is the advancement of human freedom.
> I believe that only reactionary resistance to social change will make a Jacobin, or armed revolution inevitable, but that in a democratic society, revolution is of necessity, constitutional, peaceful, and legal.
> I believe that while we have utilized the presidential powers to dismantle the violent revolution and its communist apparatus, we must not fail our people; we must replace the

61

violent revolution with the authentic
revolution--liberal, constitutional, and
peaceful.

I believe that even if a society
should be corrupted by an unjust
economic or social system, this can be
redressed by the people, directly or
indirectly, for democracy has the powers
of self-rejuvenation and self-
correction.

I believe that in this troubled
present, revolution is a fact, not
merely a potential threat, and that
if we value our sacred rights, our
cherished freedoms, we must wrest the
revolutionary leadership from those who
would, in the end, turn the democratic
revolution into a totalitarian regime.

I believe that in our precarious
democracy, which tends towards an
oligarchy because of the power of the
wealthy few over the impoverished many,
there remains a bright hope for a
radical and sweeping change without the
risk of violence. I do not believe that
violent revolution is either necessary
or effective in an existing democracy.

I believe that our realization of
the common peril, our complete understanding of our national condition, will
unite us in a democratic revolution that
will strengthen our democratic institutions and offer, finally, our citizens
the opportunity of making the most and
the best of themselves.

I believe that democracy is the
revolution, that it is today's
revolution.[29]

The Revolution as Reality: The Students
Take the Lead

In the student sector there was also talk
about revolution, but the rhetoric was in no way
similar to Marcos'. In fact the thrust of the
student activists' analysis was that the immediate
enemy was "the Marcos fascist government," and that
the twin evils which needed to be exorcised were
those of imperialism and feudalism. To the students, "revolution" became reality on 26 January

1970, less than one month after Marcos' second
inauguration, on the occasion of the customary
"State of the Nation" address before a joint session
of Congress.

Just who were these student rebels? Were the
student revolts of January, February, and March,
1970 and the sporadic uprisings of the ensuing
thirty months spontaneous phenomena? Or were these
calculated acts "to force the contradictions"
between the government and the students in order to
justify the subsequent adoption of draconian and
repressive measures, and finally, the declaration of
martial law itself? In any case, what was the
student movement like?

The Philippine Student Movement:
A Factious Interest Group

If the term "student movement" is taken to
mean a united and cohesive group motivated by a
common ideology or principle, then there was no
student movement in the Philippines prior to Proclamation 1081. What did exist was a proliferation
of discrete student organizations each committed to
its own set of goals, following its own separate
strategies to achieve those goals. As an interest
group, the student movement was badly fragmented and
therefore generally ineffectual. This was especially true in the early and middle 1960's, when the
older major student organizations such as the
Conference Delegates Association (CONDA), Student
Councils Association of the Philippines (SCAP),
National Union of Students of the Philippines
(NUSP), and the College Editors Guild (CEG) broke up
into opposing factions, with each faction holding
its own annual conference and electing its own set
of officers. For the most part, these organizations
were devoted to junketing, fund raising (with
politicians and big business being the most frequent
contributors), and other activities geared to
symbolically reinforce the status quo.

Because of the "corruption" and factionalism
of the CONDA, NUSP, and CEG, another national
student organization, the National Students League,
(NSL) was organized in 1964. Membership in the
National Students League was limited to state-owned
schools and was founded, oddly enough by a non-
student, Nemesio E. Prudente, who was president of
the state-owned Philippine College of Commerce.[30]
The NSL was basically reform oriented and intended

63

as a counterpoise to the sectarian National Union of Students of the Philippines.[31] By 1970, however, the National Students League had also disintegrated into no less than three factions.[32] Politically, the CONDA, SCAP, CEG, NUSP, and NSL were either right or left of center or centrist, with NUSP, with its sectarian orientation, perhaps the farthest to the right.

The Student Left: The Radicals Prevailed

Although relatively better organized and united, the student left was not exempt from the factionalization and bickering which afflicted the more conventional student organizations. Most of the leftist student organizations were either organized from, or based at, the Diliman campus of the University of the Philippines. The Kabataang Makabayan, (Patriotic Youth), Samahan ng Demokratikong Kabataan, (Democratic Youth Organization), and the Bertrand Russell Peace Foundation later expanded to the privately-owned Lyceum of the Philippines and the state-owned Philippine College of Commerce, both of whose campuses were located in downtown Manila.

The relative success of the KM and SDK in organizing in the Lyceum of the Philippines and the Philippine College of Commerce, was due to the tolerant attitude taken by the administrative authorities in both schools to "nationalist" organizations and to the transfer to these two schools of erstwhile activist leaders at the University of the Philippines either as teachers or students.[33] Moreover the Lyceum of the Philippines was owned by the Laurel family and the Philippine College of Commerce was under the leadership of Nemesio E. Prudente, one of the most articulate supporters of nationalist and activist student organizations among Philippine educators at that time.[34]

In addition to the KM, SDK, and the BRPF, there were other left-leaning student organizations. The Students Cultural Association of the University of the Philippines (SCAUP) was originally organized in 1962 to coordinate resistance to the "infringement on the academic freedom" of the university by the Committee on Anti-Filipino Activities (CAFA) of the now-defunct Philippine Congress in its investigation of alleged subversive activities at the University of the Philippines.[35] Also playing a major role in the politicization of the larger student body of the University of the Philippines, and the students of neighboring institutions were the UP Student Council and the official student publication of the University of the Philippines, the Philippine Collegian. Except for brief intervals in school year 1966-67, the UP Student Council and the Philippine Collegian were at the forefront of organizing, funding, and publicizing the cause of the student loft.[36]

The Ascendancy of the Student Left

The end of Marcos' first term in 1969 saw an increase in the mass appeal of the student left and some of their more popular demands, such as a reexamination of Philippine-American relations with the end-in-view of eliminating the inequalities in the relationship; meaningful and effective agrarian reforms; the diminution of the influence of vested interests in the formulation and conduct of public policy; and solving the problems of runaway inflation, unemployment and underemployment. As the political situation deteriorated, more and more students were drawn to the student left. By 1970, one prominent Filipino political scientist observed that the "prestige of the student movement [had] grown in its potential for either supporting or undermining the political leadership."[37]

A crisis atmosphere in the Greater Manila area was further aggravated by a widespread fear that Marcos wanted to "prolong his rule by manipulating the 1971 Constitutional Convention as he had exploited government resources to ensure his reelection."[38] Moreover, there were the disastrous after-effects of massive election spending; the tightening squeeze of controls on imports, credit, foreign exchange, and travel; personnel layoffs in government and in the private sector; and the sudden cutbacks in the budgets of state colleges and universities. There was a series of unusually violent demonstrations in the metropolitan area from January through March, and ensuing brutal government repression. All these helped to accelerate the politicization of heretofore indifferent or apolitical students not just in the greater Manila area but throughout the country, especially in central and northern Luzon, the Bicol region and western Visayas.

It was primarily this climate of crisis and the perception of a common foe, rather than ideology, that galvanized the fragmented and amorphous student left. Seymour Martin Lipset put it as follows:

> On a comparative level, it is clear that the extent of potential concern among students in different countries is in part a function of the degree of tension in the larger polity. In societies that have a stable democratic order with legitimate government and opposition . . . students may be disproportionately to the left of non-students of a similar strata, but on the whole they exhibit much less interest in politics and give less support to extremist groups than do students in those nations that have unstable patterns.[39]

In a comparative context, the pattern of the Philippine students' rapid politicization was in many ways similar to the "participation explosion" among Indonesian university students after the attempted Communist coup of 30 September-1 October 1965.[40] Before the attempted coup and the so called "30th of September Movement," Indonesian students were generally apolitical, tending to shun overt political activity especially where such activity involved physical risks.

This disinterest in leftist political activity was in fact found by Robert O. Tilman to be the norm among Filipino students in Cebu City in eastern Visayas in early 1970.[41] Tilman found that while the "university students of [the] area . . . [were] politically discontented and frustrated," the fact is that "the many universities outside of the Manila metropolitan area have been quiet, and non-Manila students have shown little revolutionary fervor thus far."[42] Tilman also concluded that "Filipino students in Cebu view[ed] themselves as potential reformers, not revolutionaries. Discontent with the basic structures of Philippine politics [was] fairly low, and support for the idea of democracy [was] impressively strong."[43]

The violent student demonstrations of 26 and 30 January 1970, the latter resulting in the loss of six student lives--the first deaths of their kind Philippine history--and the brutal government repression that followed, served to unite, even if only temporarily, the Beijing-oriented Kabataang Makabayan (Patriotic Youth) under the leadership of Jose Ma. Sison, Nilo Tayag and Monico Atienza, and the Samahan ng Demokratikong Kabataan (Union of Democratic Youth) led by Sixto Carlos, Jr. and Gary B. Olivar; with the Moscow-oriented Bertrand Russell Peace Foundation led by Professor Francisco Nemenzo, Jr., the SCAUP, and a peasant-based organization called the Malayang Pagkakaisa ng Kabataang Pilipino (Free Filipino Youth Union) led by Ernesto Macahiya and Ruben D. Torres, under an umbrella organization called the Movement for Democratic Philippines (MDP) with Nelson A. Navarro a former editor of the <u>Philippine Collegian</u>, as its secretary-general and spokesman. The other elements in the MDP were a faction of the now-fragmented National Students League, and the Samahang Molabe (Molabe Organization) of the Philippine College of Commerce, a Moscow-oriented organization founded by Professor Teodosio A. Lansang, a Filipino expatriate in the Soviet Union for more than three decades before he was allowed to return home by President Marcos in 1967. The new battle cry was <u>makibaka</u>, <u>huwag matakot</u> (fight, dare to struggle, fear no sacrifice) and the common objective was the ouster of the Marcos "fascist" government.

As the students became more violent and firmer in their demands, so too did the Marcos administration respond with more repression and brutality. When Marcos proclaimed limited martial law on 21 August 1971, suspended the privilege of the writ of habeas corpus and ordered the arrest and incarceration of student leaders, educators, and other critics of the administration, the students remained adamant.[44] Joined by civic groups and prominent politicians and civil libertarians such as former senator Jose W. Diokno[45] the students succeeded in bringing pressure on Marcos until he lifted the martial law proclamation and ordered the release of most of the political detainees.[46]

The Strategy of the Student Left Failed

Violent student protest escalated after 26 January 1970 and included such incidents as the Siege of Malacanang Palace, the "Battle of Mendiola" (which resulted in six student deaths, scores of injured and massive destruction of property), and the takeover of the University of the Philippines' Diliman campus. These evidently were intended by the student left to force the Marcos regime into escalating its level of brutality, thus justifying charges of fascism and politicizing more people. The strategy of forcing the government's hand meant that the extremists, the proverbial "hotheads" and "adventurists" had taken over the leadership of the movement. The amateurish and brief takeover of the University of the Philippines' Diliman campus by the student rebels, during which they fought army helicopters with fire-crackers and harmless warning flares, would have looked ludicruous had it not been for extensive damage to university property.

In retrospect, the adventurism of the student left and the triumph of the extremists, doomed the "student revolt." Instead of enhancing their image in the eyes of the public, the strategy of confrontation seemed to have had the opposite effect of alienating the general public. The irony of the whole situation was that the government did respond as the student leftist extremists hoped--with guns, truncheons, and brutality. But the extremists who chanted "revolution now" and hoped that the conduct of the military would inspire a spontaneous response from the student left's natural allies--the masses of peasants and workers--overestimated the popularity of their cause. Conversely, they underestimated the determination of Marcos to stay in power by proclaiming absolute martial law and curtailing all civil liberties.

Absolute Martial Law:
How the Decision was Made

As it turned out, the declaration of limited martial law (Proclamation No. 889) on 21 August 1971, and the affirmation of its constitutionality by the Supreme Court proved to be a decisive factor in the issuance of Proclamation No. 1081.[47] Ironically, the experience derived from Proclamation No. 889 convinced Marcos that half-way measures did not suffice; at the same time those elements which thought the time was ripe for a bloody revolution apparently interpreted Marcos' lifting of limited martial law on 11 January 1972, as a sign of weakness. Moreover, the Supreme Court's decision gave Marcos an effective weapon against well-meaning civil libertarians and the mass media who charged that Proclamation No. 889 had no basis in law and that it constituted an abuse of executive authority.

Two months after the lifting of limited martial law and the restoration of the privilege of the writ of habeas corpus, a rash of new bombings rocked the metropolitan area.[48] Three months later, on 18 June, the Philippine Constabulary obtained possession of an alleged blueprint of the planned revolutionary activities of the Communist Party of the Philippines (CPP). If authentic, the document, entitled "Regional Program of Action 1972," seemed to identify the bombings in the metropolitan Manila area as parts of a well-coordinated revolutionary offensive. The alleged "Regional Program of Action 1972" read in full as follows:

The following Regional Program of Action for 1972 is prepared to be carried out as part of the overall plan of the [Communist] party to foment discontent and precipitate the tide of nationwide mass revolution. The fascist Marcos and his reactionary members of Congress [are] expected to prepare themselves for the 1973 [election] hence:

January-June

1. Intensify recruitment of new party members especially from the workers-farmers class. Cadres are being trained in order to organize the different regional bureaus. These bureaus must concentrate on mass action and organization to promote advancement of the mass revolutionary movement. Reference is made to the <u>Borador ng Programa sa Pagkilos at Ulat ng Panlipunang Pagsisiyasat</u> as approved by the Central Committee.
2. Recruit and train armed city partisans and urban guerrillas and organize them into units under Party cadres and activists of mass organizations. These units must undergo specialized training on explosives and demolition and other forms of sabotage.

69

3. Intensify recruitment and train-
    ing of new members for the New
    People's Army in preparation for
    limited offensive in selected
    areas in the regions.
4. Support a more aggressive pro-
    gram of agitation and propaganda
    against the reactionary armed
    forces and against the Consti-
    tutional Convention.

July-August

During this period the party expects
the puppet Marcos government to allow
increase in bus rates thus aggravating
further the plight of students, workers
and the farmers.

1. All Regional Party Committees
    must plan for a general strike
    movement. The Regional Opera-
    tional Commands must plan for
    armed support if the fascist
    armed forces of Marcos will try
    to intimidate the oppressed
    Filipino masses.
2. Conduct sabotage against
    schools, colleges, and univer-
    sities hiking tuition fees.
3. Conduct sabotage and agitation
    against puppet judges and courts
    hearing cases against top party
    leaders.
4. Create regional chaos and dis-
    order to dramatize the inability
    of the fascist Marcos government
    to keep and maintain peace and
    order through:
    a) Robbery and hold-up of
        banks controlled by
        American imperialists
        and those belonging to
        the enemies of the
        people.
    b) Attack military camps,
        US bases, and towns.

September-October

Increase intensity of violence, disorder and confusion:

1. Intensify sabotage and bombing of government buildings and embassies and other utilities:
   a) Congress
   b) Supreme Court
   c) Con Con
   d) City Hall
   e) US Embassy
   f) Facilities of US Bases
   g) Provincial Capitols
   h) Power Plants
   i) PLDT
   j) Radio Stations
2. Sporadic attacks on camps, towns and cities.
3. Assassinate high government officials of Congress, Judiciary, Con Con [Constitutional Convention] and private individuals sympathetic to puppet Marcos.
4. Establish provisional revolutionary government in towns and cities with the support of the masses.
5. With the sympathetic support of our allies, establish provisional provincial revolutionary governments.

CENTRAL COMMITTEE,
COMMUNIST PARTY
OF THE PHILIPPINES

The military authorities linked the Regional Program to the seizure at Digoyo Point, Palanan, Isabela, of a substantial quantity of weapons, including thirty-five hundred M-14 rifles, several dozen 40-millimeter rocket launchers (reportedly Chinese copies of a Russian prototype rocket launcher), large quantities of 30-millimeter rockets and ammunition and other combat paraphernalia. The government also claimed that the New People's Army (NPA), the military arm of the revitalized Communist Party of the Philippines, had expanded its total strength from 6,500 on 1 January to approximately

7,900 on 31 July, and had increased its troop
strength by more than one hundred percent in just
six months--from 560 to 1,028--thereby posing a
direct military threat.

A different view was taken by the International Institute for Strategic Studies which said
in its Strategic Study, 1972:

> The NPA in rural Luzon may also be
> growing in confidence and size;
> President Marcos claimed in September
> that its active strength was now 7,900
> with 1,028 regulars and 1,800 in combat
> support. But the NPA, whose scope is
> still constricted within ethnic and
> religious boundaries, has yet to deny
> any area, even within Luzon, to the
> security forces. Its style suggests a
> disciplined gradualism, and it may well
> consider itself to be still in the early
> stages of development as an insurgent
> force, primarily concerned to mobilize
> popular support.[49]

A similarly skeptical view was taken by a
number of Filipino and foreign observers who claimed
that the bombings blamed by Marcos on the "subversives" and "Maoists" were actually carried out by
Marcos' operatives. Even the "ambush" of National
Defense Secretary Juan Ponce Enrile on 22 September
1972 (the proverbial "last straw" that triggered the
implementation of Proclamation No. 1081)[50] was
according to a long-time student of Philippine
politics, "created" by Marcos to "permit a more
forceful intervention while he still possessed the
precious advantage of incumbency."[51]
Whatever the truth about the alleged Communist
Party of the Philippines' "Regional Program 1972"
and the seriousness of the threat posed by the New
People's Army to the security of the Republic,
Marcos' decision, even if motivated by other than
noble purposes, did stabilize peace and order which
had by then reached a new nadir. One pro-Marcos
commentator described the situation in August and
September as follows:

> Confusion and anarchy assumed apoca-
> lyptic proportions. The media and the
> radicals accused the government of
> instigating the bombings; the govern-
> ment, on the other hand, insisted that

the terrorist acts were the work of subversives. It was impossible to distinguish truth from falsehood. . . . Marcos had to act--and act fast.[52]

Proclamation No. 1081: Its Thrust and Rationale

Although Proclamation No. 1081 was signed on 21 September its contents were not announced to the public until approximately 7:15 p.m. on 23 September a Saturday. The delay was deliberate and intended to give the military authorities time and an advantage of surprise in making arrests, presumably, with the least possible publicity. The delayed release of Proclamation No. 1081 did catch a lot of those arrested by surprise, especially since many of the arrests were made in the dead of night and carried out with military precision, replete with armored cars and machine guns.[53]

In his formal statement announcing Proclamation No. 1081, Marcos assured the people the "proclamation of martial law [was] not a military takeover;" that it would be "implemented by the military authorities to protect the Republic of the Philippines and . . . democracy."[54] Marcos said the legal basis of Proclamation No. 1081 was Article VII, section 10, paragraph 2 of the 1935 Constitution.[55] Officials and employees of the national and local governments would remain in office and "continue to discharge their duties as before within the limits of the situation," as clarified by "subsequent orders which shall be given wide publicity."

To minimize fears about the military establishment's emergence as the most dominant and possibly even uncontrollable force in the "New Society," Marcos announced that he had directed "the organization of a military commission to investigate, try, and punish all military offenders immediately." As Marcos put it, "more than any other man, the soldier must set the standard of nobility."

Alluding to the "oligarchs" and "influence peddlers" in previous administrations, Marcos warned that "no man who claims to be a good friend, relative or ally [should] presume to seek license because of [the] relationship . . . if he offends the New Society, he shall be punished like the rest." The full force of martial law, Marcos went on, would be unleashed on those "who have actively participated in the conspiracy and in operations to overthrow the duly constituted government of

73

the Republic of the Philippines by violence."
Conversely, those "who [have] nothing whatsoever
to do with such conspiracy and operations to
overthrow the Republic of the Philippines [have]
nothing to fear."

On the question of the press, Marcos announced
the imposition of censorship on all mass media and
all "other means of dissemination of information as
well as all public utilities," and a massive crack-
down on loose and illegal firearms. The carrying of
firearms "outside residences without the permission
of the Armed Forces of the Philippines," Marcos
warned, "will be punishable with death." Travel
abroad by Filipinos except "those [on] official
missions" was also "temporarily suspended;" and
public gatherings proscribed.

In the pursuit of societal and political
reforms, Marcos said that he would shortly "issue
all the orders which would attain reforms in . . .
society." These contemplated reforms included
"the proclamation of land reform all over the
Philippines, the reorganization of the government,
new rules of conduct for the civil service, the
removal of corrupt and inefficient public officials
and their replacement and the breaking up of
criminal syndicates."

The remainder of the statement was devoted to
a documentation of what was claimed as a "state of
rebellion . . . in the Philippines." Marcos invoked
the decision of the Supreme Court in Lansang (see
note 47, supra) to support his claim that a state of
rebellion existed. "The ordinary man in the streets
of our cities know it, the peasants and the laborers
know it . . . industrialists know it . . . so do the
government functionary . . . they have all been
affected by it," Marcos said.

Going into specifics to prove his contention
that there was an ongoing "state of rebellion,"
Marcos cited once again the rash of bombings,
robberies, gunrunning, and other such crimes during
most of 1971 and 1972 and the "battles that [were]
going on between the elements of the Armed Forces of
the Philippines and the subversives in the island of
Luzon at Isabela, Zambales, Tarlac, Camarines Sur,
Quezon; and in the island of Mindanao at Lanao del
Sur, Lanao del Norte, Zamboanga del Sur, and
Cotabato." Marcos also called attention to the
supposedly phenomenal increase in the size of the
membership of the CPP and in the strength of the
CPP's military arm, the NPA, as well as the expansion of "communist front organizations" like the

74

Kabataang Makabayan ("Patriotic Youth") and the Samahan ng Demokratikong Kabataan ("Union of Democratic Youth").

Another item cited by Marcos as proof of a state of rebellion was the so called M/V Karagatan or "Palanan Incident" off the coast of Palanan, Isabela in Northern Luzon on 4 and 5 July, when a large cache of weapons and assorted equipment supposedly intended for the NPA was intercepted and recovered by the Armed Forces of the Philippines. Marcos suggested that the M/V Karagatan incident proved: "(1) that the claim of the New People's Army that they are well-funded has basis in fact; (2) that they now have sources of funds and equipment not only inside the Philippines but also outside the country; and (3) that the Communist Party and the New People's Army [were] capable of landing armaments, military equipment and even personnel in many points off the long seacoast of the Philippines which is twice the seacoast of the United States."

Concluding his statement, Marcos reminded the people that he proclaimed martial law only after all other measures had failed; that the decision was "not a precipitate" one and that he had "weighed all the factors" involved. Then in an almost concilia-tory tone he declared:

> All other recourses have been unavail-ing. You are all witnesses to these. So we have fallen on our last line of defense.
>
> You are witnesses to the patience that we have shown in the face of provocation. In the face of abuse and license we have used persuasion. Now the limit has been reached. We are against the wall. We must now defend the Republic with the stronger powers of the Constitution.
>
> To those guilty of treason, insur-rection, rebellion, it may pose a grave danger. But to the citizenry whose primary concern is to be left alone to pursue their lawful activities, this is the guaranty of that freedom.
>
> All that we do is for the Republic and for you. Rest assured we will continue to do so.
>
> I have prayed to God for guidance. Let us all continue to do so. I am confident that with God's help we will

attain our dream of a reformed society,
a new and brighter world.

As stated in Proclamation No. 1081 the
imposition of martial law was not only to "save the
Republic" but also to build a "new society."   To
"save the Republic," Marcos used   the Armed Forces
of the Philippines to destroy the New People's Army
in Luzon and the Visayas and the Moro Bangsa Army in
Mindanao and Sulu.   The apparent logic behind
Marcos' overall plan was that with the dissident
military threat gone, he would then be able to
concentrate upon building a "new society," conceivably one along the lines of Walter Lippmann's
"liberal state," a model Marcos repeatedly alluded
to in Today's Revolution[56].   The reformation of
society would be much easier and less cumbersome
with the elimination of former institutionalized
sources of opposition--Congress, the mass media,
student activists, and trade unions--and with the
executive as the sole locus of power.

Summary

By 1965, the year he began his first term as
president, Marcos had begun to evolve a more-or-less
coherent body of "revolutionary" ideas.   Even as he
called for radical change, however, Marcos continued
to curry favor with the economic elite.   Being a
pragmatic politician, Marcos realized he needed the
financial suport of the wealthy families--the
Lopezes, Zobel de Ayalas, Elizaldes, Jacintos, and
the Roxas-Chuas--if he wanted to be reelected
president.   Because of Marcos' continued and open
alliance with the economic elite then, his repeated
calls for the restructuring of society were never
taken seriously, especially by militant students,
peasants, workers, and intellectuals.

An unprecedented second term in 1969 (and by
an overwhelming mandate at that) seemed to
strengthen Marcos' position as well as his "radical"
rhetoric.   To a large extent, the escalation of
Marcos' denunciations of the "privileged few" was
influenced by what had, by that time, emerged as a
nascent but articulate anti-Marcos student movement.
For Marcos knew that if he did not act decisively
soon enough, the student-worker-peasant alliance
could very well wrest the initiative away from him
and destroy whatever credibility he still had.

When student demonstrations became violent in
early 1970, Marcos tried to negotiate with the
students. Sensing victory, the students became even
more daring until it was apparent that the leadership of the student movement had been taken over by
revolutionary extremists. What the students failed
to realize was that Marcos was only feigning defeat,
dissembling, and biding his time, waiting for the
opportune moment to strike back. Ironically, the
students provided Marcos with the justification he
needed to resort to repressive measures, culminating
in the proclamation of limited martial law on 21
August 1971. Proclamation No. 889 which had
declared martial law and suspended the writ of
habeas corpus in thirteen provinces including the
Greater Manila area, turned out to be a "dress
rehearsal," for Proclamation No. 1081. The
subsequent affirmation by the Supreme Court of the
constitutionality of Proclamation No. 889 rendered
Marcos' position even more solid.

Also by 1971, Marcos had firmed up a rather
ecclectic theory of "revolutionary change." Marcos'
"revolution" was supposedly "non-violent" (in
contrast to a Jacobin-type revolution); "nationalist," or rooted in the history and traditions of the
Filipino people; and "constitutional," or sanctioned
by the fundamental law itself. Democracy is by its
very nature revolutionary, according to Marcos, and
will be so, for as long as democracy's full potentials have not been achieved.

Marcos then proceeded to identify the
"oligarchs" as the enemy of the people, and the
"oligarchic society" as the nation's most serious
malady. The unbridled use of wealth and influence
to pervert the political authority, and enrichment
at the expense of the poor, was a version of a "new
barbarism," according to Marcos. In order for a
just society to develop, the oligarchy must be
dismantled and private wealth "democratized" and
regulated, but not taken over, by the state. For
their part, the poor must purge themselves of
corrupt ways and modes of thinking, because the
democratic revolution could only come to a successful denouement if it was preceded by an "internal
revolution."

If one took Marcos' rationale on its face
value, the immediate cause of Proclamation No. 1081
and the radical restructuring of Philippine government and politics was an alleged communist-led
conspiracy to overthrow the duly-constituted government. The government simply acted in self defense.

The larger and more deep-seated cause was the
iniquitous social and political structure and
martial law was merely a vehicle to redress
inequities and bring about the creation of a
"progressive and just society." The opposition's
view on the other hand, held that martial law was
declared in order to suppress the people's legitimate grievances against the government, to sabotage
the authentic democratic revolution, and to
perpetuate Marcos and his family in power, over and
beyond what was constitutionally permissible.
Instead of creating a "just society" Marcos had
created a one-man dictatorship, or as one writer
chose to call it, a "proscribed hothouse apery of a
revolution."

Chapter 5

THE AFTERMATH OF CHANGE

The advent of the New Society radically reshaped the governmental structure of the Philippines. It transformed a presidential system closely patterned after that of the United States which functioned under the principle of separation of powers into a virtual one-man rule or as Marcos preferred to call it, "constitutional authoritarianism."[1] As a consequence of this transformation, congress--heretofore a coequal branch of the presidency--was abolished, and the judiciary especially the Supreme Court, reduced to a subordinate status, apparently to provide legitimacy to the edicts and proclamations of the New Society.[2] In order to better understand the scope of the changes wrought by Marcos, it is instructive to review the structure of government before martial law.

Government Before Martial Law

When the Philippine founding fathers met to frame the 1935 Constitution as authorized by the Tydings-McDuffie Act, they decided to pattern the government of the future Republic of the Philippines after that of the United States. The founding fathers adopted a unitary presidential system consisting of three coequal branches: the presidency, congress, and the judiciary, each with its own set of primary powers and functions, and each with the ability and power to check and balance the other.

The National Government

The president and vice-president were elected by direct popular vote and served for four years at a time. The presidential term was specifically limited to not more than two consecutive four-year terms or a maximum of eight years.[3] The legislative branch, like its American counterpart, was bicameral with the number of congressional seats determined on the basis of the principle of proportional representation and the number of senatorial seats fixed at twenty-four.[4] Congressmen served for four years with no limits to the number of times they were eligible to seek reelection, while senators served six-year terms. Senatorial elections were held biennially. As in the United States, the terms of Philippine senators were staggered and the Philippine Senate, also like the American Senate, was a continuing body with a third of the Senate's membership up for election every two years.

Judicial power was vested in "one Supreme Court and in such inferior courts as may be established by law."[5] Examples of the "inferior courts," the workhorses of the judicial system, referred to in Article VIII were the Court of Appeals (an intermediate appellate court roughly similar to the thirteen appellate courts in the American federal judiciary), the Courts of First Instance (again, roughly the equivalent of the ninety-five federal district courts in the United States). All judges were appointed by the president of the Philippines with the "consent" of the Commission on Appointments, a bicameral and bipartisan committee of the legislative branch. They served during "good behavior" until the age of seventy years. In addition to the Supreme Court, Court of Appeals, and the Courts of First Instance, there were specialized courts such as the Court of Agrarian Relations, Juvenile and Family Relations Court, and numerous municipal and city courts of specialized or lesser jurisdiction.

Elections

Elections were always hotly and keenly contested. While outside observers have often described Philippine elections as violent, disorganized, and characterized by fraud and irregularities, elections have generally served not only as a means for selecting government officials but also, and perhaps more importantly, as safety valves for the Filipino's proverbial volatile temper.[6] Moreover, election irregularities (except perhaps during the Quirino-Laurel presidential contest in 1950) have tended to be the exception rather than the rule, and were quite often sensationalized by a licentious Philippine press. Whether or not Filipinos voted according to "issue orientation" more than "candidate orientation" or "party identification,"[7] it cannot be denied that Filipinos on the average, exhibited a higher degree of politicization than their American counterparts.[8] Voters especially during presidential elections usually trooped to the polls in appreciable numbers. The great majority of the people tended to be active "spectators" if not themselves "gladiators." The percentage of "apathetics" was considerably less than the thirty-three per cent Lester W. Milbrath found in his study of political participation in the United States.[9]

Political Parties

The Philippines, like the United States, adhered to a two-party system. The two dominant parties were the Nacionalista and Liberal, with the latter starting as a splinter group of the Nacionalista party. Critics of the two parties have often pointed out that the so called two-party system was "artificial," that the Liberal and Nacionalista parties were in reality factions of one party and were alike in every respect.[10] Even within the parties, factionalization was rampant. It was not unusual especially in the context of the Philippines' personalistic value system for members of one party to jump to the opposition party for expediency or "reasons of principle." Both Magsaysay and Marcos were members of the Liberal party before the elections but ran as official standard-bearers of the Nacionalista party. Third parties, although frequently organized during the twenty-six years prior to the declaration of martial law, never quite made it although they tended to perform very well in the urban areas, especially in the metropolitan Manila area.[11]

With the American-style presidential system dismantled, political parties and public gatherings outlawed, and free and open biennial elections supplanted by occasional national referenda through the so-called barangays (citizen assemblies), what did the New Society governmental structure look like? What specific changes and governmental "reforms" were instituted? Was the 1973 Constitution ever really operational? What were the disparities, if any, between what was stated in various provi-

81

sions of the 1973 Constitution and what obtained in fact?

Government Under Martial Law

In analyzing the structure of government under the New Society one has to distinguish between what was formally stated in the new Constitution and what actually obtained in practice. This is necessary in light of the fact that while the new Constitution (which was supposed to have been ratified on 17 January 1973 and was therefore operational) provided for a parliamentary system of government[12] with the locus of power being the National Assembly,[13] no "permanent" parliament was constituted until 1981, and President Marcos ruled the country from 1972, through 1981 primarily by proclamation, edict, and decree. A paradox in the governmental structure of the New Society was that it functioned basically through the various offices and departments of the old bureaucracy.

The ten executive departments of the Second Philippine Republic[14] remained basically the same with the addition of a few constitutional commissions and councils,[15] a central economic planning body (the National Economic Development Authority), and six other departments: Agrarian Reforms, Tourism, Industry, Natural Resources, Local Government and Community Development, and Public Information. The Department of Local Government and Community Development was recast from the old Office of Presidential Assistant on Community Development (PACD) while the Department of Public Information was an expanded version of the Office of Press Secretary (a cabinet-level post without portfolio in the Second Philippine Republic). The Department of Natural Resources used to be part of the Department of Agriculture; the Department of Industry in like manner used to be part of the Department of Commerce. The branches of the government which were substantially altered were the judiciary and of course, the Department of National Defense. These two governmental units which were central to the New Society and highly visible will be examined thoroughly later on.

The 1973 Constitution

The 1973 Constitution instituted numerous and radical changes not just in the structure of government but also in the country's underlying political principles. Article II (Declaration of Principles and State Policies), for instance, spelled out some traditionally-held democratic principles, for example, the subordination of the military to civilian authority, and added new ones such as the primacy and importance of the family as a basic social institution. Specifically, the new or modified provisions were as follows:

> Section 4--The state shall strengthen the family as a basic social institution. The natural right and duty of parents in the rearing of the youth for civic efficiency and the development of moral character shall receive the aid and support of the Government.
>
> Section 6--The State shall promote social justice to ensure the dignity welfare, and security of all people. Towards this end, the State shall regulate the acquisition, ownership, use, enjoyment and disposition of private property, and equitably diffuse property ownership and profits.
>
> Section 8--Civilian authority is at all times supreme over the military.
>
> Section 9--The State shall afford protection to labor, promote full employment and equality in employment, ensure equal work opportunities regardless of sex, race, or creed, and regulate the relations between workers and employers. The State shall assure the rights of workers to self-organization, collective bargaining, security of tenure, and just and humane conditions of work. The State may provide for compulsory arbitration.
>
> Section 10--The State shall guarantee and promote the autonomy of local government units, especially the barrio, to ensure their fullest development as self-reliant communities.[16]

Section 6 and Section 9 reflected the 1970 Constitutional Convention's new level of social consciousness and identification with the plight of the working man while Section 4 served to make the preservation and strengthening of the Filipino family a governmental concern.

The Bill of Rights also expanded and clarified heretofore ambiguous and broad guarantees. An example of the latter was Section 4, sub-sections 1 and 2 of Article IV which provided as follows:

> Section 4 (1)--The privacy of communication and correspondence shall be inviolable except upon lawful order of the court, or when public safety and order require otherwise.
> (2)--Any evidence obtained in violation of this or the preceding section shall be inadmissible for any purpose in any proceeding.

Section 4, particularly sub-section 2, incorporated some of the key developments in jurisprudence on the Fourth Amendment (of the American Constitution) including the United States Supreme Court's rulings in Mapp v. Ohio (367 U.S. 643, 1961) and Katz v. United States (389 U.S. 347, 1967).

An entirely new provisionwas Article V, "Duties and Obligations of Citizens." Among some of the more interesting items were the following: the obligation of an individual to exercise his rights "responsibly and with due regard for the rights of others;"[17] the "duty of every citizen to engage in gainful work [and] to assure himself and his family life worthy of human dignity;"[18] and the "obligation of every citizen qualified to vote to register and cast his vote."[19] Also new was the provision (Article VI, Section 1) on suffrage which lowered the voting age to eighteen and abolished the literacy requirement, a prerequisite to voter registration since 1946. It is significant to note that Marcos originally opposed the lowering of the voting age then turned around to support it when it became apparent that the idea had widespread support not just in the Constitutional Convention but among the people.[20]

As a consequence of the shift to a parliamentary system, the position of president was downgraded to a mere symbolic role.[21] The powers of the president were to (1) "address the National Assembly at the opening of its regular session"; (2) "proclaim the election of the Prime Minister"; (3) "dissolve the National Assembly and call for a general election as provided (for)"; (4) "accept the resignation of the Cabinet as provided (for)"; (5) "attest to the appointment or cessation from office of members of the Cabinet, and of other officers as may be provided by law"; (6) "appoint all officers and employees in his office in accordance with the Civil Service Law"; and (7) "perform such other duties and functions of state as may be provided by law."[22]

As was the case with other parliamentary systems, the locus of power in the New Society was the unicameral National Assembly. The term of office of members of the National Assembly was fixed at six years (Article VIII, Section 3, sub-section 1); membership was restricted to natural-born Filipinos (Article VIII, Section 4), an "improvement" over a similar provision in the 1935 Constitution which specified that only natural-born Filipinos were eligible to serve in either the Senate or the House of Representatives. This is in contrast to the United States Constitution which allows other than natural-born citizens to serve in the United States Congress.

The National Assembly could withdraw its confidence from the Prime Minister by simply electing a successor by a majority vote (Article VIII, Section 13, sub-section 1). It also had the power to ratify treaties, with such ratification being a prerequisite to the treaty's becoming effective (Article VIII, Section 14, sub-section 1). Still in the area of foreign policy, it had the "sole power to declare the existence of a state of war," with such action requiring the two-thirds vote of all of the National Assembly's members (Article VIII, Section 14, sub-section 2). The rest of Article VIII defined the various steps involved in the legislative process, and other related organizational details. One interesting provision was Section 20, sub-section 2, which gave the Prime Minister the "item veto" in respect to "an appropriation, revenue, or tarriff," an enlargement of a similar provision (Article VI, Section 20, sub-section 2) of the 1935 Constitution.[23]

The provisions on the judiciary--in so far as the role of the Supreme Court relative to the National Assembly, the cabinet, and the entire judicial system, was concerned--remained basically the same. A major change in the structure of the judiciary was the enlargement of the Supreme Court from eleven (Article VIII, Section 5 of the 1935 Constitution) to fifteen. Article X Section 2, sub-section 1, of the 1973 Constitution provided that "the Supreme Court shall be composed of a chief justice and fourteen associate judges." The court could function as one body, en banc, or in two divisions. The nature of the jurisdiction of the Supreme Court--the types of cases which it could review and the procedure for appeals to it--were the same as those in the 1935 Constitution.

Another entirely new provision was Article XI (Local Government) which seemed to reflect a tendency toward decentralization of government, a perennial item in the platforms of the Liberal and Progressive parties in the mid-and late 1960's.[24] The two most important sections of Article XI seemed to be Sections 2 and 3 which stated as follows:

> Section 2--The National Assembly shall enact a local government code which may not thereafter be amended except by a majority vote of all its Members, defining a more responsive and accountable local government structure with an effective system of recall, allocating upon the different local government units their powers, responsibilities and resources, and providing for their qualifications, election and removal, term, salaries, powers, functions, and duties of local officials, and all other matters relating to the organization and operation of the local units. However, any change in the existing form of local government shall not take effect until ratified by a majority of the votes cast in a plebiscite called for the purpose.
>
> Section 3--No province, city, municipality, or barrio may be created, divided, merged, abolished, or its boundary substantially altered, except in accordance with the criteria established in the local government code, and subject to the approval by a majority of the votes cast in a plebiscite in the unit or units affected.

Article XI strengthened local governments in relation to the national government and afforded them a greater measure of authority and autonomy. It is significant that under the Second Philippine Republic, local government autonomy (or whatever local government autonomy there was) came as a

86

result of specific statutory enactments, not from an express constitutional provision.

The "new morality" in politics or, in any case, an apparent perception of it by the majority of the delegates, could very well have been behind Article XIII (Accountability of Public Officers). Through the years, politicians in the Philippines have gained international notoriety for their alleged propensity toward graft and corruption; indeed it will be recalled that one of the major justifications offered by President Marcos to justify the declaration of martial law was the "necessity" of putting an end to corruption in public office. The adoption of Article XIII, however, may have also been influenced by two internal and external events, the "payola" scandal which rocked the Constitutional Convention in mid-1972, and the "Watergate crisis" in the United States.[25] Both events were widely publicized in the Philippines and while the true extent of the Watergate controversy had not yet been fully grasped at the time, it is reasonable to assume that most of the delegates were able to apprecate its implications. Article XIII, Section 1 set the tone of the "new morality," thus:

> Public office is a public trust. Public officers and employees shall serve with the highest degree of responsibility, integrity, loyalty, and efficiency, and shall remain accountable to the people.

It is equally noteworthy that "graft and corruption" was specifically listed as one of the grounds for the impeachment of the president, members of the Supreme Court, and members of constitutional commissions.[26] This contrasted with the counterpart provision in the 1935 Constitution (Article IX, Section 1) which simply listed "culpable violation of the Constitution, treason, bribery or other high crimes" as grounds for impeachment.

An even more novel feature incorporated under Article XIII was the creation of a special court called Sandiganbayan (roughly translated, "people's refuge" or "people's tribunal") which "shall have jurisdiction over criminal and civil cases involving graft and corrupt practices and such other offenses committed by public officers and employees, including those in government-owned or controlled corporations."[27] To receive and investigate complaints of possible graft and corruption and

87

other related problems, the National Assembly was directed to create "an office of the Ombudsman, to be known as _Tanodbayan_, (roughly translated, "people's sentinel") which shall receive and investigate complaints relative to public office . . . make appropriate recommendations, and in case of failure of justice as defined by law, file and prosecute the corresponding criminal, civil, or administrative case before the proper court or body."[28]

As any student of contemporary Philippine politics and history will readily recall, one of the most controversial political issues of the 1950s and 1960s was the question of economic independence; whether foreign nationals, especially Americans, would be eligible to own property, operate vital public utilities, or engage in the exploration and development of natural resources. The Parity Amendment to the 1935 Constitution gave American citizens and corporations the right not only to own property, explore and develop natural resources, and operate vital public utilities, but also to engage in business and compete with Filipino entrepreneurs.[29]

The resurgence of Filipino nationalism in the mid-1960's created widespread awareness of the issue of economic independence. It was this awareness and the presence in the 1973 Constitutional Convention of such well-known nationalists as Jesus G. Barrera, Salvador Araneta, and E. Voltaire Garcia II, which undoubtedly led to the inclusion of a new concept in Philippine constitutionalism, a separate provision (Article XIV) on "The National Economy and Patrimony of the Nation."

Article XIV, Section 2 empowered the state to prohibit or regulate "private monopolies", while Section 3 "reserve[d] to citizens of the Philippines or to corporations or associations wholly owned by such citizens, certain traditional areas of investments when the national interest so dictate[d]." Reflecting a position diametrically opposed to the spirit which led to the passage and ratification of the Parity Amendment in 1947, the 1973 Constitution explicitly prohibited the granting of any "franchise, certificate or any other form of authorization for the operation of a public utility" to any person "except to citizens of the Philippines or to corporations or associations . . . at least sixty _per centum_ of the capital of which [was] owned by such citizens."[30]

The obvious rationale behind this provision was to make sure that vital public utilities remained under the control of Filipinos and that this was funded by Philipine capital. The "disposition, exploration, development, exploitation, or utilization of any of the natural resources of the Philippines" was also limited to citizens of the Philippines or corporations sixty per cent of whose capital belonged to Filipinos.[31] Moreover, as a reflection of concern for conservation and ecology, the National Assembly was authorized to limit the size of lands of the public domain which may be developed or leased to private corporations to one thousand hectares, and to individual citizens to five hundred hectares.[32]

Some of the more controversial and suspect provisions of the 1973 Constitution were in Article XVII (Transitory Provisions). Perhaps the most controversial was Section 2 which provided as follows:

> The Members of the <u>interim</u> National Assembly shall be the incumbent President and Vice-President of the Philippines, those who served as President af the nineteen hundred and seventy-one Constitutional Convention, <u>those Members of the Senate and the House of Representatives who shall express in writing to the Commission on Election within thirty days after the ratification of this Constitution their option to serve therein,</u> and those <u>Delegates to the nineteen hundred and seventy-one Constitutional Convention who have opted to serve therein by voting affirmatively for this Article.</u> They may take their oath of office before any officer authorized to administer oaths and qualify thereto, after the ratification of this Constitution. [Emphasis mine.]

It does not take much to figure out that this was intended to "persuade" the Constitutional Convention delegates to approve the proposed Constitution, including Article XVII. The very small minority who voted against the provision were consequently excluded.[33] As one student of Philippine constitutional law rather wittily observed: "Given the fact that members of the interim National Assembly were to have received a windfall of 260,000 (pesos) per year for salary and expenses, the attractiveness of this self-induced offer must have been more than what the most patriotic of delegates could resist!"[34]

Since the Constitutional Convention had not finished its work by the time martial law was declared in 1972, Marcos supporters in the Convention pushed for and secured approval of Section 3 which legitimized President Marcos' numerous orders, decrees, proclamations and acts. The salient portions of Section 3, sub-sections 1 and 2 read as follows:

> The incumbent President of the Philippines shall initially convene the interim National Assembly and shall preside over its sessions until the interim Speaker shall have been elected. He shall continue to exercise his powers and prerogatives under the nineteen hundred and thirty-five Constitution until he calls upon the interim National Assembly to elect the interim Prime Minister, who shall then exercise their respective powers vested by this Constitution.
>
> All proclamations, orders, decrees, instructions, and acts promulgated, issued or done by the incumbent President shall be part of the law of the land, and shall remain valid, legal, binding, and effective even after the lifting of martial law or the ratification of this Constitution, unless modified, revoked, or superseded by subsequent proclamations, orders, decrees, instructions, or other acts of the incumbent President, unless expressly and explicitly modified or repealed by the regular National Assembly. [Emphasis mine.]

Five years after the declaration of martial law and his assumption of plenary executive-legislative powers, Marcos scheduled elections to the interim National Assembly for 7 April 1978. Marcos, however, refused to lift martial law and indicated that if things did not work out, he would not hesitate to dissolve the interim National Assembly even as he continued to exercise the concurrent powers of president and prime minister.

Observers pointed out that no one in the Philippines could have won over Marcos in his home province of Ilocos Norte or in the interim National Assembly itself. The opposition led by former president Diosdado P. Macapagal, former senators Jovito R. Salonga, Benigno S. Aquino, Jr., Francisco "Soc" Rodrigo, Jose W. Diokno, and Lorenzo M. Tanada, were unable to agree on whether to contest the elections. Only Salonga and Aquino (who was still in detention at that time) announced their intention to stand for office, "depending on the election ground rules." The opposition Liberal party on the other hand, refused to present a slate of candidates, calling the proposed elections an "expensive, useless farce."[35]

In retrospect, the Transitory Provisions have had the net effect of validating and legitimizing President Marcos' martial law regime. Through a complicated set of Supreme Court decisions, edicts, referenda, and clever and astute political maneuvers, Marcos was able to discharge the powers of president under the 1935 Constitution and those of prime minister under the 1973 Constitution. In short, he was the legislative and executive, all rolled into one.

The Judiciary in the New Society

There was very little doubt that the judiciary, specifically the Supreme Court, played a central role in the New Society. For instance, while Marcos did not have any hesitation in abolishing Congress, he very carefully tried to project an image of an independent judiciary. Why this meticulous concern to project an image of constitutionalism and an operational checks-and-balances process? Again del Carmen seemed to provide a credible answer:

> One can suggest converging explanations. Obviously, the admission of a blatant power grab would be dysfunctional and impolitic for foreign as well as domestic consumption. The spectre of the Philippines, long ballyhooed as the 'show window of American democracy in Asia' unreservedly repudiating constitutional niceties would have been traumatic to Americans as well as to Filipinos. Rejection of the American

91

brand of democracy--yes, but the total
absence of a constitutional process--no.
There is need for a veneer of constitutionality for everybody's peace of
mind--including perhaps that of the
President. Images and symbols become
more important than reality, particularly in the Philippines.[36]

What were the specific changes in the Philippine
judiciary--both structurally and in the role of
judges as public officials--in the New Society?

The Structure of the Supreme Court

As mentioned earlier, the membership of the
Supreme Court was enlarged to fifteen. This number
could not have been increased or decreased by
legislative enactment or by executive fiat, because
the Supreme Court derived its existence from the
Constitution. The Supreme Court existed for as long
as the Constitution itself survived. The inferior
courts did not enjoy the same degree of permanence
with the possible exception of the newly-established
Sandiganbayan, a constitutional court designed to
try public officials charged with graft and
corruption.

The organization of the inferior courts
remained the same since the National Assembly had
not been convened and consequently has not had a
chance to reexamine and possibly modify the old
structure. It must be pointed out, however, that
under the Transitory Provisions (Article XVII), the
president acting as the legislative branch could at
any time have revamped or even abolished the lower
courts. In fact, he had already done this to a
limited extent when by executive order he removed
from the jurisdiction of the civil courts the
following types of cases:

1. Those involving the validity,
   legality or constitutionality of
   any decree, order or acts
   issued, promulgated or performed
   by [him] or by [his] duly designated representatives pursuant
   to Proclamation No. 1081, dated
   September 21, 1972.
2. Those involving the validity,
   legality or constitutionality of

any rules, orders or acts
issued, promulgated or performed
by public servants pursuant to
decrees, orders, rules and
regulations issued and promulgated by [him] or by [his] duly
designated representative
pursuant to Proclamation No.
1081, dated September 21, 1972.
3. Those involving crimes against
national security and the Law of
Nations.
4. Those involving crimes against
the fundamental laws of the
State.
5. Those involving crimes against
public order.
6. Those crimes involving usurpa-
tion of authority, rank, title,
and improper use of names, uni-
forms, and insignia.
7. Those involving crimes committed
by public officers.[37]

The obvious intent of General Order No. 3, was
to provide blanket immunity from civil or criminal
charges to all public officials responsible for
carrying out President Marcos' orders pursuant to
Proclamation No. 1081. As Secretary of National
Defense Juan Ponce Enrile admitted later, General
Order No. 3 placed virtually all types of cases
enumerated in the order under "the exclusive mantle
of military tribunals."[38]

Appointment and Tenure

A notable modification of the qualifications
of justices to the Supreme Court was that they
should be natural-born citizens. Otherwise the
other qualifications remained the same: at least
forty years of age, ten or more years of experience
as judge in a court of record or in the practice of
law. The qualifications for judges in the inferior
courts were to be determined by the National
Assembly. A major change in the appointment of
judges was the removal of legislative checks on the
appointing powers of the chief executive. (Under
the 1935 Constitution nominees to the bench were
subject to the advice and consent of the Commission
on Appointments, a bipartisan, bicameral committee

of the legislature.) Under the 1973 Constitution the appointment power was vested solely in the prime minister.

On the other hand, disciplinary power over judges of inferior courts was taken away from the chief executive and given to the Supreme Court. This was obviously intended to transform the judiciary into a non-political and non-partisan governmental branch, the assumption being that the justices of the Supreme Court would be less vulnerable to political pressure than, say, the prime minister who was a politician. Justices of the Supreme Court were guaranteed security of tenure until they reached the mandatory retirement age of sixty-five, five years earlier than that provided for in the 1935 Constitution.

This guarantee of tenure, however, seemed to be negated--at least for as long as martial law remained in force--by Section 10 of Article XVII (Transitory Provisions) which provided that the incumbent justices could continue in office "unless sooner replaced." Since the Transitory Provisions went into effect as of 17 January 1973, "any judge or justice of any court [were subject to dismissal] by the President at any time by appointment of his successor without the official being told the reason for such removal. Hence justices of the Supreme Court and all members of the judiciary [had] become, to use a Filipino parlance, 'casual employees'--a decidedly derogatory level previously reserved for partisan manual laborers who somehow managed to find employment during the height of the pork barrel season!"[39]

Jurisdiction

The Supreme Court had both original and appellate jurisdictions. Like the United States Supreme Court after which it was initially patterned, the Philippine Supreme Court had "original jurisdiction over cases affecting ambassadors, other public ministers, and consuls, and over petitions for certiorari, prohibition, mandamus, quo warranto, and habeas corpus; and had, on the appellate side, the power "to review, revise, reverse, modify, or affirm on appeal or certiorari" final judgements or decrees of inferior courts in five specific areas.[40] The Supreme Court also had the power of judicial review, to declare a treaty, executive agreement, law, ordinance, or executive order unconstitutional. For this, ten affirmative votes were needed and the court must decide the question en banc. It was noteworthy that the appellate jurisdiction of the Supreme Court was restricted to "cases in which only an error or question of law [was] involved."[41] This differed from the counterpart provision in the 1935 Constitution which gave the Supreme Court appellate jurisdiction over "all cases in which an error or question of law [was] involved."[42] The interposition of the phrase "only an" before the phrase "error or question of law" in the 1973 Constitution, while apparently innocuous and harmless, actually constricted the jurisdiction of the new Supreme Court.

Procedure and Administration

An added feature to the Supreme Court's rules of procedure was that it may review or hear cases in two divisions of seven or eight members, with five votes being needed to arrive at a decision. If the necessary number of votes was not obtained, the case was decided by the entire Supreme Court sitting en banc where the affirmative votes of eight justices are required. Section 2, sub-section 1 of Article X also specified that an "executive agreement" may be declared unconstitutional by the Supreme Court only if ten members concurred, a change from Article VIII, Section 2, sub-section 1 of the 1935 Constitution.[43] Some students of the Philippine judiciary felt that this raised doubts concerning the power of the court to pass on the constitutionality of executive agreements."[44] If anything, it reduced the flexibility of the court as the final arbiter of legal issues of national importance especially during periods of strong and absolute executive rule.

Administratively the Supreme Court was vested with disciplinary power over judges of inferior courts--a change which as mentioned earlier seemed salutary. The Supreme Court was also empowered to order the transfer of judges of inferior courts to "other stations as public interest require[d] . . . provided that such assignment shall not last longer than six months without the consent of the judge concerned."[45] Moreover the Supreme Court was authorized to order a "change of venue or place of trial to avoid a miscarriage of justice."[46]

A section of Article X, however, which could have had long-term implications on the status of the Supreme Court as a coequal branch of government was that which required it to submit to the president, prime minister, and National Assembly an "annual report on the operations and activities of the judiciary" within thirty days from the opening of the National Assembly. This seemed to indicate, at least on the surface, a diminution of the judiciary into a subordinate branch in relation to the executive and legislative branches.

The Supreme Court's Martial Law Decisions

The new Supreme Court seemed to behave along two basic patterns in the New Society. The Supreme Court through certain key decisions tended to support the martial law regime, in effect providing the legal and judicial basis for its existence. It also assumed an active role in "selling" the regime to audiences both at home and abroad. The latter phenomenon was unprecedented in the annals of the Philippine judiciary especially since there were still cases pending before the high tribunal challenging the legality of some of the official acts of the martial law regime.

Perhaps the first major decision made by the Supreme Court in favor of the New Society was the dismissal on 22 January 1973 of ten identical petitions challenging President Marcos' right to order a substitute plebiscite on the new Constitution.[47] The ten-man Supreme Court in a nine-to-one decision declared as "moot and academic" the petition filed jointly by among others, Senators Diokno, Roxas, and Aquino and National Press Club President Eduardo Monteclaro, questioning the legality of Presidential Decree No. 73.[48] The only justice who dissented was Calixto Zaldivar who with Chief Justice Roberto Concepcion and Justice Querube Makalintal were the only three non-Marcos appointees to the high court. The rest of the justices who voted to uphold Marcos' Proclamation No. 1102-- Enrique Fernando, Antonio Barredo, Felix Antonio, Felix Makasiar, Jesus Esguerra, Fred Ruiz Castro, and Claudio Teehankee--were all appointed to the court by President Marcos.[49]

Because the decision of 22 January 1973 did not deal squarely with the legality of the new Constitution, four suits were filed by the same petitioners and two private citizens, this time

96

asking the Supreme Court to void the new charter and prohibit key government officials from carrying out its provisions.[50] The petitioners in an impassioned plea asked the court to "save the Republic from the stark reality of a dictatorship."[51] Without challenging the provisions of the new charter, the petitioners asked that a new plebiscite in accordance with the 1935 Constitution, which they claimed was still legally in force, should be ordered by the court. The government warned through Solicitor General Estelito Mendoza against judicial intervention in an "essentially political question" and maintained that the ratification of the new charter by Citizen's Assemblies was in "substantial compliance" of the provisions of the 1935 Constitution.[52] A similar position was taken by former Senator Arturo M. Tolentino who appeared as counsel for corespondents former Senate President Gil J. Puyat and former Senate President Protempore Jose Roy. Tolentino, a highly regarded expert on constitutional law, further contended that the "Marcos revolution" was a "real revolution which had the distinction of being achieved without bloodshed," and should be regarded as having succeeded since there was no proof of large-scale public opposition to it and that it had the support of the military.[53]

In a complicated decision handed down on 31 March 1973, the Supreme Court speaking through Chief Justice Concepcion ruled (by a six-to-four vote; there was one vacancy in the Court at that time) to dismiss the petitions, and declared the new charter operative, even as it held that the "ratification process" was not in "substantial compliance" of the law. If the court's decision appeared contradictory, it was intended to be so; indeed, it was "strongly reminiscent of Justice [John] Marshall's judicial technique employed in Marbury v. Madison where that great Chief Justice adroitly obtained pragmatic legal results without unduly provoking powerful enemies or forsaking idealistic allies."[54]

In a 245-page decision the Supreme Court reduced the issues involved in the case into the following five questions:

1. Whether the court had jurisdiction over the validity of the proclamation which declared the charter ratified by the people;
2. Whether the Constitution was validly ratified with sub-

97

stantial compliance of the
people;
3. Whether the Filipino people had
acquiesced in the new Constitution;
4. Whether the petitioners were
entitled to relief by an
injuction against the executive
branch; and
5. Whether the new charter was in
force.[55]

The justices voted on each question
separately. On the first question the justices
voted six to four that the Supreme Court did have
jurisdiction over the case; on the second question
the Court said, also by a six to four vote, that the
new charter had not been ratified in substantial
compliance of applicable constitutional and
statutory provisions. The justices skirted the
third question by invoking the curious logic that
since the new charter was already in force de facto,
six votes were required to declare Presidential
Proclamation No. 1102 unconstitutional. The court
fell short by two votes.

This happened because two of the six justices
(Justices Castro and Makalintal)[56] who voted that
the "ratification" was not in substantial compliance
of the law also said there were other germane and
unavoidable extra-judicial considerations beyond the
competence of the court to deal with, such as "the
President's own assessment of the will of the people
as expressed through the Citizens Assemblies and the
importance of the 1973 Constitution to the successful implementation of the social and economic
reforms he had started or envisioned."[57] Because of
Castro's and Makalintal's turn-around, the court
voted negatively on the fourth question and
dismissed the petitions accordingly. The high
tribunal's position vis-a-vis the last question was
that the new charter was operational, de facto.
Since there were not enough votes to throw it out
(only four Justices voted for the outright
unconstitutionality of Proclamation No. 1102) the
new charter was therefore also operative, de jure.

Very clearly President Marcos' "beating the
gun" if one might be allowed the cliche, on the
court by proclaiming the new charter ratified by the
so called Citizens Assemblies, gave the Supreme
Court very little room within which to operate, and
foreclosed what might have been an adverse decision.

The Supreme Court's ambivalent and almost resigned posture vis-a-vis the new constitution was an open acknowledgment of the fact that even if it had declared Proclamation No. 1102 unconstitutional, and the new charter null and void, it would have been powerless to implement the "nation-wide plebiscite participated in only by duly qualified voters voting secretly and preceded by free and open discussion" alluded to in its decision.

It was apparently this long and tedious process and its possible repercussions on the martial law regime which President Marcos sought to avoid when he postponed the nationwide plebiscite scheduled for 15 January 1973, and proclaimed the constitution ratified instead by what one editorial in a major newspaper called a "show of hands."[58] The Supreme Court must be given credit, however, in that even as it realized its relative impotence, it nevertheless excoriated the executive branch's willful and patent disregard of constitutional processes.

Chief Justice Concepcion resigned from the court two months before his compulsory retirement age at seventy. Although the official reason given was that of "health," there were speculations that he was "just being consistent with his principles."[59] As the author of the court's majority opinion on the new charter, Concepcion was one of four justices who believed that the new charter had not been legally and properly ratified. If he had accepted the reorganization of the Supreme Court under the new charter he would have gone against his own stand.

In September 1973, President Marcos appointed Makalintal as the new Chief Justice. Makalintal was one of two justices who had voted to uphold the new charter even if not properly ratified because of its importance for the "successful implementation of [Marcos'] social and economic reforms." Also named to the high court were former Senator Estanislao Fernandez, Court of Appeals Justice Cecilia Munoz Palma, and University of the Philippines' law professor Ramon Aquino. With the resignation of Concepcion and the appointment of Fernandez, Palma, and Aquino, all of the incumbent justices of the Supreme Court, with the exception of Zaldivar, were Marcos appointees. In 1976, Chief Justice Makalintal also retired and Castro was appointed to replace him.

This latest group of Marcos appointees figured prominently in the court's decision of 17 September

1974, "upholding the government's right to rule under martial law, detain persons without charges and restrict freedom once released from jail."[60] This particular decision resulted from a petition for writ of habeas corpus filed by thirty-one political prisoners including former senators Diokno and Aquino, Jr., and had been pending since the declaration of martial law. Chief Justice Makalintal, who wrote the opinion for the court, responded to the petitioners' contention that at the time martial law was declared no actual state of rebellion or insurrection existed, by indicating that "such a claim ignore[d] the sophisticated modern setting [which] include[d] subversion of the most subtle kind, necessarily clandestine and operating precisely where there [was] no actual fighting."[61]

On the issue of restricting the freedoms of former detainees even after their release, Makalintal wrote that "the power to detain persons even without charges for acts related to the situation which justifie[d] the proclamation of martial law necessarily implie[d] the power to impose upon released detainees conditions and restrictions which [were] germane and necessary to carry out the purposes of the proclamation."[62] The decision was concurred in by Justices Makasiar, Esguerra, Fernandez, Munoz-Palma, Aquino, Teehankee, Barredo, Castro, and Antonio. Of Marcos' appointees to the court only Fernando--a well-known civil libertarian before his appointment to the high tribunal--filed a "qualified dissenting opinion" although he concurred with the decision as a whole."[63]

The 17 September decision of the Supreme Court, therefore, accorded legitmacy to the martial law government and its various acts, including the arrest and indefinite detention of alleged subversives. The decision was immediately used by the martial law regime to counter criticisms, especially from abroad, that Marcos had become a "dictator." In a world-wide press conference via satellite on 20 September the eve of the second anniversary of the proclamation of martial law, Marcos must have been thinking of his most recent victory before the Supreme Court when he remarked as follows:

> the power of the President is not absolute. For one thing, before I proclaimed martial law I sought to establish what would have been a

coalition government. I asked the
opposition parties to join me in the
fight against rebellion, but my offer
was rejected peremptorily. I submitted
myself to the Supreme Court, not only
once but several times. I would like to
know if any dictator would do that.
[Emphasis mine.][64]

The government-controlled The Times Journal (the
paper was owned by Benjamin Romualdez, Marcos'
brother-in-law) echoed the same viewpoint when it
wrote in an editorial the following day:

Last week's decision of the Supreme
Court on martial law settled once and
for all the constitutionality of Proclamation No. 1081 which the President
issued as a self-defense measure for the
nation in view of a state of rebellion
existing at the time. The legal ground
for the present Government was thus
firmly established by no less than the
highest tribunal of the land.[65]

What the long-term implications of these decisions were on the future of the Supreme Court and
the nation was uncertain for a while. Interestingly
enough, former Justices Anontio and Fernandez (both
involved in the controversial holding) travelled
throughout the United States, particularly in
Filipino-American communities in Honolulu, San
Francisco, Los Angeles, Chicago, and New York, not
long after the decision promulgating, martial law
government and drumming up support for it.[66] In a
speech in Honolulu, Antonio said that "institutions
like the judiciary can now function as they ought to
in view of the 'elimination' of politics from the
system."[67] "In the past," Antonio continued, "the
power and interference of politicians impeded the
swift and smooth flow of justice."[68]

For his part, Justice Fernandez wrote a letter
to Donald Fraser (Democrat, Minnesota), chairman of
the Subcommittee on International Organizations of
the United States House of Representatives, at the
time claiming "there [had] been no violation of
human rights by the government because our Supreme
Court [had] already declared that the proclamation
and continuance of martial law [was] in accordance
with our Constitution and that, therefore, those
arrested and detained by virtue thereof, [were]

legally under detention and cannot be said to have been deprived illegally of their constitutional rights."[69]

The Military Establishment

One of the most powerful--if not in fact the most powerful--single organization in the New Society was the Armed Forces of the Philippines (AFP). The AFP was not only the enforcer of the various edicts, proclamations, and decrees of Marcos, it was also responsible for keeping the peace, suppressing dissent, and guaranteeing the existence of the regime. The military establishment showed no signs of wanting to grab power for itself. There was little doubt, however, that any major change in the position of the military would have had a profound impact on the regime and could very well have precipitated its downfall. In neighboring Indonesia, Thailand, and other Third World countries, the military on numerous occasions has wrested political power away from the civil authorities.

The Philippines falls under S. E. Finer's "democratic competitive" prototype of politics and military establishments.[70] The great bulk of the military--including the officer corps--was recruited from middle and lower classes, and as Morris Janowitz suggested, "drawn mainly from the rural hinterlands."[71] Consequently the Philippine military establishment, like its counterparts in other developing polities, "[did] not have a strong allegiance to an integrated upper class which it accepts as its political leaders nor [did] it have a pervasive conservative outlook."[72] Civilian supremacy over the military was a well entrenched principle in Philippine politics and law; the 1935 Constitution guaranteed it and the 1973 Constitution listed it as one of its underlying tenets. There was little or no exaggeration in the claim made by the New Society that despite the enhancement of the "Army's prominence as a disciplined locus of national power," Marcos "remained in control as constitutional commander-in-chief and president."[73] The reason for this restraint can be summed up as follows:

> the remarkably high standard of profes-
> sionalism, in the political American
> tradition, that had been inculcated into

102

the AFP officer class since the early 1900's when the nucleus of the Army was founded. Subordination to constitutional authority remains the creed of the career officers at its highest commands, many of whom had, as young soldiers, fought alongside Americans at Bataan--as Mr. Marcos, himself a much-decorated war hero, had done."[74]

Marcos' martial background and the great esteem in which he was held by the officer corps and rank and file of the AFP was largely responsible for the survival of the New Society and of Marcos himself. As T. J. S. George put it:

> Any future set-up in the Philippines will be safe from a military takeover only as long as the Constitutional bond between the civilian leadership and the military is maintained in its present form. True, the orientation of the Philippine military remains strongly democratic. There are no known hawks in the top echelons. But it is also true that it is Marcos' personal acceptibility to the military that has smoothed the present experiment in civil martial law. If Marcos were absent from the scene, it would have been conceivable to think of the military gradually developing political ambitions of its own.[75] [Emphasis mine.]

There were reportedly three factions within the AFP during martial law. One faction was headed by General Fabian C. Ver, who headed the elite Presidential Security Command; the second faction was headed by General Fidel V. Ramos who was chief of the Philippine Constabulary; the third faction was headed by Defense Secretary Juan Ponce Enrile, a civilian.[76] Of the three, Ver was supposed to have had the greatest accessibility to Marcos and both he and Ramos reportedly had Marcos' complete trust.[77] Incidentally, both Ver and Ramos are blood relatives of Marcos while all three, Ramos, Ver and Enrile, are Ilocanos as were most of the flag- and general-level officers of the AFP.[78]

The Armed Forces of the Philippines in Brief

The Armed Forces of the Philippines consists of three service branches--the Army, Navy, and Air Force. A fourth "branch," the Philippine Constabulary (the closest approximation to a national police) was at the forefront of the counter-insurgency and anti-smuggling campaigns and was responsible for organizing and equipping the so-called "Local Self-Defense Forces," who numbered about 25,000 in 1977. The Philippines appropriated P3.08 billion ($419 million) for defense in fiscal year 1977-1978.[79] As of FY 1977-1978, the total troop strength of the AFP (including the Philippine Constabulary and the so-called Self-Defense Forces) was 164,000 officers and men, representing an increase of 113,326 from the 1972 total of 50,674.[80]

The Philippine Army (PA) consisted of 63,000 officers and men in the active force, and it was organized into four infantry divisions and one independent infantry brigade (the presidential security brigade). The PA was equipped with twenty-one Scorpion and seven M-41 tanks, thirty-five M-113 armored personnel carriers (with thirty-three more on order), one hundred 105mm and five 155mm howitzers, and Hawk surface-to-air missiles (SAMs).[81] In addition, the PA had a reserve force of 17,000, bringing the total to 80,000. While the Philippine Army had been primarily engaged in fighting the Bangsa Moro Army (BMA) in Mindanao and the New People's Army (NPA) in Luzon and the Visayas, it was also deeply involved in the New Society's infrastructure program.[82]

The Philippine Navy (PN) had 20,000 officers and men including 7,000 marines and naval engineers.[83] In terms of equipment, the PN had seven frigates, two command ships, four coastal mine-sweepers, three destroyer escorts, forty-six patrol crafts (including twenty-four under one hundred tons), thirty three landing craft (mostly medium LSTs), and one search and rescue squadron. Because of the archipelagic nature of the Philippines and its unusually long coastline, the Philippine Navy was woefully short on equipment and manpower. Moreover, most of its vessels were of World War II vintage, donated to the Philippines by the United States under the RP-US Military Assistance Agreement. With a reserve force of 12,000, the PN's total strength came up to 32,000.[84]

The smallest of the three services in terms of active troop strength was the Philippine Air Force (PAF), with only 16,000 officers and men and 104 combat aircraft.[85] The PAF was modernized and strengthened in the 1960's to meet its commitments under the SEATO and of course later, to make it more effective against the BMA in Mindanao and Sulu (in April 1974, the BMA actually shot down a supersonic F-5 fighter). As of 1977, the PAF had twenty fighter and ground attack (FGA) F-5A/B jets (two squadrons) and a similar number of the out-moded Korea-vintage F-86F all-weather fighters. Eleven of the modern FGA F-5E jets were on order from the United States. The PAF also hads a wide variety of helicopters, gunships, transport, and reconnaisance aircraft, and a reserve force of 16,000.[86]

The present Armed Forces of the Philippines had its beginnings in 1901 when the president of the Second Philippine Commission ordered the U.S. Army to create an "insular police force to protect the lives and properties of the people."[87] This meant the waging of mopping up operations against remnants of the Philippine armed forces of General Aguinaldo who took to the hills after the formal capitulation of the short-lived First Philippine Republic in 1900.

For three decades this arrangement was sufficient for the purposes of the state. The Philippine Constabulary (which was what the political force was subsequently called) success-fully quelled peasant uprisings and performed a variety of police duties. As war between the United States and Japan became imminent, another item, that of "national defense" was added to the Philippine Constabulary's duties. This led to the expansion of the Philippine Constabulary into the Philippine Scouts under the command of General Douglas MacArthur. The further growth of the Armed Forces of the Philippines may be summarized thus:

> After the World War II episode the
> military establishment was maintained,
> in keeping with the notion that an
> 'independent country' should have its
> own army. However, the threat of war
> with external forces was gone, except in
> the rhetoric of ideologists; instead,
> civil disorder became widespread. To
> this task of quelling the rebellion the
> entire armed forces turned. Thus the
> constabulary function now applied not

105

only to the constabulary organization, but to its allied services--the Army, the Navy, and the Air Force. But gradually, the internal situation stabilized, and the government gained more control. The PC was left to continue the maintenance of 'peace and order' while the Army returned to its barracks, the Navy and the Air Force to their assorted tasks. Nevertheless, the situation remained basically the same: no serious external threat, but with a continuing possibility of widespread civil disorder. And despite all the soundings-off about professional duties, the underlying concern of the AFP as a whole also remained the same: control of civil disorder and the enforcement of the authority of the central government over the population.[88]

The Armed Forces of the Philippines' non-political military tradition is attributed by David O. Wurfel to the fact that "because the Philippines won her independence peacefully, the army was never really glorified as the leader of the nationalist revolution." Qualifying the statement, Wurfel hurried to add that while it was true there were individual officers during past administrations who were involved in politics, their political participation was of a "personal and extra-military" nature.[89]

If as claimed by various commentators and knowledgeable observers, the military establishment had indeed emerged as the most dominant force, the "new elite" in the New Society's scheme of things, it is worthwhile to closely examine this "new elite" in retrospect. Was the entire military establishment--including non-commissioned officers and enlisted men--the "new elite"? Or was the "military elite" synonymous with the AFP officer corps? If so, was the AFP officer corps a monolithic and singularly- motivated entity (reminiscent of Floyd Hunter's elites in mythical Regional City)[90], or was it a plural, competitive, and even fragmented group akin to Robert A. Dahl's "influentials" in New Haven, Connecticut?[91] What were the social backgrounds of the men who constituted the "new elite"? What motivated them into choosing military careers?

The Officer Corps: A Fragmented Elite

There was a great deal of ambiguity extant in attempts to isolate the elite within the military establishment. At best the attempted definitions were arbitrary and limited, for example that the "elite" were specific groups within the officer corps. One such commentary was that of Captain Danilo P. Vizmanos, PN, a former faculty member of the Philippine National Defense College:

> The closest to a 'military elite' that one can find in this country is the PMA [Philippine Military Academy] group in the AFP. However, I would not really consider it as such compared to other countries because of the presence of countervailing factors both within and outside the AFP. The dominant group in the AFP is of course the senior officers group (field grade officers). But within this group are certain sub-groups with their respective interests. The most prominent are the PMA group, the integrees, and the reserve officers. Because of their limited number in key positions in the AFP, the senior field grade reserve officers have a tendency to gravitate towards the integrees. So actually there are two major groupings that contend with each other in the military hierarchy, the PMA and the integrees-reserve groups. What is happening now is that while these two groups have certain things in common, for example social and financial improvement, the means to achieve this plus the desire to achieve power and authority have resulted in conflicting interests between these two major groups.[92]

Captain Vizmanos called the hierarchy of the Armed Forces of the Philippines an "unholy alliance" of both common and conflicting interests in a precarious state of equilibrium. Conflicting interest groups, whom Vizmanos referred to as "countervailing forces," carefully considered the reactions and responses of each other before resorting to any drastic measures or action. And while there were minor and petty conflicts and rivalries, these were not significant enough to threaten the stability of the entire military establishment.

The equation of the Philippine Military Academy (PMA) group with the military elite was disputed by a young U.S. Navy officer who served in the Philippines as Flag Lieutenant and Aide to the Commander of U.S. Naval Forces in the Philippines, Rear Admiral Draper L. Kauffman, from 1969 to 1972. In a solicited comment, then Lt.(jg) Charles G. Untermeyer, USNR, submitted that:

> Elitism in the Philippines is similar to that in the United States--high rank does confirm a measure of eliteness. A PMA, USMA, or USNA graduate does not have any decided advantage. World War II performance and political affiliation and backing seem to carry more weight with the present flag and general officer selection boards. As of the present, only General Manuel T. Yan (the AFP Chief of Staff at that time)--among all the general staff--is a Philippine Military Academy graduate.[93]

Despite the disagreement between Vizmanos and Untermeyer, it can be assumed that the military elite in the Philippines was indeed the officer corps in all four branches of the Philippine Armed Forces--Army, Navy, Air Force, and the Philippine Constabulary. This officer corps was fragmented into contending groups, the most prominent of which were the PMA graduates, the integrees-reservists, and graduates of the three United States service academies.

The Military and Civilian Establishments Compared

Even as the Armed Forces of the Philippines suffered from a number of defects and shortcomings, it was generally regarded as a "better organization" when compared to other non-military or civilian offices. A possible explanation for this was as follows:

> Military organizations in new states tend to be more advanced than their co-institutions in this regard: ritualized relationships characterized

by hierarchy and clearcut lines of authority create a degree of organizational cohesion and conformity that enables the armed forces to act more effectively and more rationally than their co-institutions. Thus the military inevitably seems to assume the character of an elite organization among inefficient, ineffective, and ever-corrupt civilian institutions.[94]

A similar observation was made by Amos Perlmutter in a study of civilian-military relations in Israel:

In developing states, breakdowns in modernization, an uneven development in social and political mobilization, or inadequate integration have often created situations where the army must assume tasks of managing and directing economic, agricultural and educational enterprises. In such situations, the army usually intervenes because of the absence, impotence, or indifference of other elites.[95]

In the Philippines there was widespread public satisfaction with the AFP's active participation in the infrastructure program during Marcos' first four years in office. Furthermore, both before and after the declaration of martial law, military personnel especially the officer corps have generally been well-treated and have achieved higher living standards than their counterparts in the civil service.

Motivations for Entering Military Service

Another aspect of any analysis of the military establishment is that of career motivation. A study on the "career motivations of the Philippine military elite" by Quintin R. de Borlaa, found that "educational opportunity" was the single most powerful motivation for entrance into military service (twenty-two respondents or 40.7 per cent of the total sample). Other motivations cited were "boyhood ambition," "patriotism," and "careerism."[96]
The following are illustrations of the responses elicited by de Borja:

Respondent No. 18, said in part:

> After graduation from high school, I
> taught in a public high school to
> support my younger sisters who were in
> the high school also. Although I was
> determined to continue my studies,
> somehow after the graduation of my
> sisters, I foresaw some financial
> difficulties. My luck in getting a
> nomination and in passing the cadetship
> entrance examination to the Philippine
> Constabulary Academy [this was renamed
> the Philippine Military Academy some
> years later] provided the good and
> timely solution, as the schooling in the
> Academy was--and still is--financed by
> the government,[97]

The perception that cadetship in the
Philippine Military Academy and a subsequent
military career could serve as a ladder for social
mobility was revealed in this response by respondent
No. 66:

> Graduating as an honor student from the
> Manilal South High School in 1929, I
> tried to be a self-supporting student by
> getting employed in the Metropolitan
> Water District as a 'peon' then as a
> casual time keeper. Dropped as a
> 'casual laborer,' I enlisted in the 50th
> PC Company in Pasig, Rizal because I was
> informed that high school graduates
> after a year or so would be given the
> chance to become a PC officer. I did
> take the cadet examinations for three
> times until I was No. 5 and ten were
> taken as in the past yeras. . . . Had I
> not been able to get into the Academy, I
> would have settled as a Sergeant-Major
> in the PC. We must consider also that
> primarily because of the last World War,
> my contemporaries were accelerated in
> rank, otherwise we would be retiring
> only as full colonels at most.[98]

That a military career was a "childhood
ambition" was reflected in this candid, if maudlin
account:

The idea [of military service] entered my mind in my early childhood from my mother when one strong desire is [sic] to see me wear the immaculate Constabulary officer's uniform (boots, Sam Brown belt, and shoulder strap) a symbol of 'power and success.' From the age of nine my dream of becoming a constabulary officer (has) never escaped my mind. . .

When I was in the intermediate grades we had a neighbor who was a cadet in the Philippine Constabulary Academy . . . Whenever he came home for vacation he was wearing [sic] the cadet uniform. My ambition was further strengthened and my desire became even greater to be like him who was idolized by everyone . . . especially the girls. I was always following him as if he were a hero to me.[99]

Patriotism in its more romantic and idealized from also served as a motivation for some respondents:

When the Commonwealth Army was organized, there was a call for professionals to join the Reserve Force to fill the void that could not be filled by the smal officer's corps of the Constabulary. I was then holding a good paying job in the Meralco [Manila Electric Company]. But a personal appeal was made to me by a ranking colonel of the Philippine Army, that my country needed me. I responded.[100]

The above responses suggest that many of the senior officers of the AFP were influenced to enter military service by careerist reasons, and others by notions of heroism, mission, honor, and other military shibboleths. De Borja's findings validate one of Morris Janowitz' theses that in most underdeveloped countries, the officer corps was usually recruited from the lower social classes, with the military establishment serving as an "opportunity structure" for "underclasses" to achieve social mobility.

111

The Military in the New Society

The members of the Armed Forces of the Philippines have been the beneficiaries of numerous presidential decrees and proclamations since 21 September 1972. On 29 December 1973, President Marcos announced by decree that he had upgraded by one level the ranks of all senior AFP officers. Specifically, the decree called for the promotion of the AFP vice chief-of-staff to the three-star rank of lieutenant general and the deputy chief of staff and the commanders of the major services to the two-star rank of major general.[101]

On 15 January 1974, the Philippine Times reported that the following other benefits to the AFP had been decreed: (1) an increase in the daily subsistence allowance of every member of the military by six pesos; (2) the organization of a Veterans Investment Development Company with the president making an initial contribution of P1 million; (3) the creation of a regular appropriation for the retirement of military personnel in the amount of P200 million; (4) free educational benefits to the dependents of servicemen killed in action or incapacitated in action; (5) the establishment of a system of college-level scholarships; and (6) organization of a Veterans Assistance Commission.[102] The decree also provided for an annual special group insurance for members of the Armed Forces in addition to compulsory insurance in the Government Service Insurance System; even cadets in the service academies were included.[103]

Military personnel also replaced several provincial governors and municipal mayors throughout the country during the lifetime of martial law. While the formal titles have not been taken away from civilian provincial and municipal officials, the military authorities have been known to "call the shots." A report which originated from the Philippines on 15 October 1972 indicated that as follows:

> Out in the provinces of the Philippines, military men are playing a much more important role under martial law than before, but governors, mayors, judges and other civil authorities continue to function and to administer their areas of responsibility with little change.
> The military is more prominent than ever in matters concerning security,

subversion and expression of public opinion.[104]

A possible upshot of the AFP's favored status in the New Society was the proliferation of cases of graft and corruption involving military men. In the "old society" the grafters were usually civilian personnel in such government bureaus as Internal Revenue and Customs. Bernard Wideman made the following observation:

> From all accounts, corruption in the military is among the most serious abuses in the New Society. The most common offence among corrupt military officers is the ordering of goods and services and then not paying. According to a high-ranking military source, this tactic has resulted in numerous generals and colonels supplying new cars and big houses for their wives. The source added that with the declining authority of civil officials, there are no longer any checks on the military and a government lawyer confirms that people are afraid to voice complaints against military abuses. However, the new JAG [Judge Advocate General] is seeking ways of ending the spread of corruption in the military.[105]

Needless to say, the corruption-free image that the New Society tried hard to project was badly tarnished by these alleged corrupt practices.

The pampering of the military by Marcos may be interpreted in two ways: first, that he was trying to make a military career as financially and socially rewarding as other professions, and second, that he was repaying the military for its loyalty to him and for guaranteeing the existence of his regime. In the context of the Philippine value system, especially that of utang na loob, the second possibility seemed more plausible.[106]

Summary

The government of the Second Philippine Republic was patterned after that of the United States and consisted of three coequal branches--the executive, legislative, and judiciary--whose

113

relationships with each other were guided by the principles of separation of powers and checks and balances. The president, vice-president, and members of Congress were elected by the people in biennial nationwide elections. The justices of the Supreme Court and judges of inferior courts were appointed by the president with the advice and consent of the Commission on Appointments, a bipartisan, bi-cameral committee of the legislature. Judges served during "good behavior" or until the mandatory retirement age of seventy years, and like the president and vice-president could be removed from office only by impeachment. The 1935 Constitution limited the term of the president and vice-president to not more than eight consecutive years; the term of office of senators was fixed at six years, and that of congressmen at four years. The House of Representatives was organized every four years while the Philippine Senate like its American counterpart, was a continuing body with senatorial terms staggered in such a way that one third of the body's membership was elected every two years.

Elections were free and popular and invariably keenly and hotly contested. Voter turnout even in off-year presidential elections was consistently high, and, despite sensationalized stories about election frauds and irregularities, these were more of the exception rather than the rule. Like the United States, the Second Philippine Republic also subscribed to a two-party system, the two parties being the Nacionalista and Liberal. At the time of the declaration of martial law in 1972, the Nacionalista party had been in power for the previous seven years. Marcos was a Nacionalista although before his nomination as the Nacionalista standard bearer in 1965, he was president of the opposition Liberal party. Hopping from one political party to the other was quite common in the Philippines then.

With the declaration of martial law and the ratification, by presidential decree, of the new Constitution on 17 January 1973, the Philippines theoretically became a parliamentary system of government. The shift from the American-style presidential system to the parliamentary form was formalized by a Constitutional Convention assembled in 1971 to revamp the 1935 Constitution and supposedly bring it up to par with present-day conditions. Under the parliamentary system, the office of president was downgraded to that of a ceremonial and symbolic role, while real executive and legislative power was vested in a unicameral National Assembly. Under the 1973 Constitution, Marcos was eligible to become either president or prime minister. Under the 1935 Constitution he was forbidden from seeking a third consecutive term.

In actual practice, executive and legislative power were concentrated in Marcos, who ran the country from 1972 to 1981, through proclamation, decree, edict, and "letters of instruction." The civilian courts were left intact, at least structurally, in spite of the fact that certain types of cases were removed from their jurisdiction and transferred to military tribunals. In an apparent bid to counter mounting domestic and international criticism of his martial law regime—especially the freeze on elections and the alleged mistreatment of political prisoners—Marcos announced on 27 January 1978, that elections for the interim National Assembly would be held on 2 April 1978 (later postponed to 7 April 1978). He also ordered a relaxation of restrictions on public political debate and rescinded a little-known decree (PD No. 1052) issued in November 1976, which barred individuals who had unresolved charges of "subversion" or "rebellion" against them from standing for office. Marcos also resurrected the Nacionalista and Liberal political parties which had become inoperative upon the declaration of martial law.

The 1973 Constitution contained a number of novel ideas and provisions, such as the creation of a special court called the Sandiganbayan (roughly translated, "people's court" or "people's refuge") to hear cases involving official misconduct, graft, and corruption, and the corollary office of Ombudsman or Tanodbayan to prosecute cases before the Sandiganbayan. Graft and corruption were listed as one of the grounds for impeachment of the president, prime minister, judges, and members of the constitutional commissions. The 1973 Constitution also contained various provisions relating to domestic and family relations, the environment and ecology, and the nation's patrimony. Voting was made compulsory, and the voting age was reduced to eighteen; literacy was abolished as a prerequisite for voter registration. Compared to the 1935 Constitution, the 1973 Constitution appeared to be more nationalistic in that it restricted the exploration, development, and exploitation of natural resources to Filipino citizens or corporations sixty per cent of whose capital was owned by citizens of the Philippines.

Other than the creation of three constitutional commissions, the national bureaucracy remained basically the same. The ten cabinet departments under the Second Philippine Republic were retained; a new department was that of Local Government and Community Development, an expanded version of the former Presidential Assistant on Community Development (PACD). There were new and powerful offices under the Executive Office, including the National Economic Development Authority (NEDA), the Board of Investments (BOI), the Department of Tourism, the Department of Agrarian Reforms (DAR), and the ubiquitous Department of Public Information which included the National Media Production Center. These offices were headed by Marcos' "go-ahead technocrats" and were at the forefront of rule-making and rule-implementation.

Two institutions stood out in the New Society: the judiciary, especially the Supreme Court, and the armed forces. While the size of the Supreme Court was expanded from eleven to fifteen, and the tenure of judges made less certain (under the "Transitory Provisions" of the 1973 Constitution, incumbent judges may continue in office "unless sooner replaced"), it was quite obvious that Marcos tried very hard to project the image of an independent judiciary. The reason behind this appeared to be the desire to convince the Filipino people, and the rest of the world as well, that the decisions of the martial law regime were legitimate, and did have legal and judicial bases; that the New Society was a government of laws and not of men. Significantly, the Supreme Court sustained all of Marcos' official acts including the declaration of martial law itself and the continued incarceration of alleged subversives without the benefit of charges being specified against them or the certainty of ever being brought to trial. Some members of the Supreme Court even went as far as to travel through the United States praising and drumming up support for the Marcos regime.

The Armed Forces of the Philippines was not only the main enforcer of all the edicts, proclamations, decreesd, and "letters of instruction" of the New Society, it was also its chief protector. There were supposed to be three factions within the AFP in the New Society although the leaders of all three factions were either blood relatives of Marcos or fellow Ilocanos, and were all intensely loyal to him

116

and his family.   The AFP which consisted of three
service branches--the Army, Navy, and Air Force--and
the Philippine Constabulary was 52,674 strong in
1972; in 1977 it was 164,000.   The elite of the AFP,
the officer corps, is fragmented.   Graduates of the
Philippine Military Academy constitute one faction;
integrees-reservists, another faction; and graduates
of United States service academies, still another.
As a group the AFP was been the recipient of
numerous rewards and benefits from Marcos, including
wage increases and other fringe benefits, special
insurance coverages, and the upgrading of the ranks
of general- and flag-level officers.

Chapter 6

CHANGE AND PUBLIC POLICY: TWO EXAMPLES

While the armed forces and judiciary were the
New Society's most significant institutions, the
policy areas to which Marcos accorded top priority
were foreign affairs and land reform.   A more
detailed analysis of these two policy areas will
contribute to a better comprehension of the nature
of public policy in the New Society, as well as the
manner in which key decisions were made.
Perhaps a good indication of the importance
Marcos placed on foreign affairs was his designation
in late 1972, of his wife Imelda Romualdez-Marcos,
and his brother-in-law Governor Benjamin Romualdez,
as "roving" ambassadors or "ambassadors-at-large."
Apparently, the main function of Mrs. Marcos and
Governor Romualdez was to counter anti-martial law
criticism abroad, especially in the United States.
At the same time the two roving ambassadors were
also instrumental in laying the groundwork for the
subsequent expansion of Philippine foreign relations
in sub-Sahara Africa, Latin America, the Middle
East, and in the socialist bloc.   When the
Philippines and the People's Republic of China
established formal diplomatic relations on 9 June
1975 after twenty-six years of cold war enmity,
Marcos and his entire family journeyed to Beijing
with a full entourage of journalists.
The urgency of land reform, and its centrality
to the New Society's overall political blueprint,
was underscored by Marcos in Proclamation No. 1081
itself, and in his statement to the nation on 23
September 1972, explaining the reasons behind the
declaration of martial law.   Since then, the
numerous brochures and pamphlets[1] cranked out by the
National Media Production Center have invariably
featured such optimistic references to land reform
as: "[it] is expected to transform the basic
structure of social and political power . . . [and]
to create new habits and attitudes necessary to
national growth, and which were not possible under

119

the conditions of inequality and tyranny which
tenancy perpetuated until the proclamation of
martial law."[2]

Foreign Policy Under the New Society

The establishment of diplomatic relations with
the People's Republic of China, the Union of Soviet
Socialist Republics, Rumania, Yugoslavia, the German
Democratic Republic, Bulgaria, Hungary, Poland,
Czechoslovakia, Cuba, and the People's Republic of
Mongolia, the recognition of the Khmer Rouge government in Kampuchea and of the Socialist Republic of
Vietnam, the projected recognition of the government
of North Korea, the expansion of relations with the
Arab world, Latin America, and sub-Sahara Africa,
and finally, the reported movement away from the
United States toward an "independent" foreign policy
were frequently cited by Marcos' spokesmen as solid
achievements and clear proof that the Philippines
had "established [its] identity, [and was] no longer
a mere shadow, opaque and obscure."[3]   Did the
Philippines really move to "assert its identity and
its independence" from the United States?   What
factors or chain of events   brought these changes
about?   What were some of the short-term and
long-term implications of these changes?

A Brief Historical Overview

Philippine foreign policy from 1946 to 1972
was uncomplicated.   It revolved around maintaining
good relations with the United States and the
so-called free world, and conversely, pledging
eternal enmity and opposition to the countries of
the socialist bloc.   The Philippines depended on the
United States for military security, specifically
through the RP-US Mutual Defense Treaty and the
Military Bases Agreement, and later, the Southeast
Asia Treaty Organization.   The excessive military
dependence of the Philippines on the United States
was the object of sharp criticism from nationalists
of the earlier period such as the late Senator Claro
Mayo Recto and later, from various nationalist organizations such as the Movement for the Advancement
of Nationalism (MAN) and the Kabataang Makabayan.[4]
Critics of this pro-American foreign policy
pointed out that the defense treaty with the United
States and one of its adjuncts, the Military Bases

120

Agreement was lopsided in favor of the United States, and was not really intended for the protection of the Philippines but rather of American interests in the Philippines. Identified as the root cause of the United States' domination of the Philippines was the Parity Rights Amendment[5] incorporated after the Second World War into the 1935 Constitution.[6] The Parity Rights Amendment, which gave American nationals and corporations the right to own property as well as to operate vital public utilities and engage in the development and exploitation of natural resources on the same basis as Filipinos helped perpetuate the Philippines' colonial status even after the formal withdrawal of direct American political control.

In spite of these criticisms which escalated in intensity and popularity through the years, the Philippines adhered to her close economic and military ties with the United States, and in the process, virtually isolated herself from countries outside the so-called free world. There were no substantial changes in the overall foreign policy of the Philippines from President Roxas' time through the first term of President Marcos, although there were attempts during the incumbencies of Garcia and Macapagal to reexamine Philippine-American relations with the avowed goal of putting the relationship on a more equitable basis. These attempts did not get very far.

One of the consequences of the excessive dependence of the Philippines on the United States was her alienation from her Asian neighbors. For a long time, the Philippines was ridiculed by such Asian leaders as the late Jawaharlal Nehru of India as the "tail to the American kite," (or one of two anyway, the other being Thailand). The Philippines was perceived as a country geographically located in Asia but not quite Asian in her culture, religion, and foreign policy. The resurgent movement towards an Asian-oriented foreign policy began in 1961 during the Garcia presidency with the formation of the Association of Southeast Asia (ASA), an attempt to revive dreams of a Malaysia Irredenta, first articulated by the youth leader Wenceslao Q. Vinzons in the mid-1930's.

The ASA never got off the ground since two of its members, Malaya (later the Federation of Malaysia) and the Philippines, subsequently found themselves embroiled in a territorial dispute over Sabah. After the collapse of ASA, another pan-Asian union was organized in 1964. This was MAPHILINDO, an effort to bind Malaya, the Philippines, and Indonesia into one organization. Malaya eventually withdrew from the organization after the outbreak of an armed konfrontasi with Indonesia over the establishment of what is today the Federation of Malaysia. The Association of Southeast Asian Nations (ASEAN), established on 8 August 1967 in Bangkok, with Thailand, Singapore, the Philippines, Malaysia, and Indonesia as members hopes to succeed where both the ASA and the MAPHILINDO failed.

The declaration of martial law and the establishment of the New Society in 1972 formalized the Philippines' abandonment of the hard-line policy towards the socialist bloc, the expansion of relations with the Arab countries, Latin America, and sub-Sahara Africa, and the "Asianization" of Philippine foreign policy. The policy of accommodation with the countries of the socialist bloc, however, began to unfold as early as six months before the advent of martial rule. Teodoro C. Benigno observed on 2 March 1972, as follows:

> The Philippines is carefully evolving a foreign policy of accommodation with the Communist world in line with the US-China rapprochement while continuing to crush communism at home.
>
> At first blush, this policy appears bizarre in that instead of reaching towards China or any other Asian Communist country, it would establish the first such Philippine embassies this year in Rumania and Yugoslavia.
>
> Philippine foreign policy makers have obviously identified Rumanian and Yugoslavian communism as the safest to start with since these two countries are noted for their independence within the Soviet orbit.[7]

According to then Foreign Affairs Secretary Carlos P. Romulo, the new foreign policy was a response to "newly perceived needs" and "profound changes" which have occurred in the international scene. Specifically, Romulo outlined the thrust of the new foreign policy as:

1. An emphasis on regionalism as a means of assisting in aspects of national development, which the Philippines cannot achieve alone;

122

2. Diversification of markets for raw
    materials, hand-in-hand with the
    search for markets for manufactured
    products; and
3. Widening of relations with the
    socialist world.[8]

Accommodation with the Socialist Bloc

A rationale behind the Philippines' accommodation with the socialist bloc countries was provided by Marcos when he announced in his "Report to the Nation" on 21 September 1974, that:

> it shall be our policy to reach out to
> that portion of humanity, whose markets,
> capital resources, and technological
> know-how had remained inaccessible to us
> for reasons of ideology. In a small
> way, we shall seek to make our own
> contribution to the <u>detente</u> that now
> makes it possible for the big powers to
> talk of wider cooperation.[9]

To allay possible fears (especially that of the military establishment's) that the new foreign policy would lead to a weakening of the anti-communist struggle at home, Marcos suggested "that a distinction must be made between the communist insurgency . . . at home and the socialist governments who are seeking to make their own contribution to the cooperation among nations, the growth of commerce, and the progress of the world."[10]
It was fairly evident that the Marcos regime's accommodation with the socialist bloc countries was brought about not so much by an ideological re-orientation but by urgent and pragmatic economic and commercial considerations, including much-needed oil from the People's Republic of China and foreign exchange from new trading partners to replenish a badly depleted national treasury. This was admitted by Marcos himself when in the same "Report to the Nation" he said the following:

> As of today, Mrs. Marcos, acting as my
> special representative, is meeting with
> officials in the People's Republic of
> China on matters of culture and tech-
> nology. She will also sign on behalf of
> the government the purchase of oil from

123

the People's Republic. Inevitably, this should lead to our normalization of relations with that country, and also the Union of the Soviet Socialist Republics. This is a reality that cannot forever be defered, and must sooner be faced. Postponing it indefinitely can constitute a loss rather than a gain on our part.[11]

On 13 November 1974, the People' Republic of China and the Philippines signed a Trade Agreement after the two countries had exchanged trade delegations and determined the terms of export commodities. Under the agreement, the People's Republic of China agreed to supply the Philippines with 125,000 barrels of crude oil twice a month (accounting for 4.4 per cent of the Philippines' oil consumption of sixty seven million barrels per year). For her part, the Philippines agreed to sell the PRC copra, timber, copper, and possibly sugar.[12]

The expansion of relations with the Arab countries, including a condemnation of the "continued unjust occupation of lands belonging to the Palestinian people," was obviously designed to put the Philippines in the good graces of the Arab countries and to counter its image as a "lackey" to the United States, and by extension, Israel. Marcos himself confirmed this when he said that the visit by senior Arab and Islamic officials and diplomats to the Philippines was intended to "give the Muslim world a clearer picture of the problem of rebellion in Mindanao and gain for the Philippines the status of a 'friendly country' to the Arab oil-producing countries."[13]

In spite of bilateral agreements between the Philippines on the one hand, and the People's Republic of China, Mexico, and Venezuela, on the other--under whose terms these countries would supply the Philippines with crude oil--the Philippines was still largely dependent on the OPEC countries (primarily Saudi Arabia) for her petroleum needs. The Arab oil embargo sanctioned by the OPEC after the 1973 Yom Kippur War, underscored the vulnerability of the Philippines to economic strangulation and made clear the need to cultivate the goodwill of the Arab countries. This meant, among other things, the recognition of the Palestine Liberation Organization (PLO) as the only legitimate representative of the Palestinians, and a turnaround in the Philippines' stance toward Israel.

Ironically, the Philippines had originally voted in committee against the creation of the state of Israel in 1948 only to reverse its vote in the General Assembly as a result of intense pressure from the United States.[14] In addition, the Philippines felt compelled to allow a representative of the Islamic Conference to monitor the conduct of the war in Mindanao and Sulu in order to counteract Moro National Liberation Front propaganda that the Marcos regime was waging virtual genocide against Philippine Muslims.

It was obvious from Marcos' generalizations about the new shifts in Philippine foreign policy that these were motivated by a combination of economic and political considerations. By being friendly towards the socialist countries, especially the People's Republic of China, he hoped to neutralize and possibly out-flank the communist insurgency in the country. And by the same token, he hoped to neutralize the Muslim rebellion in Mindanao by being supportive of the Arab position vis-a-vis Israel and Zionism. It was widely assumed that both the New People's Army (in Luzon and the Visayas) and the Moro Bangsa Army (in Mindanao and Sulu) received varying amounts of logistical and financial support from the People's Republic of China and some of the more radical Islamic countries of the Middle East, notably Libya.

Movement Away from the United States

On 18 April 1975, Marcos announced that he was calling a meeting of the Foreign Policy Council (FPC) (the equivalent of the National Security Council of the United States) to discuss the possibility of a Philippine take-over of American military bases in the Philippines and the rescinding of the RP-US Mutual Defense Treaty.[15] Meeting on 21 April 1975, the Foreign Policy Council decided to call for the abrogation of the Military Bases Agreement and the Mutual Defense Treaty, and for the formation of a "new organization of Asian countries to include the People's Republic of China."[16] The decision was officially announced four days later and the United States was formally notified of the FPC decision. Information Secretary Francisco S. Tatad in a press briefing on 25 April 1975, said that the "status quo was no longer tenable because of present realities."[17] Tatad further told newsmen of Marcos' conviction that the power balance in Asia had been disturbed by "recent events in Cambodia and Vietnam" and that because of recent congressional restrictions (referring obviously to the 1973 War Powers Act) it was doubtful whether the United States could come to the rescue of the Philippines in case of an armed attack; the bases were therefore of doubtful military value.[18]

A segment of the international press interpreted these Marcos moves and the accommodation with the socialist bloc countries as indicative of the Philippines' movement away from American control and influence.[19] Did the Philippines indeed move away from the United States or were Marcos' moves calculated ploys to create concern in the United States, in order to generate support for the martial law regime (which had at best, been lukewarm and guarded) and improve his leverage in bargaining for increased economic and military aid?

In a testimony before the Senate subcommittee on Appropriations chaired by Daniel K. Inouye (D, Hawaii) in 1975, Daniel B. Schirmer of the Goddard-Cambridge Graduate Program in Social Change, pointed out that there was nothing new nor independent in the New Society's foreign policy, that indeed, it fit well into America's post-Vietnam Asian policy, and the United States' own rapprochement with the People's Republic of China. Speculating on Marcos' possible motives for suggesting the removal of U.S. bases from the Philippines, Schirmer suggested that this was basically intended by Marcos for "its possible effects on the U.S. Congress."[20] "Marcos," Schirmer continued, "[was] aware . . . that the threat of neutrality or a slant to the socialist nations on the part of a Third World country [was] supposed to cause members of the US Congress to be generous with grants-in-aid."[21] Summing up, Schirmer said the following:

> Ferdinand Marcos' agitation about foreign policy and bases can be seen as a double pressure. First, to silence Congressional criticism of the Philippine dictatorship so that the political atmosphere of Washington [became] more like that of Manila and aid will be forthcoming. Secondly, for payment of rent for the bases, so that should Congress fail to knuckle under the dictator's bluff, base rent will help make up the loss in aid.[22]

A similar view, that Marcos was in fact jockeying for increased military and economic aid, or in any case, substantial remuneration for the continued use of the military bases by the United States was expressed by David A. Andelman of the <u>New York Times</u>, thus:

> Senior American officials said this week that what most of the statements could mean in concrete terms would be demands for a new cash-rental arrangement for Clark Air Base, the beiggest United States base overseas, and the sprawling Subic Bay Naval Facility, as well as greater Philippine control over the bases.
> With the expanding guerrilla war against Muslim dissidents in the southern part of the country, and a rapidly expanding foreign exchange deficit because of the increasing cost of fuel oil, the country is facing some major cash needs that officials here feel may be met by a restructuring of the bases agreement.[23]

In spite all these agitations, however, it was evident that the Marcos regime did not wish a complete American pullout. This was because the Philippines could not do without the estimated $150 million which 14,000 American and 54,000 Filipino employees in the two military installations pumped into the economy each year. This constituted approximately a little over ten percent of the country's Gross National Product.[24]

Marcos' posture on the issue of the Military Bases was also geared for domestic consumption as much as it was aimed at his American critics. As an astute political strategist, Marcos knew that the preponderance of public opinion seemed to be that the Philippines' lack of jurisdiction over the military bases was inconsistent with the country's sovereign status. Filipinos were particularly sensitive to the refusal of American military authorities to turn over to Philippine courts for prosecution, American servicemen accused of committing crimes against Filipino nationals within the military bases. Indeed the jurisdictional conflict had been one of the major irritants in Philippine-American relations through the years.[25]

Through carefully timed maneuvers (all in the wake of the American debacle in Indochina) Marcos was undoubtedly driving home the point to the United States Congress that unless it came up with more economic and military aid, the United States would lose another friend and ally in Southeast Asia. It is also reasonable to assume that Marcos wanted to give the impression to the rest of Southeast Asia, especially the new governments in Indochina, that the Philippines was "no longer a vassal of the United States, as some non-aligned nations insist[ed]."[26] It was noteworthy that Marcos took time to notify President Soeharto of Indonesia of his decision vis-a-vis the military bases and that in return Soeharto expressed support for the Philippine decision.[27] Still later, Marcos and then Prime Minister Kukrit Pramoj of Thailand issued a joint communique, at the conclusion of the latter's state visit to the Philippines, calling for the phasing out of the Southeast Asia Treaty Organization.[28]

Assuming that Marcos' demand for the abrogation of the RP-US Mutual Defense Treaty was sincere and did indeed represent "a climax to the slow evolution of a policy of non-alignment . . . a reaction to the Nixon Doctrine in Asia," there was no question about the fact that continued American military and economic aid was crucial to the survival of the martial law regime.[29] In the economic front alone, the elimination of the nearly $500 million surplus in trade with the United States as a result of the contraction of the American market for Philippine products meant, among other things, the absorption by the Philippines of almost $1,000 million in payments deficit in its international foreign transactions.[30] Such an unfavorable balance of payments position "would almost certainly [have wrought] further havoc on the peso's buying power as well as its international convertibility."[31]

On the other hand, in spite of all the talk about the "self-reliance" of the Armed Forces of the Philippines[32] the AFP was still dependent on the United States for the bulk of its weapons, equipment, and military supplies. From the $235 million the Philippines spent for arms from 1963 to 1974, $232 million's worth was purchased from the United States.[33] In direct and indirect military aid (including funds, services, and equipment obtained under the Military Assistance Program, Foreign Military Sales Credit, Excess Defense Articles, Ship and Plane Transfers, Military Assistance Advisory

Group, and Officer Training categories), the Philippines received a grand total of $45.3 million in 1973, $41.2 million in 1974, and $32.2 million in 1975.[34] American military aid to the Philippines in 1973 and 1974 alone was greater than the total allocation for Africa, and those of Japan and Indonesia in East Asia, and greater than the combined allocations for Japan, Malaysia, Pakistan, India, and Sri Lanka.[35]

The continuing military effort against the New People's Army in Luzon and the Visayas and the Moro Bangsa Army in Mindanao and Sulu, as well as the announced expansion and modernization of the Armed Forces of the Philippines meant that the Philippines needed more and more new weapons and replacements for lost or captured weapons.[36] The only source for these weapons was the United States. There were no indications whatsoever that the Philippines was interested in shopping for weapons elsewhere assuming that she was in a financial position to do so. It was not surprising then that when the United States announced that military aid to the Philippines would be terminated in 1978, and that thenceforth military assistance would only be on the basis of "loans and concessional terms," Marcos immediately reassured the United States of the Philippines' continued loyalty.[37] Speaking on 12 June 1975, on the occasion of the seventy-seventh anniversary of Philippine independence, Marcos said as follows:

> The United States shall remain our good friend and firm ally and none of the negotiations we enter into, with respect to the security arrangements we have with that country, should be construed as an effort to diminish our historic relationship.[38]

Evidently, the Marcos regime became convinced that because the United States was "geopolitically a Pacific power, [she had] no way--and no reason--to retreat into sulky isolationism from Asian affairs."[39]

Notwithstanding all the rhetoric, the Philippines did not move away from the United States during the martial law period. For as Robert L. Youngblood observed:

> Both economically and militarily, the Philippines, with the possible exception

of the Laurel-Langley Trade Agreement
and the termination of the SEATO is more
dependent on the United States now than
it was in the year just prior to the
declaration of martial law. By eliminating major sources of government
criticism like the press, the Congress
and opposition leaders, President Marcos
[was] able to engage in a rhetoric of an
independent foreign policy while
continuing to rely heavily on American
investment, financial assistance and
military aid.[40]

The "Open Door" Economic Policy

The economic policies of the New Society
seemed to be geared not toward achieving independence but just the opposite. Nowhere was this
more apparent than in the "open door" policy of
the martial law regime vis-a-vis multinational
corporations. Through a succession of presidential
proclamations and decrees, the New Society tried to
attract several American and Japanese multinational
corporations with such incentives as accelerated
depreciation of fixed assets, secret numbered
bank accounts, tax breaks and exemptions, and the
freedom to repatriate their profits out of the
Philippines.[41]

Before the declaration of martial law, foreign
investors--especially when foreign equity participation exceeded thirty percent--were regulated by
various acts of Congress such as Republic Act No.
5455. With Congress no longer in existence, Marcos
and a handful of technocrat-advisers were free to
waive or relax all previous congressionally-mandated
restrictions. These technocrats were jestingly
referred to in Manila's coffee shops as the "Harvard
Mafia." They evidently enjoyed Marcos' complete
trust, and were accorded considerable latitude in
the planning and implementation of the regime's
economic programs.[42]

According to a report prepared by the
Corporate Information Center of the National Council
of Churches of Christ in the USA, American corporations in 1971 owned 30.4 percent of the equity
capital of the top two hundred Philippine corporations.[43] In strategic industries, such as the
petroleum industry, 96.3 percent of the equity
capital was foreign-owned; while in the mining

industry, the percentage of the equity capital which did not belong to Filipinos was 77 percent.[44] In 1975, it was estimated that about 80 percent of all foreign investments in the Philippines belonged to American corporations; and they were still coming in.[45] In banking alone, twenty-five foreign banks established branches in Manila including such giants as Chase Manhattan, Banker's Trust, Bank of Tokyo, Ltd., Manufacturers Hanover Trust, Crocker Bank, Chemical Bank, Wells Fargo Bank, First National City Bank of Chicago, and American Express. These banks joined the already-established Bank of America and the First National City Bank of New York, and as of 1972, owned 16.1 percent of the total assets of the Philippine commercial banking system as compared to only 7.26 percent in 1969.[46]

While there were immediate and short-term benefits which accrued from this "open door" policy--jobs for the unemployed and increased per capita purchasing power, for instance--the long-term implications are unclear. The favored status of multinational corporations with their virtually unlimited capitalization, advanced technological and entrepreneurial know-how, and worldwide market outlets, could have worked to stunt even further the growth of native capital and local industries. Most ominous of all, however, was the potential impact of these multinational corporations on the political independence and sovereignty of the Philippines. International law and economics expert Jovito R. Salonga articulated this fear when he warned:

> A sense of realism tells me that in the foreseeable future, multi-nationals will progressively dominate the economy and the social, cultural, and political life of the nation. As of April 1974, there were 75 multi-nationals operating in the Philippines. By the end of 1974, there should be around a hundred or even more.[47]

While there were not very many definitive studies on the political impact multinational corporations had on host countries, a study by Charles T. Goodsell[48] found that in Peru "the political threat embodied in foreign investment [was] believed to be real but controllable."[49] To prove his point that the political threat posed by multinational corporations was "controllable,"

Goodsell cited the "anti-investor" policies adopted by the regime of General Juan Velasco y Alvarado after the 1968 coup d'etat which swept Alvarado and his cabal of generals to power. Be that as it may, Goodsell found that "most of the corporations [did] not shy away from politics; [and did] not hesitate to involve themselves when their interests require[d] it."[50] Moreover, the "American government definitely intervene[d] in Peruvian affairs on behalf of the companies," although as Goodsell put it, "not in errand-boy fashion."[51]

Assuming that Goodsell's findings about the "controllability" of the political threat posed by multinational corporations was applicable to the Philippines, efforts to exercise control could have only come about were Marcos to be overthrown. In fact, Robert B. Stauffer even went as far as to contend that the declaration of martial law was a response to the demands of "transnational economic actors." Explaining the links between the New Society and these "transnational actors," Stauffer wrote as follows:

> In the face of rising nationalist demands for Philippine economic independence, i.e., for defeudalization, the regime responded to the counter-demands of transnational economic actors, in alliance with what is probably a majority of the Filipino economic elite, by radically altering the Philippine political system. The 'New Society' imposed authoritarian controls over the flow of information, eliminating the leadership of the nationalist movement from any possible contact with its mass base, denied all civil rights under which opposition might openly become possible, and eliminating major governmental institutions such as Congress and the Supreme Court from decision-making roles. The new system promises 'stability' and full cooperation of Philippine material resources and manpower, cooperation that signifies a new increment of refeudalization.[52]

Foreign Policy and the Domestic Structure

For any foreign policy to succeed it must have domestic support; indeed, as Romulo aptly put it, "foreign policy is a reflection of domestic policy."[53] Marcos' radical reorientation of Philippine foreign policy was calculated to secure for the regime wider public approval and legitimacy. If the new foreign policy--which even some of Marcos' severest critics[54] roundly praised--achieved its avowed objectives, Marcos' position would be further strengthened. Failure, on the other hand, would have led to a diminution of the regime's prestige and credibility. How did this new foreign policy fare, especially in those sectors of Philippine society where dissent against the martial law regime was strongest?

By and large, the new foreign policy seemed to have set quite well with the majority of the Filipino people. What was even more outstanding was it won over most of the intellectuals, the ever-militant student body of the University of the Philippines, and some leading technocrats, who had been clamoring for precisely such changes since the early 1950's. Such economic benefits of expanded trade relations as cheaper fuel costs and the infusion of much-needed foreign exchange made the new foreign policy even more palatable to the majority, since "most Filipinos were probably more concerned with a better life than they [were] with the president's trip to China or his lofty pronouncements about ASEAN or his tough talk about revising the bases agreement with the United States."[55]

One influential sector in the New Society which did express some misgivings about the new foreign policy was the military establishment. The military was particularly concerned about the establishment of friendly and cordial relations with the erstwhile "enemy country," the People's Republic of China. As early as 18 October 1974, the Far Eastern Economic Review noted that as follows:

> The President's diplomatic initiative towards China apparently did not please leaders of the Armed Forces of the Philippines who are engaged in fighting Maoist insurgents.
> The military had good reason to be wary of the coming of the Chinese, since the local Maoist-oriented New People's

133

Army has occasionally received arms from Chinese Communist sources, although these have not been linked to the Chinese government.

Evidently some senior and middle-level officers in the Armed Forces of the Philippines were apprehensive that the Chinese and the Soviets would use their newly-found access to the Philippines as an opportunity to foment and encourage subversion, or in any case, to disseminate communist propaganda. The grumblings were sufficiently muted by Marcos' reassurances about the PRC and USSR's peaceful intentions and the continued pampering of the members of the Armed Forces through increased remunerations and other attractive fringe benefits.[56]

Another source of opposition to the new foreign policy was the Catholic Church whose relations with the Marcos regime had been quite strained since the inception of martial rule. The church had repeatedly protested the New Society's alleged persecution of some of its clergy, including James B. Reuter, Jose Nacu, Francisco Claver, Edicio de la Torre, Mariano Lahoz, and Jose Blanco. The church, of course, had also been at the forefront of the campaign to stop the mistreatment of political prisoners and all other forms of torture.

The main opposition of the church to the establishment of diplomatic relations with the countries of the socialist bloc had to do with the church's traditional distaste and fear of these countries' "Godlessness." But even within the Catholic Church (both clergy and laity) the majority appeared to favor friendship and cooperation with the countries of the socialist bloc.[57] Another objection raised by churchmen (this time protestant ministers and laymen) was the morality of accommodation with the People's Republic of China even as Filipinos remained in prison for supposedly being "Maoists." Pointing out the inconsistency of the continued incarceration of alleged Maoists with Marcos' lavish praises of Mao Tse Tung and the Chinese people, the churchmen wrote the following:

> Now, if all these tributes and statements are right, our question is--how, in the name of fairness, can government conceivably justify the arrests, the investigations, and the prolonged imprisonment of so many people whose

134

only 'crime' was to have kept some
pamphlet or publication written by
others, not by them, in praise of Mao
Tse Tung and Communist China?[58]

Agrarian Reform Under the New Society

The agrarian problem, and attempts to cope
with it, antedate even the First Philippine Republic
(1898-1901). To a great extent, the problem is a
legacy from the _encomienda_ system[59] originated by
the Spaniards to reward civil and ecclesiastical
officials and certain Filipino ilustrados for
services rendered to the Spanish crown. As a
result, huge landed estates came to be owned by a
small group of wealthy families or by religious
corporations. The overwhelming majority of the
people were peasants who tilled the land for the
landowners in what came to be known in various parts
of the Philippines, but especially in central and
southern Luzon as the _kasama_ system (kasama is a
Pilipino word meaning "associate" or "comrade" or
"companion"). The relationship between the _cacique_
(landlord) and the kasama (peasant) was by and large
exploitative and oppressive in nature. In response
to various landlord excesses and the desire for
meaningful agrarian reform there were numerous
peasant uprisings such as the Kolorum, Pulahanes and
Sakdalista revolts of the early and mid-1900's and
the Huk rebellion of the latter half of the century,
all of which were invariably quelled by government
authorities.[60]

Land Reform Before Martial Law

The first serious attempt by a Philippine
president to implement a land reform program was
made by Quezon during the penultimate stage of the
Commonwealth period. Land reform was made part of a
larger "Social Justice Program" unveiled by Quezon
on 14 February 1939, and designed to give the
"common man" a better life. The salient features of
Quezon's proposed reforms were (1) fifty-fifty
sharing of the harvest and the cost of production
between the farmer and the landlord, (2) the
establishment of a Farmer's Financing Agency to
finance from Five Hundred Pesos to One Thousand
Pesos to P1000 of the farmer's share of the cost of
production, to be amortized at an annual interest

135

rate of six percent, and (3) the reduction by ten percent of the share millowners received for their sugar cane. In addition, Quezon asked the National Assembly for an appropriation of P500,000 to implement the program.[61] Although short-lived because of the advent of World War II the Quezon-initiated reforms supposedly contributed to the loosening of tensions between peasants and the government.[62]

Land reform took the backseat during the administration of Roxas, the first president of the Second Philippine Republic, because of Roxas' preoccupation with the problems of rehabilitation and reconstruction. It was Roxas who was primarily responsible for securing the passage of the Parity Amendment to the 1935 Constitution, which was in turn, tied up with the Philippine Trade Act of 1946 and the Philippine Rehabilitation Act of 1946. When Vice-President Quirino took over the presidency after the death of Roxas on 15 April 1948, the Huk rebellion was already underway. In fact, one of Quirino's first official acts was to grant amnesty to the Huks in June 1948. Taruc, the Huk Supremo at that time, was allowed to take his seat in Congress and the Quirino administration promised the surrendered Huks that the landlords' private armies would be disbanded and that a 70:30 crop-sharing system favorable to the farmers would be adopted by the government.[63] Because of strong landlord opposition, Quirino's promised reforms were aborted. Accusing the Quirino government of reneging on its commitments, Taruc and his followers returned to the hills on 15 August 1948, where they remained until 16 May 1954, when Taruc finally surrendered.[64]

It is interesting to note that the United States applied considerable pressure on the Quirino administration to institute land reform. In the so-called Bell Report, it was recommended that "a program of land redistribution be undertaken through the purchase of large estates for resale to small farmers; and that measures be undertaken to provide tenants with reasonable security on their land and an equitable share of the crops they produce[d]."[65] Two years later the Hardie Report issued under the aegis of the United States Mutual Security Agency, attributed such serious problems as poor agricultural production, slow industrial growth, the rise of communism, and even alleged threats to American security to the absence of an adequate land reform program.[66] The principal obstacle to land reform during Quirino's presidency and in later years was the presence in Congress of landlords or spokesmen for landlords who invariably managed to either defeat or waterdown various land reform proposals.

Two such watered-down versions of land reform were passed during the incumbencies of Presidents Magsaysay (R.A. 1400) and Macapagal (R.A. 3844). Earlier of course, Magsaysay had skillfully used the peasants' yearning for land of their own by combining a mailed fist policy and a "land for the landless" program to put an end to the Huk rebellion.[67] Republic Act 1400 allowed landowners to retain as much as three hundred hectares of contiguous land, while all lands in excess of the retention limit could be sold to the peasants upon the request of the majority of the peasants living on that land. Their requests were to be submitted to the Land Tenure Administration where the reallocation process would start. The final purchasing price for the land was to be negotiated between the landlords and the tenants, but the actual sectioning of the landed estate itself was left to the courts. This made final purchase virtually impossible since the landlords often tied up the proposed sale in protracted litigation, the cost of which the peasants were unable to afford.

Macapagal's Land Reform Code of 1963 (R.A. 3844) was equally rich in promise but poor in performance. While R.A. 3844 went much further than previous laws in that it completely abolished the institution of share tenancy (supplanting it with leasehold tenancy) it contained many loopholes which were fully exploited by the landed gentry, among them, the conversion of rice and corn lands into "mechanized farms" or into coconut and sugar plantations and the payment of "wages" to tenants in order to avoid expropriation since only rice and corn lands were subject to the provisions of R.A. 3844. Moreover, since the retention limit was pegged at 144 hectares for individuals and 1,024 hectares for corporations, some large landed estates were simply subdivided between and among members of the landowners' families or in the case of the corporations, among their subsidiaries. There were also the chronic inadequacy of funds to effectively implement the programs and the insolvency of the Agricultural Credit Administration which was supposed to lend low-interest loans to farmers who wanted to purchase land.[68]

The last land reform-oriented measure passed by the old Philippine Congress was Republic Act 6390 which provided for a "land to the tiller" program. This was passed on 10 September 1971, slightly more than a year before the declaration of martial law. Significantly, the "land to the tiller" concept would later be incorporated into Presidential Decree No. 27, the keystone of the New Society's land reform program.

The Rationale of Land Reform

Marcos gave an indication of his thinking about land reform in a commencement address at Central Luzon State University in the heart of what journalists used to call Huklandia, on 29 April 1968. On that occasion he made the following statement:

> To a very large extent, the general poverty and the state of economic backwardness in underdeveloped countries, not only in the Philippines, may be attributed to the unequal ownership of land. The concentration of land holdings in a few families has induced in these countries that peculiar historic rhythm of human living which has estranged whole populations from progress. Cycles of peaceful monotony and violent upheaval have perpetuated conditions of semi-feudalism in many nations on earth, notably in Asia and South America.[69]

It was presumably in order to stop these "cycles of peaceful monotony and violent upheaval" that Marcos included the prosecution of land reform as one of the "complementary concern(s) to the restoration of order and the securing of the Republic" in Proclamation No. 1081.[70]

Exactly five days after he signed Proclamation No. 1081, Marcos issued Presidential Decree No. 2, designating the entire country as a land reform area. And to make PD No. 2--described by an enthusiastic admirer as a "measure of transcendental significance . . . a historical accomplishment"-- even more dramatic, the entire document was written in Marcos' handwriting.[71] Presidential Decree No. 2 proposed among other things, to "achieve dignified existence for the small farmers, free from pernicious institutional restraints and practices

138

which have not only retarded the agricultural
development of the country but have also produced
widespread discontent and unrest among farmers, one
of the causes of the existing emergency."[72] The
decree also directed all government agencies and
offices to extend their full cooperation and
assistance to the Department of Agrarian Reform
headed by former Pangasinan Governor Conrado F.
Estrella.

There is no doubt that the New Society
accorded land reform top priority, at least if not
in substance in symbolic gestures such as
Presidential Decree No. 2 and later Presidential
Decree No. 27. Apparently Marcos was convinced that
"the land reform program was the only gauge for the
success or failure of his New Society. If land
reform failed, there is no New Society."[73] As the
thirty-one page full color advertisement in the New
York Times of 10 June 1973, put it: "no regime no
matter how benevolent, can of course, be based
indefinitely on coercive power. Mr. Marcos is
therefore building the new Filipino society on the
bedrock of land reform."[74]

The Strategy of Land Reform

What was the land reform strategy of the New
Society? In what way or ways was the strategy
different from attempts at land reform from the
Commonwealth period to 21 September 1972? What were
the obstacles if any, that stood in the way of
meaningful land reform? Is land reform really the
solution to the Philippines' agrarian and related
social problems?

The main basis of the New Society's land
reform program was Presidential Decree No. 27,
issued on 21 October 1972. The key provisions of PD
No. 27 were:

1. the emancipation of all tenant
    farmers as of 21 October 1972;
2. the tenant farmer, whether in land
    classified as landed estate or not,
    shall be deemed owner of a portion
    constituting a family-sized farm of
    five hectares if irrigated;
3. the total cost of the land, includ-
    ing interest at the rate of six per
    centum per annum, shall be paid by

> the tenant in fifteen years of equal
> amortizations;
> 4. in case of default, the amortiza-
>   tions due shall be paid by the
>   farmer's cooperative, having a right
>   to recourse against him;
> 5. title to the land shall not be
>   transferrable except by hereditary
>   succession.[75]

In short, PD No. 27 provided that the prospective
tenant-owner had to meet the following qualifications: he must pay the landowner for the land over a
fifteen-year period, pay taxes on the land, and
belong to a government cooperative (the so called
samahang nayon). The samahang nayon was not only
intended as a safeguard against possible default by
the tenant-owner on his annual amortizations, but
also as a source of assistance in the acquisition of
scientific farming techniques and methods.

According to Benedict J. Kerkvliet, the Marcos
land reform program consisted of a multi-stage
approach that did not try to redistribute large
landholdings in one swift action, but was instead
divided into three stages.[76] From October 1972, to
June 1973, the targets were landlords owning more
than one hundred hectares; from July to November
1973 to the present time, the focus was on holdings
of from twenty-four to fifty hectares.[77] The retention limit for individuals was seven hectares as
compared to 144 hectares under the 1963 Land Reform
Code (R.A. 3844).

Apart from the seven-hectare retention limit,
the Marcos land reform plan was also different from
previous programs in its direct transfer of land
from the landowner to the tiller and the mode of
payment for the land. Under Republic Act 3844 and
previous land reform laws, the procedure was for the
land to be purchased by the government and then
redistributed to deserving occupants or their
beneficiaries with the landowners being compensated
on the basis of the "fair market value" of the
property. Under Presidential Decree No. 27 "fair
market value" was replaced by a complicated formula
which called for the averaging of the value of the
harvest over three crop years prior to 1972, and
multiplying this average by a factor of 2.5.
According to a study made by the Civil Liberties
Union of the Philippines (CLUP), the resulting
amount was assuredly "well below the market value of
the land--doubtless with the idea of making the

payments of compensation well within the productive capacity of the tiller-operator."[78]

Conflicting Assessments on Land Reform

In a 1975 seminar on land reform sponsored by the Southeast Asia Advisory Group (SEADAG) of the Asia Society of New York City, the participants unanimously noted that martial law

> [had] facilitated presidential support for land reform by curtailing Marcos' dependence on landlord-based political parties and a landlord-based Congress. This [had] enabled him to advocate land reform forcefully, to create a unified Department of Agrarian Reform and to fund the department fully. It [had] enabled him to declare strong measures against bureaucrats and judges whose decisions sabotage[d] land reform. In a literal sense it [had] disarmed key opponents of land reform; the confiscation of weapons and disbandment of the so-called private armies of the biggest landlords and politicians [had] been one of the most notable accomplishments of martial law. This, in turn, [had] facilitated the organization of peasants by moderate forces such as the Federation of Free Farmers.[79]

A less favorable assessment was made by the Civil Liberties Union of the Philippines which found "key weaknesses" in the New Society's land reform program, namely, (1) the low level of compensation which it found especially unjust to small landowners who did not inherit their land but bought it out of hard-earned savings, (2) the inadequacy of the infrastructure required to provide support services to tiller-operators, and (3) the fact that it promised more than it could produce.[80] The CLUP pointed out that while PD No. 27 promised tenants at least three hectares of irrigated and five hectares of unirrigated land, the total area of tenanted corn and rice lands (according to DAR statistics) was only 1,343,217 hectares while the total number of eligible tenants was 1,078,817. Even if the retention limit for small landowners was totally eliminated, each tenant would have received, on the average, less than 1.5 hectares.[81]   The CLUP also assailed the absence of a program to improve the lot of tenants on coconut and sugar lands who numbered between 200,000 and 250,000 families, as well as the 3,000,000 or so landless peasants who aspired to become farmers but were ineligible under the terms of Presidential Decree No. 27.[82]

In his 1974 <u>Report to the Nation</u>, Marcos summarized his regime's accomplishments in land reform as follows: (1) the issuance of land transfer certificates (LTCs) to 178,000 farmers (from a total of 450,000 who were interviewed), (2) the issuance of Presidential Decree No. 450 which broadened credit sources for farmers, and (3) the initiation of a four-year cooperatives development plan designed to increase the productive capacity of farmers as a whole.   Divided into two phases, the cooperatives plan called for the organization, first, of the samahang nayon (barrio cooperative), then, of the <u>kilusang bayan</u> (national movement). Marcos claimed that there were 10,000 barrio cooperatives as of 9 September 1974.   In addition, the New Society "adopted during the year an integrated approach to agrarian reform wherein the tenurial shift [was] supported by legal assistance, farmer education, infrastructure development, electrification, land consolidation, financing and cooperative organization."[83]

There was little doubt that the claims made by Marcos in his <u>Report to the Nation</u> and by Estrella in a book entitled <u>Agrarian Reform in the New Society</u> were, on their face value, impressive.[84] Whether the farmers who were supposed to have received those titles actually received their certificates of land transfer (CLT), however, was another matter.   According to a study on the "political impact" of the New Society's agrarian reforms, a wide discrepancy between CLTs "issued" and CLTs actually "received" was discovered and documented.   Wurfel found that:

> As of 30 June 1976 DAR reported the issuance of over 307,000 CLTs to 197,973 tenants.   The term 'issuance,' however, referred only to the spewing forth by the computer, not to receipt by the tiller.   Public reports in 1975 on the wide discrepancy between CLTs 'issued' and 'received' led to a revision of the data collection system at the regional level.   A national compilation was made

> in February 1976, revealing that of
> 281,000 CLTs 'issued,' only 127,000 had
> been actually received by the farmer
> . . . At the rate of 9,000 new tenant-
> recipients in the first half of 1976, it
> [would have taken] nearly 18 years to
> distribute the certificates to all
> tenant-beneficiaries as defined in
> 1972.[85]

Wurfel also found that the land reform program was inadequately funded, and that landowner opposition remained a major stumbling block. And what was worse, "the DAR [had] almost never taken steps to penalize landlords for their many evasive and sometimes illegal, tactics. In effect it [was] the honest landlord, who complied with all regulations and [did] not ask for special favours, who [was] being penalized."[86]

But whatever the truth was, the sincerity of the leadership of the New Society in the implementation of land reform was crucial to the program's success. Was land reform an integral part of a synoptic plan for national construction, or just a stop-gap device, a "means to another end, one among several means the government [used] to foster stability and counter potential unrest?"[87] Was land reform merely another "instrument to legitimize the regime," a calculated scheme to "destroy the mass support--feudal in character--of [Marcos'] elite competitors?"[88] An even more basic question was whether over the long haul, land reform was the answer to the Philippines' agrarian problems, especially given such variables as a runaway population growth and limited hectarage of available arable land.

Summary

The New Society instituted major changes in foreign policy, in most cases, broad departures from the foreign policy which the Philippines followed from 1946 to the early 1970's. Foremost among these changes were the recognition and establishment of full diplomatic relations with the countries of the socialist bloc. The Philippines also expanded her relations with the Arab countries, Latin America, and sub-Sahara Africa. Within Southeast Asia, the Philippines extended diplomatic recognition to the Socialist Republic of Vietnam and the Khmer Rouge government in Kampuchea, and it continued to play a major role in attempts at regional development and cooperation through the Association of Southeast Asian Nations.

The new foreign policy of the Philippines appeared to have been motivated not so much by a philosophical or ideological reorientation as it was by a more pragmatic and flexible perception of the international milieu, and the Philippines' need for oil, and foreign exchange. In the case of the establishment of diplomatic relations with the People's Republic of China, an added motivation seemed to be the desire to neutralize or outflank the communist insurgency in Luzon and the Visayas.

The accommodation with the countries of the socialist bloc posed some problems for the Marcos regime in so far as its relationship with the military establishment was concerned. The strongly and fanatically anti-communist Armed Forces of the Philippines was understandably wary of the suddenly cordial relationship between the Marcos government and the People's Republic of China. Moreover, it was supposed to be to stop the "Maoist communists" that martial law was declared in the first place.

The relationship between the martial law regime and the United States exhibited little that was new. The Philippines' establishment of diplomatic relations with the People's Republic of China came only after the United States had already come into her own accommodation with that erstwhile "enemy country." Marcos' repeated calls for the reexamination of Philippine-American relations, which led to the renegotiation of the Military Bases Agreement in 1979 seemed less a harbinger of an ideological turnabout than an effort to secure adequate financial remuneration for the United States' continued use of the Subic Bay naval facility and Clark Air Base and in general, improve the Philippines'bargaining position with the United States on other matters.

The "new" foreign policy seemed to enjoy public support; its vulnerability if at all, was its perceived inconsistency with domestic policies such as the continued incarceration, and reportedly even torture, of political prisoners whose only "crime" was their espousal of certain Marxist-Leninist-Maoist ideas. Internationally, the new foreign policy won new friends and admirers from the Southeast Asian region, the Third World and the socialist bloc. Conversely, it may well have created potential foes in Taiwan, South Korea, and even Israel.

In the main, the consequences of the"new" foreign policy were salutary. The Philippines profited from expanded trade relations and she also assumed a leadership role in regional politics through active participation in ASEAN. The attraction of foreign investments resulted in new jobs for the unemployed, increased per capita income and purchasing power, and significant increments to the Gross National Product. The long-term implications of the New Society's "open door policy" on foreign investments and multinational corporations are not as clear.

Because of the multinational corporations' preferred position in the New Society, as well as their virtually unlimited capitalization, superior technological and entreprenurial know-how, and worldwide marketing outlets, their impact on local capital generation and infant industries was generally negative. If the development of native capital was one of the New Society's synoptic goals, the preferential treatment accorded by the regime to these multinational corporations seemed to have had the opposite effect.

The agrarian problem is as old as the Philippines itself. To a great extent, the Philippines' land tenure problems were inherited from the Spanish period, and the encomienda system which brought about the current feudal or semifeudal land tenure system. Attempts to cope with the problem during the Commonwealth period and throughout the Second Philippine Republic were mostly unsuccessful, because of the determined opposition of powerful landed interests in Congress and other government offices. Meanwhile peasant unrest had continuously seethed and on certain occasions exploded into open rebellion.

Macapagal succeeded in pushing through a comprehensive Land Reform Code in 1963 (R.A. 3844) which transformed the land tenure system from that of share-tenancy to leasehold. Like previous land reform laws, R.A. 3844 called for the acquisition of suitable lands by the government and their subsequent redistribution to deserving tenants and beneficiaries. The retention limit for individuals was 144 hectares, and for corporations 1,024, and payment for expropriated land was determined on the basis of the land's "fair market value." There were various loopholes in the 1963 Land Reform Act, such as the exemption of lands not planted to rice or corn and of "mechanized farms" and plantations. These loopholes were fully exploited by the landowners and all but frustrated the effective implementation of R.A. 3844.

Not long after the issuance of Proclamation No. 1081, Marcos issued two related decrees—PD No. 2 which declared the entire country as a land reform area, and PD No. 27 which spelled out the mechanics of the New Society's land reform program. Land reform under the New Society was different from previous programs in that it provided for the direct transfer of land from the landowner to the tiller. The mode of compensation was also different—identical amortizations spread out in fifteen years, computed by averaging crop yields for the three years prior to the issuance of PD No. 27, and multiplying the average by a factor of 2.5. This replaced the "fair market value" formula embodied in R.A. 3844. As a prerequisite to the finalization of the transaction, the farmer was required to become a member of a cooperative called the samahang nayon.

While positive gains were achieved in the New Society's land reform program, a number of obstacles remained. Some of these problems were inadequate funding, continued landlord opposition, and the limited hectarage of land available for transfer to farmers. Since PD No. 27 like previous land reform laws, also exempted plantations and lands planted to such export crops as abacca, sugar, and coconut, it was still possible for landowners to circumvent the law and defeat the intent of land reform. A lesser but potentially ticklish problem was the fact that many of the small landowners who owned from twenty-four to fifty hectares were military officers and government employees whose continued support Marcos needed in order to survive.

146

Chapter 7

THE REGIME IN RETROSPECT

After a thorough examination of available documents and of Marcos' public papers, it is clear that the declaration of martial law on 21 September 1972, had been under consideration for several years. The creation of the New Society--also referred to in later years as the "command society" and "crisis government"--was not a spontaneous and impulsive act. The need for a "New Society" rid of "oligarchs" and the "profligate rich" had been a perennial theme in Marcos' public pronouncements from early 1965 to the actual imposition of martial law. The partial declaration of martial law (under Proclamation No. 889) on 21 August 1971 and the affirmation of its constitutionality by the Supreme Court in Lansang v. Garcia provided Marcos with the necessary legal and constitutional support he needed to justify the subsequent imposition of absolute martial rule.

The people's initial reaction to the promulgation of Proclamation No. 1081 was generally positive. Marcos' excellent sense of timing and mastery of the Filipino psyche ensured an almost cavalier acceptance of martial rule by the majority. Had martial law been declared any sooner, or later, it is doubtful it would have been received as favorably by the Filipino people. On their face, Marcos' statements indicated a long and slow process of transformation from a "political oligarch" into a "revolutionary." However, having decided to part ways with the "oligarchy" after winning an unprecedented second term in 1969, Marcos seemed to have bided his time, waiting for the opportune moment to make his move. The violent student demonstrations of 1970 through 1972 and the state of open rebellion allegedly fomented by "Maoist Communists" were what Marcos needed to justify adopting more draconian measures, to launch a "revolution" of his own.

Marcos and the Military Establishment

Marcos was ideally suited to launch the so-called revolution because of the convincing mandates he received in the elections of 1965 and 1969, his strong-arm reputation, and his unique relationship with the military establishment. Marcos made history in 1969 when he won an unprecedented second term as president in an overwhelming electoral victory. The only other president who might have similarly succeeded was Magsaysay. The people would have followed Magsaysay; the military would have supported him. Like Magsaysay, Marcos was a charismatic personality and, like Magsaysay, Marcos had the full and unqualified backing of the military establishment.

As a legendary war hero and the most decorated soldier to come out of World War II, Marcos was held in high esteem by his former comrades-in-arms. But just in case, he also made sure that the leadership of the Armed Forces of the Philippines (all three service branches, the Philippine Constabulary, and the elite Presidential Guard Regiment) was in the hands of Ilocanos or officers personally loyal to him.[1] In a rather regionalistic Philippine polity this was significant, since Marcos had always counted on the so-called "solid north" as his main political base, and his fellow Ilocanos had never let him down.

The military establishment's perception of Marcos as a courageous and reportedly even "ruthless" man and his proven martial background served him in good stead. Whatever dissent, if any, from the military was more than adequately neutralized by presidential proclamations and edicts increasing base pay for enlisted men and non-commissioned officers, raising the ranks of flag-level officers by one grade, establishing an AFP commissary, instituting special insurance coverages for military personnel, and a variety of other fringe benefits. Indeed, in the context of the Philippines' utang na loob value system, the AFP felt beholden to Marcos. To ensure that no ambitious generals and colonels may be tempted to depose him, Marcos retired (in some instances prematurely) certain senior officers who could conceivably have served as the focal point of a coup d'etat. Marcos seemed to be particularly wary of flag-level officers who were graduates of American service academies supposedly because of the latter group's alleged links with the Pentagon and the Central Intelligence Agency.

148

With the exception of Magsaysay who also had a unique relationship with the AFP (Magsaysay was a famed and storied _guerrillero_ and as President Quirino's Secretary of National Defense was credited for "breaking the backbone" of the Huk rebellion of the early 1950s) no other president could lay claim to such excellent rapport with the officers and men of the Armed Forces of the Philippines. Moreover, the socialization of the AFP officer corps on the principle of civilian supremacy over the military was a crucial factor that worked in Marcos' favor.

While the ruling Marcos coalition included technocrats, intellectuals, "reformed" media men, and even some old-line politicians, there was little doubt that the most important element was the military establishment. Even opponents of martial law, such as Raul S. Manglapus' American-based Movement for a Free Philippines (MFP) realized the centrality of the military to the survival of the New Society. Consequently, the MFP frequently directed appeals to the officers and men of the AFP urging them to restore the constitutional system and pointing out that Marcos had been holding office unconstitutionally and illegally, his second and last lawful term of office having expired on 31 December 1973.

The AFP's monopoly of the instruments of violence, its esprit d' corps, and its tight organization and chain of command, put it in a potentially strong position to overthrow Marcos. But the AFP never attempted to seize power. Instead, the AFP successfully supressed anti-regime dissent although some of its activities such as the mistreatment of political prisoners, created a negative image for the Marcos regime abroad. Separate fact-finding missions by the International Commission of Jurists, Amnesty International, and the US State Department confirmed and documented specific incidents of torture and other human rights violations in New Society detention centers and safe houses.[2] While Marcos and some members of his cabinet, notably Information Secretary Francisco S. Tatad, Solicitor General Estelito P. Mendoza, and Defense Secretary Enrile, argued that the cases cited in the ICJ, AI, and US State Department reports were isolated incidents involving over-zealous officers and men, there was no doubt that Marcos was unhappy about the negative publicity these reports generated abroad. Consequently, Malacanang Palace made it a point to accord maximum publicity to the court-martial and separation from the service of military personnel found to have abused their powers.

The Public's Response to Martial Rule

The indications were that the majority of Filipinos accepted martial law either out of fear or as an alternative to the corrupt and inept government of the Second Philippine Republic, at least for the first three to four years. The people seemed to be particularly impressed by improved peace and order conditions, spectacular economic gains and new initiatives in foreign policy and land reform. Notwithstanding the fact that verification of the extent or genuinenes of the public's acceptance of the New Society was circumscribed by tight security rules and a ban on political research, all six referenda which were held from 1973 to 1977 and the election held on 7 April 1978 gave the Marcos regime overwhelming votes of confidence.

It may, of course, be argued that the results of these referenda and the election of 7 April 1978, were unreliable indices of the public's acceptance (or rejection) of the New Society because among other things, the referenda and election were held under martial law restrictions. According to the International Commission of Jurists, there were eleven reasons why the results of the six referenda "cannot be considered, in any way, as a true measure of the will of the people."[3] In the case of the election of 7 April 1978, on the other hand, the regime's Kilusang Bagong Lipunan (New Society Movement) not only had a monopoly of print and broadcast media coverage, but Marcos also used the immense resources of the presidency to win votes.[4]

There were also confirmed reports by foreign correspondents who covered the event of cheating and other anomalies, especially in the Metro Manila area where the First Lady, Imelda Romualdez-Marcos was one of the candidates. Metro Manila was the only constituency where an organized opposition, Lakas ng Bayan or LABAN, fielded a complete slate of candidates. It is significant that election results there were not announced until several days after the election and only after six opposition candidates were detained and arrest warrants were issued for six others who reportedly went into hiding.

Yet it was also true that a sizeable segment of the population supported Marcos and his New Society, for, as one sympathetic observer found out,

150

"the atmosphere [was] far more peaceful than it was prior to the confiscation of loose firearms . . ." and in contrast to martial law alsewhere, "the Philippine version [was] relatively benign."[5] Overseas Filipinos who returned to the Philippines for brief visits on the New Society's much-heralded balikbayan (roughly translated, "return to one's country") program also made similar observations. Many of these overseas Filipinos were impressed by cosmetic changes that had taken place in Metro Manila such as the Cultural Center, the Convention Center, the changed Manila and Makati skylines, the proliferation of multi-storey hotels, the cleanliness of Metro Manila's streets, and improved peace and order conditions.

Indeed, much of Marcos' success in selling the regime to the Filipino people had been due to tangible gains in such areas as law and order, the economy, land reform, public works, and foreign policy. It appeared that the people were willing to forego some of the freedoms they enjoyed before martial law in exchange for political stability and certain material benefits. Master political strategist that he was, Marcos tried to involve the people, if not in the actual decision-making process itself, at least symbolically, through so-called Citizen's Assemblies or barangays, and through the 7 April 1978 election. The Filipino puts a high premium on "saving face"; thus even if in reality, his vote did not matter in the New Society's scheme of things, he was evidently placated enough by Marcos' going through the motions or appearances of involving him in decision making.

Stricter enforcement of tax and customs laws and the summary dismissal of known and suspected grafters in the Bureau of Customs and in the Bureau of Internal Revenue, two of the most corrupt government offices in pre-martial law days, also resulted in unprecedented increases in government revenues. The resulting political stability plus a concerted government campaign to attract foreign investors also led to the investment in the Philippines of a considerable volume of foreign capital especially from American and Japanese multinational corporations. This in turn created new jobs for the Philippines' ample pool of skilled and unskilled labor.

Unfortunately, worldwide inflationary trends virtually negated these economic gains. Thus the Philippine balance of payments remained unfavorable due largely to the prohibitive cost of OPEC oil and

the price increases which this triggered in manu-
factured goods the Philippines imported from the
United States, Japan, and other industrialized
countries. Locally, the cost of the war against the
New People's Army nationwide and the Moro Bangsa
Army in Mindanao and Sulu strained the national
treasury to the limit. On balance, however, the
economy improved during the first five years of
martial rule--another reason for the apparent
acceptance, or in any case, toleration by the
general public of the regime.

While land reform was still a long way from
being successfully implemented, the New Society
gave it official top priority. For as long as the
peasants believed that Marcos was doing what he
could within historical and inherent limitations, he
had most of the peasants on his side. Traditionally
and historically, peasants have been the mainstay of
dissident movements in the Philippines. Realizing
this, Marcos repeatedly assured the peasantry,
through symbolic gestures and through dramatic
demonstrations, of the government's determination to
bring about meaningful agrarian reforms. Because
the peasants did not have reasons to feel betrayed,
they were generally supportive of Marcos. In fact a
political scientist from the University of the
Philippines (who refers to the New Society as a
"Bonapartist regime") conceded that "if the voting
patterns in the last referendum [were] indicative of
the people's feelings, the peasantry in traditional
areas of agrarian unrest seeme[d] to have become a
major power base of the Bonapartist regime."[6]

Dimensions of Dissent Against the New Society

With the arrest and detention of Marcos'
critics, a series of decrees and "letters of
instruction" banning public demonstrations and
strikes, and the threat of real or imagined
reprisals, dissent was effectively muted during the
first three years of martial law.[7] The only opposition consisted of a few underground newsletters
published by various church groups and Ang Bayan,
the official organ of the Communist Party of the
Philippines (CPP). Certain church leaders--from
both the laity and clergy--also occasionally
denounced the martial law regime for its deportation
of progressive priests, nuns, and protestant
churchmen, and for its mistreatment of political
prisoners. The various student groups that were

152

vocal and militant prior to martial law were
unusually quiet; for some time the most "exciting"
news that came out of the universities were inter-
fraternity "rumbles" that resulted in death and
serious injuries to participants and bystanders. By
1975, however, the Philippine Collegian, the
official publication of the student body of the
University of the Philippines, started to feature
opinion columns and editorials critical of martial
law and Marcos. The arrest, detention and subsequent death of the newspaper's editor, Abraham M.
Sarmiento, Jr., the eldest son of a member of the
university's Board of Regents, only intensified the
restiveness among students in the Metropolitan
Manila area.

Dissent under martial rule assumed two basic
dimensions--guerrilla warfare and parliamentary
struggle. The armed struggle was waged in two major
fronts, in the Minsupala region by the secessionist
Moro National Liberation Front (MNLF) and in Luzon,
Visayas, and certain areas of Mindanao, by the
revitalized Communist Party of the Philippines. The
Moro Bangsa Army, financed at one time by Libya's
Muammar Gaddafi, was fighting for the establishment
of a separate and politically autonomous Muslim
state. The territory sought by the MNLF corre-
sponded roughly to the lower half of the island of
Mindanao, the provinces of Sulu and Tawi Tawi, the
traditional home of the Tausugs, the provinces of
Cotabato, South Cotabato, Davao del Sur, Davao
Oriental, Zamboanga, Lanao del Sur, and Lanao del
Norte. These provinces, with the exception of Sulu,
Tawi Tawi, and the two Lanaos, were predominantly
populated by Christians, while Cotabato was about
evenly split between Christians and Maguindanao
Muslims.

It was uncertain whether the MNLF had formal
links to the New People's Army. The leader of the
MNLF, Tripoli-based Nurralaji Misuari (Misuari has
since relocated to Jeddah, Saudi Arabia) was a
contemporary and close friend of the former chairman
of the Communist Party of the Philippines, Jose Ma.
Sison at the University of the Philippines. At one
time in the late 1960's, Misuari and Sison were both
active in the now-outlawed "front organization"
Kabataang Makabayan and one of the factions of the
Bertrand Russell Peace Foundation. Apart from the
personal association of Sison and Misuari, however,
and their common opposition to the Marcos martial
law government, there was no evidence that the two

153

groups were waging a coordinated guerrilla war against the Marcos government.

While the activities of the NPA were, for a short while, overshadowed by the MNLF's, the NPA continued to wage limited hit-and-run operations against military targets and did not seem to have been weakened or demoralized by the arrest of their three top leaders, Bernabe Buscayno (better known as Commander Dante), Lieutenant Victor Corpus, and Jose Ma. Sison in late 1978. This was largely due to the horizontal structure of the NPA leadership in which younger and equally able military cadres simply took over after the capture or death of their erstwhile leaders. The influence of the CPP in the rural areas (especially in the Cagayan Valley-Isabela region) did not significantly diminish, and CPP-NPA propaganda units continued to proselytize and win converts. It appeared that the NPA was being very patient, faithfully adhering to the Mao Tse Tung doctrine of disciplined gradualism so successfully adopted by General Vo Nguyen Giap in the North Vietnamese's military triumphs against both the French and Americans. It was obvious that the NPA carefully avoided set-piece battles with the AFP and confined itself to quick and mobile thrusts designed to gain eventual undisputed control of the countryside.

In spite of the inevitable harm to its propaganda and recruitment activities, by the capture of virtually all the members of the central committee of the CPP in 1978-1979, the CPP did not degenerate into a Mafia-type criminal syndicate as the Marcos regime had earlier hoped. The cadres of the revitalized CPP seemed to be more ideologically-oriented than the Hukbalahaps of the early 1950's who disbanded into rival bandit groups after their leaders fell into government hands. The party simply regrouped even as its military arm, the New People's Army, continued to prosecute its strategy of protracted guerrilla warfare in the field.

The legal-parliamentary struggle against the New Society was more complex, involved more actors, and it took place both in the Philippines and abroad, especially in the United States and Canada. These anti-martial law groups differed not only in goals but also in strategies and techniques. Their common objective was the dismantling of martial law, the release of all political prisoners, the restoration of civil liberties, and the holding of free elections. Significantly, none of these groups advocated a return to the status quo ante--the freewheeling, corrupt, and patronage-oriented style of politics for which the Philippines had been noted.

Opposition Groups in Exile

One of the largest and most viable of the anti-martial law groups that operated out of the United States was the Movement for a Free Philippines (MFP) headed by Raul S. Manglapus. It was quite effective in lobbying for reduced United States military and economic assistance to the Philippines, and its centrist or moderate stance tended to attract more members from a wider spectrum of political and ideological supporters. The MFP also counted on the support--either open or tacit-- of most of the politicians of pre-martial law Philippines who were on self-exile in the United States, such as former legislator Raul Daza, former Constitutional Convention delegate Heherson T. Alvarez, and Antonio J. Villegas, former mayor of Manila.

One obstacle which the MFP had to overcome-- especially as far as the Filipinos in the Philippines were concerned--was the pro-American "imperialist" label which the more militant anti-martial law groups successfully pinned on the MFP. Even Manglapus' credentials were questioned by these groups, and there were a few who insisted that the daring escape of the Manglapus family from the Philippines in 1973 was really engineered by the CIA, and that they (Manglapus' family members) were "flown out of Clark Air Base" instead of by way of Malaysia as was generally believed. The MFP was also wracked at least twice by internal dissension and factionalism, the last being the attempt by a former pro-Marcos "student leader," Ely V. Pamatong, to disrupt the MFP national convention at St. Louis, Missouri, in 1977. Manglapus' reelection as president became possible only after the MFP Constitution was amended to enable him to seek a third two-year term, and serve beyond five years.[8]

Another anti-martial law group which operated from the United States was the International Association of Patriotic Filipinos (Pandaigdigang Samahan ng Makabayang Pilipino--IAPF) which was organized in October 1976. The IAPF was highly ideological and primarily concerned with the mobilization of broad popular support, both in North America and in the Philippines for the "national democratic struggle" being waged by the CPP/NPA. On the same ideological wavelength as the IAPF was the Anti-Martial Law Coalition (ALLC), an umbrella group, which was founded in 1975. The AMLC organized a number of public demonstrations and pickets against the New Society in various American cities.

The National Committee for the Restoration of Civil Liberties in the Philippines (NCRCLP) was founded by concerned Filipinos and Americans in late September 1972. The NCRCLP purchased advertisement space in major national newspapers calling for the restoration of civil liberties in the Philippines and pointing out abuses perpetrated by Marcos partisans in the name of national security. The NCRCLP attracted well-known anti-war activists as well as some internationally known literary and political figures who were outraged by the suppression of civil liberties in the Philippines.

The NCRCLP was dissolved in 1973 and replaced by the Katipunan ng mga Demokratikong Pilipino (Union of Democratic Filipinos--KDP). Primarily based in the West Coast, the KDP had chapters in fourteen cities in the United States and Canada and was responsible for putting out the newspaper Ang Katipunan which carried stories either glossed over or suppressed by Philippine newspapers and news bureau reports emanating from the Philippines. In addition to its opposition to the New Society the paper also featured commentaries on such social issues as human rights and articles on international political events such as the downfall of Indira Gandhi's Congress Party in India, the racial riots in Soweto (South Africa), and Ian Smith's white supremacist government in Rhodesia.

A fifth anti-martial law organization, also based in the United States, was the Friends of the Filipino People (FFP). The FFP was an association of progressive American intellectuals and academicians who were oppposed to the New Society. Individual members such as Daniel B. Schirmer of the Goddard-Cambridge Graduate Program in Social Change and Benedict J. Kerkvliet of the University of Hawaii testified before United States congressional committees in opposition to the martial law regime (Schirmer on foreign policy and Kerkvliet on land reform). The FFP also prepared and circulated an Information Bulletin focusing on specific topics and refuting some of the more lavish claims of the Marcos government. Another FFP publication which has since become extinct was Pahayag. Pahayag showcased well-researched and documented articles by specialists on the Philippines and even some reproductions of documents suppressed by officials of the New Society.

Opposition Groups at Home

For a while it seemed as if no single individual or group would dare to openly organize against the New Society. With the two pre-martial law political parties (Nacionalista and Liberal) virtually nonexistant, the leader of the erstwhile opposition Liberal party (former Senator Benigno Aquino) in jail, and other former opposition leaders coopted into the "crisis government," prospects for a viable opposition group being organized seemed dim. Yet on 21 September 1977, the eve of the fifth anniversary of the imposition of martial law, a group of 130 leaders of various anti-martial law organizations formed the People's League for Freedom.[9] In a way this was due to a gradual "easing up" on Marcos' part--his lifting of the travel ban, the relatively benign way in which demonstrators were dealt with on 21 September 1977, his repeated announcements about "phasing out" martial law, and his scheduling of elections to the interim National Assembly on 7 April 1978. This ad hoc group of religious leaders, politicians, professionals, students, peasants, and workers elected Jovito R. Salonga as their president.

The founding of the People's Convention on Human Rights also featured Salonga as the main speaker. Salvador P. Lopez, former University of the Philippines' president and another well known Marcos critic, gave the keynote address.[10] The People's Convention on Human Rights was intended both as a supplement and an alternative to the World Law Conference held in Manila in August 1977. The conference was boycotted by a number of prospective participants, including former US Attorney General Ramsey Clark who described Manila as a "heart breaking choice for a conference on human rights."

The People's Convention on Human Rights adopted the following alternatives to the policies and programs of the New Society: (1) workers should have the right to organize free trade unions and to strike, as well as to security of employment; (2) farmers should have the right to free association and expression, including the right to refuse to join government programs without fear of government reprisal; (3) students should have their own student councils and a free campus press; (4) the urban poor should have the right to a decent dwelling near their places of employment without fear of arbitrary government relocation; and (5) unconditional and absolute amnesty should be granted to all political detainees whether provisionally released or still under detention.[11] The convention also affirmed the right of every citizen to free religious expression and the crucial role that a free and untramelled press plays in a democratic society.

The Catholic Church: Critical Collaboration

The Philippines is the only country in Southeast Asia which is predominantly Christian--about ninety-four percent of a population estimated at fifty-six million in 1987. Roughly eighty-four percent are Roman Catholic and the rest of the Christian population belong to various protestant denominations including two home-grown churches, the Philippine Independent Church (also known as the Aglipayan Church) and the Iglesia ni Kristo (Church of Christ), a more recent but politically monolithic religious sect. Because of its very large size and deep roots in Philippine history (the Philippines was converted to catholicism in the middle of the sixteenth century), the Roman Catholic Church was the most significant organization (religious or otherwise) which could have served as a counterpoise to the New Society.

There were three basic groups within the Roman Catholic hierarchy in the Philippines, the traditionalists, moderates, and radicals. The traditionalist group was led for a long time by the late Julio Cardinal Rosales, the second Filipino prelate to be elevated to the College of Cardinals. Cardinal Rosales came from a well-known political family in Samar (his brother Decoroso Rosales was a long-time member of the old Philippine Senate). He took over the "traditionalist" mantle from the late Rufino J. Cardinal Santos. Like his predecessor, Cardinal Rosales believed that the Catholic Church must eschew non-ecclesiastical concerns and confine itself instead to spiritual matters. Cardinal Rosales' view was shared by most of the older secular clergy who remained aloof from politics.

Except for a small minority of younger clergy, many of whom were Jesuits, the Catholic Church chose to generally collaborate with the New Society. To a great extent, this was due to the leadership of the

158

Archbishop of Manila, Jaime Cardinal Sin, the other Filipino member of the College of Cardinals. Cardinal Sin headed the moderate faction of the Catholic Bishops Conference of the Philippines (CBCP), the ecclesiastical body which formulated policy for some 5,000 priests in fifteen autonomous dioceses throughout the country. Cardinal Sin was also the principal author of the policy of "critical collaboration" vis-a-vis the Marcos "crisis government."

The policy of critical collaboration held that the form of government--whether democracy, dictatorship, or monarchy--was not important, provided that the church was allowed to exercise its functions freely. The Catholic Church supported the government when "it move[d] to safeguard the fundamental rights of all, particularly the less fortunate and underprivileged . . . but denounce[d] government actions which violate[d] human rights, conscience in particular, or obstruct[ed] the observance of justice and the realization of human development." Cardinal Sin did not see himself in the role of a Marcos adversary but as a "catalyst to prick the conscience of the people who were responsible for those things." [12] The moderate faction within the CBCP counted on the support of fifty-six prelates, a clear majority in a body of eighty-one.

Numerically smaller but very vocal, the so-called radicals were headed by then Bishop Francisco Claver, S.J., who also headed the central Mindanao diocese of Bukidnon. Bishop Claver who has a doctorate in Anthropology from the University of Colorado wanted the Catholic Church to take a less ambivalent stance towards martial law. Claver's supporters within the CBCP who numbered about fifteen contended that the Catholic Church should oppose the degradation of the dignity of the individual and his manipulation by government for such ends as national security and economic development. While conceding that five years of martial law did yield such salutary results as the improvement of peace and order, dramatic economic growth, the lowering of inflation from forty percent in 1974 to ten percent in 1977, Bishop Claver pointed out that on balance, "the negative aspects far outweighed the positive aspects."[13]

Because of the preponderance of the moderates and traditionalists within the CBCP, Bishop Claver and his followers spoke out instead under the aegis of the Association of Major Religious Superiors (AMRS), an organization made up of some 2,500 priests and 7,000 nuns. The AMRS expressed its opposition to the New Society through prayer rallies and vigils, symposia (usually held in convent schools to minimize the likelihood of government raids), and through leaflets and other assorted publications. On 5 December 1976, martial law authorities closed down two newsletters, The Signs of the Times and the Communicator, the latter edited by James B. Reuter, S.J. Less than a month before, on 19 and 20 November, two radio stations, one of which was operated by Bishop Claver's diocese, were also barred by military authorities from further broadcasting. In both instances the government charged the clergymen involved with disseminating "subversive information." After the seizure of the two newsletters and the closure of their radio stations, Bishop Claver and his sympathizers resorted to pastoral letters denouncing specific New Society abuses. One such pastoral letter was issued on 8 January 1977 and excommunicated all those who had engaged in the torture of political detainees.[14]

An even smaller group than Bishop Claver's was a faction critical of all three groups. This fourth faction which the Marcos regime often referred to as the "Christian Left," was typified by young and highly politicized priests such as Father Edicio de la Torre and Father Jose Nacu, both subjected to protracted detention and torture for alleged subversion. Father de la Torre suggested that the Catholic Church was remiss in its obligation to the Catholic faithful by failing to "denounce injustice and promote human development." While not openly advocating that the Catholic Church take up arms to combat the "oppression" and "exploitation" of the people, Father de la Torre noted that the very least the Catholic Church could have done was "to raise its voice in protest at every violation of human rights . . . better be accused of politicking than cowardice."[15]

Individual Opposition Leaders

In addition to the various anti-martial law organizations in exile and the militant wing of the Catholic Church, there were a few prominent individual critics who boldly spoke out against the New Society. One of the most eloquent among these was Salvador P. Lopez, former Ambassador to the United States and the United Nations, Secretary of Foreign Affairs, and President of the University of the

Philippines. As early as 30 October 1974, Lopez called on Marcos to "dismantle martial law." It was Lopez' thesis that two years of martial law was enough and its continuation was unnecessary. Prolonging martial law, Lopez cautioned, could lead to the stultification of the Filipino's initiative, and in the long run render him incapable of self-government.[16]

In his keynote speech before the People's Convention on Human Rights on 20 August 1977, Lopez argued against Marcos' theory that political-civil rights were only meaningful if the people had enough to eat and were adequately clothed and sheltered; in other words, that "economic rights" preceded political-civil rights. Lopez pointed out that the relationship between economic rights and political-civil rights in a democratic society was not a disjunctive "either-or" relationship but a conjunctive relationship of mutual support, and that the choice was not between food or freedom but food with freedom or food without freedom. Lopez also assailed the "corruption of impoverished scholars and researchers by generous subventions and seductive offers of preferment" suggesting that "a cowed university with timorous professors and frightened students [was] not the best place to train men and women of ability, intelligence, and imagination for public service," because it took "free men to produce free men."[17]

Other individuals who openly opposed the New Society were former senators Jovito R. Salonga, Jose W. Diokno, Lorenzo M. Tanada, Francisco "Soc" Rodrigo, and Eva Estrada Kalaw. Macapagal, a former president, and Laurel, a former speaker of the old House of Representatives, and a long roster of lesser but equally courageous former government officials by 1978 had begun to denounce martial law. In addition to public statements, Salonga, Diokno, and Tanada also repeatedly served as legal counsel in habeas corpus petitions before the Supreme Court in behalf of several political prisoners as well as for foreign clergymen and journalists threatened with deportation for various acts allegedly inimical to the New Society.[18] Salonga was also an outspoken critic of the Marcos government's policy on multinational corporations, contending that while the MNCs did offer short-term benefits (jobs, wages, and technological skills), their domination of the national economy was disadvantageous to the Philippines in the long run. Salonga was particularly concerned about the potential these MNCs had for undermining national sovereignty.[19]

Macapagal, Marcos' immediate predecessor in office, had also advocated the lifting of martial law. Macapagal's credibility and stature as a leader was hurt, however, when he sought political asylum at the United States Embassy in Manila on 1 April 1976 (Romulo, Marcos' Secretary of Foreign Affairs at the time, referred to Macapagal's bid for political asylum as an "April Fool's Day joke"), and by his earlier cooperation with Marcos, as the presiding officer of the 1971 Constitutional Convention. Laurel, on the other hand, called for an end to martial law on 21 August 1977, pointing out that "national unity could never be forged unless people were liberated from the compulsions and restrictions of the regime."[20]

The Prospects for Dissent

Five years after the imposition of martial law and the subsequent establishment of the New Society (rather conspicuously Marcos and his spokesmen deliberately avoided the term "martial law" to describe the regime, opted instead for the neutral phrase "crisis government"), the voice of dissent got louder and louder. In so many ways Marcos caused this to happen by public declarations about phasing out martial law, the election of 7 April 1978 and its aftermath, and his claims before world gatherings such as the Conference on the Law of the World that all political prisoners would be granted amnesty. Not to be discounted, however, was the effect of external pressures including US President James E. Carter's accent on human rights, the finding of the International Commission of Jurists that the continuation of martial rule "[was] to perpetuate the personal power of the president and his collaborators," and of course, the report of an Amnesty International investigating team which documented cases of the torture of political prisoners held in various New Society detention centers and "safehouses."[21]

In retrospect, the anti-martial law groups in exile were also quite effective in bringing to American and worldwide attention some of the excesses of the New Society. More specifically, these anti-martial law groups also succeeded in getting the United States Congress to carefully scrutinize military and economic aid to the

Philippines. What these groups were not able to do was to get themselves heard by the Filipino people whose support was, in the final analysis, what mattered most. In general, the impact of these groups in the Philippines was effectively neutralized by the New Society's propaganda apparatus. The irony of the situation was that the longer these groups remained expatriate, the more difficult it was for them to reestablish their links with Filipinos in the Philippines.

In like manner, dissent had also grown dramatically among students in the Philippines' several hundred universities and colleges. Students who seemed intimidated during the first four years of martial rule had, by 1978, resumed their so-called parliament in the streets, first demonstrating on such bread and butter issues as tuition hikes but later, demanding an end to martial law itself. Noticeably, many of the demonstrators came from Catholic schools, and eyewitness accounts told of student demonstrations led by, or participated in, by nuns and priests. This was significant in and of itself since in the years before martial law, anti-regime demonstrators generally hailed from state universities and colleges and some nonsectarian private universities while the counter-demonstrators (pro-regime) were mainly from catholic educational institutions.

The growing militance of a substantial segment of Catholic clergy and laity was a logical offshoot of the spirit of reform which had swept the Catholic Church during the previous thirty years, beginning with the ascension to the papacy of the late John XXIII. Pope John XXIII's successor, Paul VI, not only continued the reforms initiated by the Second Ecumenical Council (Vatican II)—changes in dogma, the liturgy, and in the Catholic Church's relations with other religions and churches—but added his own conception of the role the Catholic Church must play towards the amelioration of the lives of the world's destitute and underprivileged. In his famous encyclical Poppulorum Progressio, Paul VI took the view that the Catholic Church must not only minister to the spiritual needs of its flock but to their temporal needs as well.

Apart from the Armed Forces of the Philippines, the Catholic Church was the only organization which had the potential of mobilizing mass action against the martial law regime and working for the full restoration of civil liberties. Given the philosophical split between the conservative and

163

moderate groups, on the one hand, and the progressive and liberal factions on the other, however, the Catholic Church collaborated with the Marcos regime. From beginning to end, Marcos was understandably reluctant to risk a head-on collision with the Catholic Church. What Marcos sought and got was an accommodation with the conservative-moderate faction, offering as quid pro quo for the church's maintenance of its policy of "critical collaboration" a guarantee that government plans to legalize abortion, institute absolute divorce, and tax church properties be unconditionally and permanently abandoned.

Since the majority of the bishops who constituted the CBCP stood firm on their decision to eschew politics, the progressive faction's criticisms of the New Society remained a minority viewpoint and did not get parlayed into official ecclesiastical policy. What would have happened had a substantial number of the church's leadership and rank-and-file openly rebelled against the group ruled by Cardinal Sin? If de la Torre's assessment that seventy percent of the Catholic Church's flock was exploited and oppressed was accurate, then the progressive faction might well have prevailed. It is noteworthy that out of the fifty or more universities and other institutions of higher learning in the Metropolitan Manila area, nineteen including the oldest and third largest (the University of Santo Tomas) and two of the most prestigious (the Ateneo de Manila University and De La Salle University) were owned and administered by Roman Catholic religious organizations.

With the possible exception of the 7 April 1978 election, Marcos dealt with dissent against his crisis government rather well. Foreign policy initiatives such as the opening of diplomatic relations with countries of the socialist bloc and repeated calls for the reexamination of Philippine-American relations (including the radical restructuring of the Military Bases Agreement) deprived the radical left of one of its stock accusations, that Marcos was a "puppet" of the United States. Ironically, during the campaign for the interim National Assembly election, Marcos repeatedly accused the United States (particularly Mrs. Pat Derian, Undersecretary of State for Human Rights and Humanitarian Affairs at the time) and "some Japanese corporations" of interference in the domestic affairs of the Philippines. The martial law government, through then Defense Secretary Enrile, also attempted to link opposition leader Benigno Aquino to the US Central Intelligence Agency.

Improved relations with the People's Republic of China, Malaysia, and Libya also served to undercut support for the CPP and MNLF, respectively. Marcos' announcement during the ASEAN Heads of State Conference in Kuala Lumpur, Malaysia, in August 1977, that the Philippines was "unconditionally dropping" her claim to Sabah was obviously the high point of the conference and undoubtedly won the admiration of Malaysia and the new Kuala Lumpur-oriented leadership of Sabah. This in turn served to undermine the MNLF's "Sabah connection" even though the renunciation of the claim has yet to be formalized.[22]

The New Society leadership's apparent casual disregard of the Movement for a Free Philippines and other expatriate anti-martial law groups was also just short of masterful. The inter- and intra-group rivalries which beset these anti-martial law organizations in the United States clearly benefitted Marcos; the more divided these anti-Marcos groups were, the easier it was for Marcos' propagandists to neutralize their collective impact. After the spectacular escape of Eugenio Lopez, Jr. and Sergio Osmena III to the United States on 2 October 1977, for instance, Marcos' reaction was unexpectedly low-key. Instead of demanding that the United States returned the fugitives to the Philippines-- the US and the Philippines do not have an extradition treaty--Marcos announced that he "did not want them back" and that as far as he was concerned, their relatives could "even visit them there." Predictably, Marcos' statement downgraded the headline potential of the story and saved the crisis government further embarassment.

The New Society and Philippine-American Relations

American military and economic aid was crucial to the survival of the New Society. In spite of his strong anti-American rhetoric during the campaign for the interim National Assembly, Marcos knew only too well that he needed the United States more than the United States needed him. The Philippines was almost entirely dependent on the United States for weapons and other military hardware. Even the proclaimed self-reliance of the AFP in the manufacture of small arms and other munitions was being partly financed by the United States and done by

licensed subsidiaries of American manufacturers.
The organization, training, and military tactics of
the AFP are replicas of their American counterparts'. Had the Philippines decided to go shopping
elsewhere for weapons, assuming that she could
afford to do so, this would have meant the complete
retraining and retooling of the entire Armed Forces
of the Philippines.

The Philippines was also dependent on the
United States economically. Even after the 4 July
1974 expiration of the Laurel-Langely Agreement, and
with it preferential treatment of Philippine
exports, the United States along with Japan,
remained the primary market for Philippine products.
Had the United States decided to restrict or ban
Philippine products, as a retaliatory action, the
Philippines' balance of payments picture would have
gotten even worse, the convertibility of the peso
(already quite precarious) even more dubious, and
the payments deficit so great that the Philippine
economy may not have been able to absorb its impact.
An even more effective perpetuator of Philippine
economic dependence on the United States, especially
in the long-run, was the active participation of
American multinational corporations in the nation's
capital development. It must be noted that the
influx of American multinational corporations after
1972 was brought about by the New Society's
liberalized policies on foreign investments as well
as specific incentives drawn up by the Department of
Commerce and the Board of Investments.

But what about Marcos' denunciations of the
United States during the campaign for the interim
National Assembly? Did not Marcos accuse the United
States, "whites," and other "foreigners" of inter-
fering in the domestic affairs of the Philippines?
There were at least three possible explanations for
Marcos' anti-American tirades: first, he was
exploiting what he perceived as a strong resurgence
of nationalism, and second, Marcos was applying
pressure on the United States to yield to Philippine
demands when negotiations over the Military Bases
Agreement resumed the following year. Imelda Marcos
confirmed this when she told a political rally on 1
April 1978, that "the government needed a massive
victory in the election to strengthen its hand in
military bases negotiations with the United
States."[23]

A third possible explanation is that Marcos
was reacting to official Washington's lukewarm
attitude toward his regime. It was widely known

that President Carter and several influential
congressional leaders were unhappy about the New
Society's record on human rights and the liquidation
of the American-style democracy introduced to the
Philippines in 1901. In spite of these developments, however, the New Society continued to
maintain good relations with the United States,
since, notwithstanding the resurgence of nationalism
in the 1960's and 1970's, there was no gainsaying
the continued moral and political influence of the
United States over the Philippines and the Filipino
people.

Marcos and the Technocrats

Especially in the early years, much of the
prestige and strength of the New Society derived
from its successful cooptation of the professional-
technocratic elite. Some of the most influential
and respected men in the New Society were not
politicians but technocrats--highly skilled and
well-trained professionals with graduate degrees
from some of the best universities in the United
States and Europe. These technocrats were cabinet
secretaries, heads of government corporations and
think-tanks, as well as middle-level managers in the
New Society apparatus.[24] Some of them did not stand
for election on 7 April 1978, but retained their
positions in the government by presidential (or
prime ministerial) appointment. They obviously had
Marcos' complete trust.

In addition to the cooptation of these professional managers, Marcos also won over surrendered or
captured dissidents and somehow induced them to work
for the New Society. Many of the professors from
the University of the Philippines who were arrested
or went underground after 22 September 1972, were
reinstated at the university, and were evidently
left alone except for occasional security evaluations. In fact some of these former anti-Marcos
academics constituted themselves into a stable of
writers helping put together a seventeen-volume
history of the Philippines. As one University of
the Philippines critic noted:

> Under the Bonapartist regime the
> intelligentsia--or at least a section of
> it: the technocrats--never had it so
> good. Great opportunities for fabulous
> incomes . . . [had] suddenly been opened

to them with the entry of multi-national
corporations and the proliferation of
new government agencies. Furthermore,
the suspension of political institutions
previously dominated by the traditional
oligarchy [had] immensely enhanced their
influence in the making of public
policies and programs.[25]

Under the previous government system, these technocrats complained about being hamstrung by members of
Congress and having to struggle against considerable
bureaucratic red tape in order to get anything
accomplished. Under the New Society, they were only
accountable to Marcos and generally remained in
office as long as they produced results Marcos
liked.

To be sure, there were technocrats and intellectuals who opposed the Marcos regime. Some of
them--including Teofisto Guingona, Ernesto Maceda,
Fernando Barican--stood for election on 7 April
1978, but all were defeated by Kilusang Bagong
Lipunan candidates amidst charges and counter-
charges of massive fraud and cheating. Others
simply kept quiet or refused to be drawn into
contesting the election which key opposition leaders
like Salonga and Diokno dismissed as a "sham" and a
"farce." Had Marcos succeeded in coopting the rest
of the intelligentsia, overall anti-regime dissent
would have been considerably weakened, if not
eliminated altogether.

A problem Marcos repeatedly had to deal with
in relation to his technocrat advisors and managers
was that of controlling latent rivalries and
jealousies between and among these men. These
rivalries occasionally flared up and threatened the
cohesion of the New Society's inner ring of power,
e.g., when Alejandro Melchor was ousted as Executive
Secretary and his entire office abolished in 1975,
after the failure of a Melchor-initiated purge of
Defense Secretary Enrile. Late in 1977 another
highly placed technocrat, Horacio Morales, Jr.,
Vice-President of the government think-tank,
Development Academy of the Philippines, defected to
join the National Democratic Front, an alleged
communist front organization.

168

Some Concluding Observations

The literature on Philippine politics, especially as it related to the pre-martial law period, was full of negative references to its supposedly freewheeling, irresponsible, and "bazaar-like" nature. To a large extent, these criticisms were valid. Filipinos under the Second Philippine Republic did indeed often take politics too seriously and did dilute specific western political institutions to suit native habits and predilections. The results were not always pleasant to behold; the improvisations, in some cases, downright ludicrous. Nevertheless, Filipinos never lacked in their enthusiasm for constitutionalism, the idea that a government must derive its authority from the consent of the governed and that man's fullest potential can only be realized in an atmosphere of freedom. Thus the western concept of civil liberties and rights appealed to most Filipinos and inspired numerous exemplary achievements in politics, law, and in the arts and humanities. The Philippines has a long and viable democratic tradition dating back to pre-Hispanic times.

The problems that have beset the Philippines since the restoration of its independence by the United States in 1946--widespread poverty, unemployment, lopsided distribution of wealth, inflation, and armed dissidence--are similar to the problems that trouble many other developing nations. Also typical was the search for alternative political formulas and solutions to replace institutions inherited from former colonial masters. Efforts such as Soekarno's "Guided Democracy," Ne Win's "Burmese Road to Socialism," and Marcos' "Constitutional Authoritarianism," are illustrative of the difficulties these new nations experienced with the political systems they inherited. Two of Marcos' early braintrusters, Romulo and Corpuz, suggested that western democratic institutions and their overlay of individual freedoms and civil liberties would not work in the Philippine setting. Romulo and Corpuz contended that the value system of the Filipino was personalistic not universalistic, and certain indigenous institutions such as <u>utang na loob</u>, <u>compadrazgo</u>, kinship, and <u>hiya</u> militated against the full flowering of western-style democracy; that civil liberties were luxuries which the people in their economically depressed state could not afford.

The implications of the Corpuz-Romulo thesis was that for the Philippines to achieve development or modernization she must abandon the idea that this could be done in a setting similar to that of the United States where power is shared by three branches of government. Moreover, individual freedoms granted to people who did not fully comprehend why and how to exercise them could, in fact, be destructive to the well-being of the state in the long run. The argument makes sense if one defined development narrowly in terms of the building of factories, infrastructure and other public works, the maintenance of peace and order, and the raising of the Gross National Product and per capita income.

If one defined development holistically, however, as "that process of change through which a society evolves the values, political leadership and other forms of social organization necessary to mobilize and utilize resources in such a way as to maximize the opportunities available to the majority of its members, for the realization to the fullest possible extent of their potential as human beings," one wonders whether protracted regimentation is desirable.[26] Even orthodox Marxists concede as axiomatic, the transitory nature of the command society; they posit that in the end, the state will "vanish and wither away." Because of the Filipinos' previous socialization into democratic values, individual freedoms, and civil liberties, it was particularly hard to tolerate an indefinite prolongation of the command society.

It cannot be denied that many beneficial and commendable changes did take place after the declaration of martial law in 1972. In fact, the declaration of martial law and the assumption by Marcos of virtually all the powers of government were initially received by the public as the proverbial "shot in the arm" which the polity needed to restore its sense of balance and perspective, and a reaffirmation of the capacity of democracy for self-rejuvenation. As the New Society's immediate goals were achieved--and Marcos and his spokesmen claimed this to be the case--the need for its continued existence should have diminished as well. Otherwise, the "authoritarian ruler of [the] 'crisis government' must then contend with the inevitable transformation of the 'command society' into a 'spectator society' composed of citizens who, believing that indifference [was] the perfect

170

policy, are quite content to let the government do everything for them."[27]

As evidenced by the absence of widespread popular rebellion during ten years of martial rule, the people seemed to appreciate even if only grudgingly, the reforms and other tangible achievements of the New Society especially during the first five years. The results of the six referenda and the 1978 interim National Assembly election (even assuming that the people voted under duress) indicated that Marcos did have substantial grassroots support. His Kilusang Bagong Lipunan (KBL) won impressively in the rural areas although it met with significant opposition (as much as forty percent according to Marcos himself) in Metro Manila.

If Marcos' principal objective in calling the interim National Assembly election was to establish his regime's legitimacy, then he was only partly successful. The opposition's impressive showing, notwithstanding the advantages of incumbency which Marcos exploited, must have come as a surprise to the New Society leadership. Moreover, the harsh way in which the New Society authorities dealt with the opposition party and its supporters after the election cast doubt on the willingness of Marcos to relinquish his plenary powers to the National Assembly as a prelude to the return to "normalcy." As one long-time student of Philippine affairs put it, Marcos' political skills were practically unequalled in Philippine history and, in fact, he rank[ed] high among Asian power-holders . . . in the sophistication of his tactics--indeed one of Machiavelli's most apt disciples."[28]

NOTES

Chapter 2

1. Proclamation No. 1081, "Proclaiming a State of Martial Law in the Philippines."
2. Philippine Times, 30 September 1972, p. 1.
3. See "Statement of the President on the Proclamation of Martial Law in the Philippines, in a Nationwide Radio and Television Broadcast," 21 September 1972.
4. General Order No. 15, "Prohibition of Ostentatious Display of Wealth and Extravagance."
5. Presidential Decree No. 2, "Proclamation, Declaring the Entire Country as Land Reform Area."
6. Presidential Decree No. 27, "Decree on the Emancipation of the Tenant From the Bondage of the Soil."
7. Letter of Instruction No. 35, "Take Over and Control of Certain Firms Owned or Controlled by Fernando Jacinto."
8. General Order No. 1, "Proclamation of President Marcos That He Will Govern the Nation and Direct the Operation of the Entire Government."
9. General Order No. 5, "Ban on Group Assemblies Including Strikes and Picketing in Vital Industries."
10. For a behaviorally-oriented study on the 1971 Constitutional Convention as a "political formula," see Roth, "The Choice of a Political Formula in a Third World Nation: The Case of the Philippines, 1971-1973."
11. Proclamation No. 1102, "Announcing the Ratification by the Filipino People of the Constitution Proposed by the 1971 Constitutional Convention."
12. The barangays were created by Presidential Decree No. 229, "Providing for the Manner of Voting and Canvass of Votes in Barangays (Citizens Assemblies)."
13. Ibid.

14. The term _Bagong Lipunan_ (or "New Society") is how the martial law regime is officially known.

15. Almond, _Political Development_; Almond and Coleman (eds.), _The Politics of Developing Areas_; Almond and Powell, _Comparative Politics: A Developmental Approach_; Apter, _The Politics of Modernization_; Riggs (ed.) _Frontiers of Development Administration_; Huntington, _Political Order in Changing Societies_; Heeger, _The Politics of Under-development_; Eisenstadt, _Modernization, Protest, and Change_; Montgomery and Siffin (eds.) _Approaches to Development: Politics, Administration and Change_; Pye, _Aspects of Political Development_; and Shils, _Political Development in the New States_.

16. See Antonio E. Lapitan, "Citizens Assemblies: Structures for Socio-Political Mobilization in the Philippines," a paper presented at the 1974 Midwest Conference on Asian Affairs, University of Kansas, Lawrence, Kansas, 1-2 November 1974.

17. Tucker, "Towards a Comparative Politics of Movement-Regimes," p. 283.

18. For an application of the paradigm of the "transitional society" to field research in the Philippines, see Douglas, "Modernization in a Transitional Setting: A Philippine Case Study," pp. 204-31.

19. Riggs (ed.), _Frontiers_, p. 5.

20. Tucker, "Towards a Comparative Politics," p. 283.

21. Ibid., p. 286.

22. Ibid., p. 286.

23. Ibid., p. 288.

24. Ibid., p. 286.

25. Ibid., p. 289.

26. Ibid., p. 289.

27. Alfred Diamant, "Bureaucracy in Developmental Movement Regimes," in Riggs (ed.) _Frontiers_ pp. 516-20.

28. Ibid., pp. 516-20.

29. Ibid., p. 521.

30. Ibid., p. 522.

31. Kautsky, _The Political Consequences of Modernization_, p. 172.

32. Ibid., p. 172.

33. Manfred Halpern, "The Revolution of Modernization in National and International Society,"

in Jackson and Stern (eds.), Issues in Comparative Politics, p. 43.

34. Ibid., p. 43.
35. Grossholtz, Politics in the Philippines, and Averch, Koehler, and Denton, The Matrix of Policy in the Philippines.
36. Milliken and Blackmer (eds.), The Emerging Nations: Their Growth and United States Policy, p. 86.
37. Corpuz, The Philippines, pp. 87-88.
38. Ibid., p. 89.
39. "Political culture" as used in this study means "the pattern of individual attitudes and orientations toward politics among members of a political system." For an elaboration of this point, see Almond and Powell, Comparative Politics, p. 50.
40. Palmer, Dilemmas of Political Development, p. 39.
41. Jorgen Rasmussen, The Process of Politics: A Comparative Approach (Chicago: Aldine Publishing Company, 1969), p. 35.
42. Riggs, Administration in Developing Countries, p. 268.
43. Lawrence C. Mayer, Comparative Political Inquiry: A Methodological Survey (Homewood, Illinois: The Dorsey Press, 1972), p. 254.
44. Riggs, Administration in Developing Countries, p. 36.
45. Marcos, Today's Revolution: Democracy, p. 2; Cf., Marcos, Notes on the New Society of the Philippines.
46. Marcos, Today's Revolution, p. 2.
47. See The Philippine Collegian (Issues from 26 January - 20 September 1972); Pingkian, December 1971; Kalayaan, (Issues from 26 February 1972 to February 1973).
48. Huntington, Political Order in Changing Societies, p. 264.
49. Ibid., p. 265.
50. Ibid., p. 266.
51. Johnson, Revolution and the Social System.
52. Ibid., p. 27.
53. Ibid., p. 31.
54. Ibid., p. 35.
55. Ibid., p. 40.
56. Ibid., p. 48.
57. Ibid., p. 48.
58. Ibid., p. 50.
59. Ibid., p. 50.
60. Ibid., p. 57.

61. For an excellent Marxist reinterpretation of Philippine history and a presentation of the Communist Party of the Philippines' (CPP) revolutionary program, see Amado Guerrero (pseudonym for Jose Ma. Sison, founder and putative chairman of the CPP), _Philippine Society and Revolution_ (Hong Kong: Ta Kung Pao, 1971).
62. Johnson, _Revolutionary Change_.
63. Ibid., p. 65.
64. Ibid., p. 65.
65. Ibid., p. 65.
66. Peter Calvert, _A Study of Revolution_ (Oxford: Clarendon Press, 1970), p. 4.
67. Johnson (ed.) _Change in Communist Systems_, p. 9.
68. _The Philippine Times_, 15-31 October 1974, p. 4.
69. _Ex parte Milligan_ 4 Wall 475 (1866).
70. _Moyer v. Peabody_ 212 U.S. 78 (1909).
71. Chavez, "Martial Law: Scope, Problems and Proposals," p. 238.
72. Ibid., p. 238.
73. Charles Fairman, "Martial Rule and the Suppression of Insurrection," _Illinois Law Review_, 23 (March 1929), pp. 766-88. See also Frederick Bernays Weiner, _A Practical Manual of Martial Law_ (Harrisburg, Pa.: The Military Service Publishing Company, 1940), p. 10; Archibald King, "The Legality of Martial Law in Hawaii," _California Law Review_, 30 (September 1942), p. 604.
74. Story, _Commentaries on the Constitution of the United States_, Vol. 2, p. 206.
75. Ibid., p. 206.
76. Ibid., p. 208.
77. _Constitution of the Philippines_ (Manila: Bureau of Printing, 1969), p. 22.
78. Chavez, "Martial Law," p. 236.
79. For an extended discussion of the political and constitutional ideas that animated the framers of the constitution of 1898 (the Malolos Constitution), see Majul, _The Political and Constitutional Ideas of the Philippine Revolution_.
80. Public Law No. 240, 64th Congress, Organic Act for the Philippine Islands is reproduced in full in Kalaw, _The Present Government of the Philippines_, Appendix, p. 156.
81. Kalaw, _The Present Government of the Philippines_, p. 13.

82. Aruego, <u>The Framing of the Philippine Constitution</u>, Vol. 1.
83. Ibid., p. 430.
84. Ibid., p. 430.
85. Ibid., p. 431.
86. Ibid., p. 431.
87. Ibid., pp. 431-32.
88. Romani, <u>The Philippine Presidency</u>, pp. 78-79.
89. The "Huk threat" used by President Elpidio Quirino to justify the suspension of the privilege of the writ of habeas corpus in 1950 refers to the aborted bid of the Communist Party of the Philippines (CPP) to forcibly overthrow the government. The Huk (short for "Hukbong Mapagpalaya ng Bayan" or "People's Liberation Army") was the military arm of the <u>Partidong Komunista ng Pilipinas</u> (PKP). The writ was restored in fifteen provinces in February 1951, and in all other parts of the Philippines before President Quirino left office in December 1953.
90. Cited by Romani, <u>The Philippine Presidency</u>, p. 79.
91. "High Court Dismisses Petitions," <u>The Philippine Times</u>, 31 January 1973, p. 1.
92. "By Show of Hands," Editorial, <u>St. Louis Post Dispatch</u>, 18 January 1973; <u>Cf.</u>, "The Philippine Tragedy," Editorial, <u>Washington Star News</u>, 26 January 1973. For more editorial comments on President Marcos' "ratification" proclamation of 17 January 1973, see "Totalitarianism in the Philippines," <u>Los Angeles Times</u>, 19 January 1973; "Sad Farce in the Philippines," <u>Chicago Tribune</u>, 19 January 1973; "RP--and US--In Passage," <u>The Washington Post</u>, 22 January 1973; "Time to Speak Up," <u>Christian Science Monitor</u>, 22 January 1973; and Marcos of the Philippines," in the <u>Chicago Daily News</u>, 22 January 1973.
93. "High Court Dismisses Petitions," p. 1.
94. "High Court Dismisses Petitions," p. 20.
95. Ibid., p. 20.
96. Aruego, <u>Know Your Constitution</u>, p. 128.
97. Fernando, <u>The Constitutional Government of the Philippines</u>, p. 260.
98. Chavez, "Martial Law," p. 237.
99. <u>Ex parte Milligan</u>.
100. Romani, <u>The Philippine Presidency</u>, p. 83.
101. Rossiter, <u>The Supreme Court and the Commander-in-Chief</u>, p. 126.

102. Ibid., p. 127.

Chapter 3

1. See the section on "Comparative International
    Statistics,"in U.S. Bureau of the Census,
    Statistical Abstract of the United States:
    1985, 105th Edition (Washington, D.C., 1984).,
    p. 840.   See also U.S. Department of State,
    Background Notes: Singapore (Washington, D.C.:
    Government Printing Office, 1984), p. 1.
2. Tilman (ed.), Man, State, and Society in
    Contemporary Southeast Asia, p. 12.   With the
    establishment of socialist regimes in Vietnam,
    Kampuchea, and Laos in 1975 and the reunifica-
    tion of the "two Vietnams" in 1976, however,
    Tilman's typology has become dated and
    inaccurate.
3. New York Times, 26 September 1972, p. 13.
4. Agoncillo and Alfonso, A Short History of the
    Filipino People, p. 69.
5. Jose P. Rizal is the Philippines' foremost
    national hero.   In addition to two great
    novels, Noli Me Tangere and El Filibusterismo,
    he wrote scores of polemical essays including
    the "The Indolence of the Filipino" in which
    he refuted the Spanish allegation that the
    Filipino was backward and miserable because he
    was naturally lazy and indolent.
6. Mecham, Church and State in Latin America,
    Revised Edition, p. 3, also Chapter II, pp.
    38-60.
7. Agoncillo and Alfonso, A Short History of the
    Filipino People , pp. 93-95.
8. Ibid., p. 106.
9. Ibid., pp. 154-55.
10. Gregorio F. Zaide, Philippine Political and
    Cultural History, Vol. I (Manila: Philippine
    Education Company, 1957), p. 343.
11. Agoncillo and Alfonso, A Short History of the
    Filipino People, pp. 155-56.
12. The Katipunan (short for Kataastaasan
    Kagalanggalang na Katipunan ng mga Anak ng
    Bayan or Highest and Most Exalted Society of
    the Sons of the People) was a clandestine
    association founded by Andres Bonifacio in
    1892.   For an excellent and fascinating
    account of the Katipunan and Bonifacio's role
    in the revolution, see Agoncillo, Revolt of
    the Masses.

13. Agoncillo and Alfonso, A Short History of the Filipino People, pp. 209-21.
14. "Treaty of Peace Between the United States of America and the Kingdom of Spain," Papers Relating to the Foreign Relations of the United States (Washington: Government Printing Office, 1901), pp. 831-40.
15. See Frank L. Klingberg, "Historical Periods, Trends, and Cycles in International Relations," Journal of Conflict Resolution, 14 (December 1970), pp. 506-11.
16. For a detailed discussion of this and related points, see Grunder and Livezey, The Philippines and the United States, p. 29.
17. See Grayson L. Kirk, Philippine Independence: Motives, Problems and Prospects (New York: Farrar and Rinehart, Inc., 1936), pp. 29-30.
18. For two excellent works on the circumstances which led to the Filipino-American War of 1898, see James H. Blount, The American Occupation of the Philippines, 1898-1912 (New York: G. P. Putnam's Sons, 1912); and Leon Wolff, Little Brown Brother: How the United States Purchased and Pacified the Philippine Islands at the Century's Turn (Garden City, New York: Doubleday & Company, Inc., 1961), pp. 218-77.
19. President William McKinley's instructions to the Second Philippine Commission, and eventually, the civil government were that "the Commission should bear in mind that the government they are establishing is designed not for our satisfaction or for the expression of our theoretical views, but for the happiness, peace, and prosperity of the people of the Philippine Islands, and the measures adopted, should be made to conform to their customs, their habits, and even their prejudices." For the complete text of the instructions and other pertinent documents, see U.S. Department of War, Bureau of Insular Affairs, Reports of the Philippine Commission, the Civil Governor and the Heads of the Executive Departments of the Civil Government of the Philippine Islands, 1900-1903 (Washington: Government Printing Office, 1904).
20. Mamerto S. Ventura, "Philippine Post-War Recovery: A Record of United States-Philippine Cooperation and Cross Purposes" (unpublished Ph.D. dissertation, Southern Illinois University, 1966), pp. 38, 40, 45. See also

Ventura, <u>United States-Philippine Cooperation and Cross Purposes</u>, pp. 37-45.

21. For President Quezon's version of the controversy, see Manuel Luis Quezon, <u>The Good Fight</u> (New York: D. Appleton-Century Company, Inc., 1946).

22. Grunder and Livezey, <u>The Philippines and the United States</u>, p. 200. See also Robert Aura Smith, <u>Philippine Freedom</u>, 1946-1958 (New York: Columbia University Press, 1958), p. 68.

23. George F. Kennan, <u>American Diplomacy</u>, 1900-1950 (Chicago: University of Chicago Press, 1951), pp. 18-19.

24. Grossholtz, <u>Politics in the Philippines</u>, p. 27.

25. Kirk, <u>Philippine Independence</u>, p. 127.

26. Agoncillo and Alfonso, <u>A Short History of the Filipino People</u>, p. 448.

27. As quoted in Agoncillo and Alfonso, <u>A Short History of the Filipino People</u>, p. 456.

28. Agoncillo and Alfonso, <u>A Short History of the Filipino People</u>, p. 460. For a detailed account of the three years of enemy occupation, see A.V.H. Hartendorp, <u>The Japanese Occupation of the Philippines</u>, Vol. II (Manila: Bookmark, 1967), and Teodoro A. Agoncillo, <u>The Fateful Years</u> 3 vols. (Quezon City: University of the Philippines Press, 1968).

29. Agoncillo and Alfonso, <u>A Short History of the Filipino People</u>, p. 460.

30. For a sympathetic biography of Manuel A. Roxas, see Marcial F. Lichauco, <u>Roxas</u> (Manila: Kiko Printing Press, 1952).

31. For a very well researched and objective presentation of the various facets of the collaboration issue, see David Joel Steinberg, <u>Philippine Collaboration in World War II</u> (Ann Arbor: The University of Michigan Press, 1967);<u>Cf.</u>, Hernando J. Abaya, <u>Betrayal in the Philippines</u> (New York: A. A. Wyn, Inc., 1946); and Claro M. Recto, <u>Three Years of Enemy Occupation: The Issue of Political Collaboration in the Philippines</u> (Manila: People's Publishers, 1946).

32. Three excellent books that address themselves to this sensitive issue are Shirley Jenkins, <u>American Economic Policy Toward the Philippines</u> (Stanford: Stanford University Press, 1952); Frank H. Golay, <u>The Philippines: Public Policy and National Development</u> (Ithaca: Cornell University Press, 1961); and

George E. Taylor, _The Philippines and the United States: Problems of Partnership_ (New York: Praeger Publishers, 1964).

33. The vote was 1,696,753 for parity and only 222,665 against or an overwhelming ratio of 8 to 1 in favor of ratification.

34. Agoncillo and Alfonso, _A Short History of the Filipino People_, p. 502.

35. For a firsthand account of the Huk armed struggle and the underlying reasons for it, see Luis M. Taruc, _Born of the People_ (New York: International Publishers, 1953).

36. See _Montenegro v. Castaneda_, L-4331, 30 August 1952.

37. Harold F. Gosnell, "An Interpretation of the Philippine Election of 1953," _The American Political Science Review_, 48 (December 1954), pp. 1128-39 as cited by Grossholtz, _The Philippines_, p. 41.

38. For a good account of, and discussion of the Magsaysay strategy vis-a-vis the Huks, see Alvin Scaff, _The Philippine Answer to Communism_ (Stanford: Stanford University Press, 1956).

39. For a good biography of Magsaysay, see Carlos Quirino's _Magsaysay of the Philipinnes_ (Manila: Phoenix Press, Inc., 1958); _Cf._, Francis Lucille Starner, _Magsaysay and the Philippine Peasantry: The Agrarian Impact on Philippine Politics, 1953-1956_ (Berkeley and Los Angeles: The University of California Press, 1961).

40. For an excellent case study on the creation of, and the philosophy behind the PACD as well as on the political style of Ramon F. Magsaysay, see Jose V. Abueva, _Focus on the Barrio_ (Manila: Institute of Public Administration, University of the Philippines, 1959).

41. For an analysis of the "tangled political drama of this period" and Magsaysay's disillusionment with the old guard politicians of his own party, see Francis Lucille Starner, _Magsaysay and the Filipino Peasantry_, pp. 127-31. See also Carlos P. Romulo and Marvin M. Gray, _The Magsaysay Story_ (New York: The John Day Company, 1956), p. 305.

42. Grossholtz, _Politics in the Philippines_, p. 45.

43. For the rest of Macapagal's life, see his autobiography, _The Incorruptible_ (Manila: Phoenix Press, 1963).

44. R. A. No. 3844, enacted in 1963.
45. For an excellent discussion of the nature of political parties and interest groups in the Philippines before the imposition of martial law, see Lande, Leaders, Factions and Parties. See also Grossholtz, Politics in the Philippines, pp. 136-56.
46. For two interesting and favorable biographies of Marcos, see Spence, For Every Tear a Victory: The Story of Ferdinand E. Marcos, and Spence, Marcos of the Philippines: A Biography.
47. For a detailed account of Marcos' war exploits, see the "Saga of Ferdinand E. Marcos," in Baclagon, Military History of the Philippines, pp. 269-308.
48. The Philippine Times, 31 August 1973, p. 1.
49. For two definitive works on the political and constitutional ideas of Apolinario Mabini and the influence these ideas had on the First Philippine Republic, see Cesar Adib Majul, Mabini and the Philippine Revolution (Quezon City: The University of the Philippines Press, 1960) and The Political and Constitutional Ideas of the Philippine Revolution.
50. Title II, Article 4 of the Malolos Constitution. For the genesis of this particular article, see Majul, The Political and Constitutional Ideas, pp. 160-63.

Chapter 4

1. Marcos, A Dialogue With My People, a collection of selected speeches from September 1972 through September 1973. See also Marcos, Notes on the New Society of the Philippines, and Ferdinand E. Marcos, "The Conquest of Poverty," in Development for the New Society (Manila: Department of Public Information, 1974).
2. From Marcos' first inaugural address delivered on 30 December 1965. For the complete text of the speech, see Consuelo V. Fonacier and Leticia R. Shahani (comps.), At the Helm of the Nation: Inaugural Addresses of the Presidents of the Philippine Republic and Commonwealth (Manila: National Media Production Center, 1973), especially pp. 114-23.
3. Ibid., pp. 114-23.

4. From Marcos' first "State of the Nation" address delivered on 24 January 1966, before a joint session of the first session of the Sixth Congress.

5. The per capita GNP in 1972 was $134, a dollar less than that of the preceding year. Only 2.6% of Filipino families earned 10,000 ($1,538) or more a year; 6.8% earned 5,000-9,999 ($461-$769). The rest of the population--77.1%--earned far below 3,000 ($461), with 11.7% making less than 500 ($76) annually. For the rest of the "economic profile" for 1972, see "The Philippines," in Far Eastern Economic Review, 1973 (Hong Kong: Far Eastern Economic Review, 1973), pp. 251-58. Cf., United Nations Economic and Social Survey of Asia and the Far East, 1972 (New York: United Nations Publications, 1973), pp. 172-75.

6. Crisostomo, Marcos the Revolutionary, p. 108.

7. From Marcos' second inaugural address delivered on 30 December 1969. For the complete text of the speech, see Fonacier and Shahani (comps.), At the Helm, pp. 123-28.

8. Ibid.

9. Ferdinand E. Marcos, Today's Revolution: Democracy (Manila: Marcos Foundation, Inc., 1971).

10. Crisostomo, Marcos the Revolutionary, p. 154.

11. Richard Critchfield's favorable review of Marcos' book was reprinted in full by the Philippines Daily Express, 14 October 1972.

12. Marcos, Today's Revolution, p. 64.

13. Ibid., p. 64.

14. For a very well written and thorough analysis of the political ideas of Apolinario Mabini, often referred to in Philippine history books as the "Brain of the Revolution" or the "Sublime Paralytic," see Majul, Mabini and the Philippine Revolution.

15. Marcos, Today's Revolution, pp. 65-66.

16. Ibid., p. 59.

17. Ibid., p. 59.

18. Ibid., p. 96.

19. Ibid., p. 96.

20. Ibid., p. 96.

21. Ibid., p. 73.

22. Ibid., pp. 118-19.

23. Ibid., p. 137.

24. Ibid., p. 119.

25. See Marcos, "The Conquest of Poverty," p. 6.

26. Marcos, <u>Today's Revolution</u>, p. 16.
27. Ibid., p. 23.
28. Ibid., p. 19.
29. Ibid., pp. 138-39.
30. Nemesio E. Prudente was a charter member of the Movement for the Advancement of Nationalism (MAN) and was mainly concerned with the reexamination of Philippine-American relations. He was one of those arrested and detained when limited martial law was proclaimed on 21 August 1971. Later released, he went underground immediately before the proclamation of absolute martial law on 21 September 1972. He was subsequently rearrested and returned to government custody. For a comprehensive look at his political views, see Prudente, <u>Sa Mga Kuko Ng Limbas</u>.
31. Since its founding in the late 1950's the National Union of Students of the Philippines had been dominated by an alliance of Catholic Schools, including Ateneo de Manila University, De La Salle University, San Beda College, Maryknoll College, St. Theresa's College, St. Paul College, and similar institutions. During the school year 1970-71 when student-initiated political disturbances began, the president of the NUSP was Edgar Jopson of the Ateneo de Manila University. Jopson joined the CPP-NPA in the mid-1970's and was slain in an encounter with a Philippine Constabulary unit in Davao a few years later.
32. Rodolfo Tupas, "The Rebels on Campus," <u>The Sunday Times Magazine</u>, 22 February 1970, pp. 10-11. On the factionalism of the nationalist movement itself, see Martin Meadows, "Colonialism, Social Structure and Nationalism: The Philippine Case," <u>Pacific Affairs</u> 44 (Fall, 1971), pp. 337-53.
33. Some of those who moved to the Lyceum of the Philippines as teachers were Jose Ma. Sison, founder of the Kabataang Makabayan and putative chairman of the Communist Party of the Philippines (apprehended by the authorities on 8 November 1977) and Jose David Lapuz, former chairman of the Bertrand Russell Peace Foundation (Philippine Chapter). On the other hand, some of those who were recruited to teach at the Philippine College of Commerce by Nemesio E. Prudente (see Note 30, supra) were Vivencio R. Jose, Ramon Sanchez, Dante

Simbulan, Ricardo Ferrer, and Benjamin N. Muego, all charter members of the Movement for the Advancement of Nationalism and active student leaders or faculty members at the University of the Philippines at some point.

34. The Laurel family of Batangas province was one of the most influential and dominant families in the Philippines before the declaration of martial law. Jose P. Laurel, Sr., was president of the wartime Japanese-sponsored republic, and was on various occasions a member of the Supreme Court and President of the Senate. Of his sons, Jose B Laurel, Jr., was speaker of the House of Representatives for two terms; Salvador H. Laurel served two terms in the now-defunct Philippine Senate; and Sotero Laurel was President of the Lyceum of the Philippines (see Note 33, supra). There was an apparent "falling out" between the Laurels and Marcos toward the end of Marcos' first term as evidenced by Marcos' support of the ouster of Jose B. Laurel, Jr., as Speaker of the House of Representatives in favor of a defector from the opposition Liberal party, Cornelio T. Villareal. Laurel, Jr. broke his silence on 22 August 1977 and called for an end to martial law saying "national unity could never be forged unless people were liberated from the compulsions and restrictions of the regime."

35. The CAFA (which bore an uncanny resemblance to the infamous Committee on Un-American Activites of the United States Senate during the Joseph McCarthy era), later renamed the Committee, on Un-Filipino Activities, was chaired by then Representative Leonardo B. Perez (N, Nueva Vizcaya). After the abolition of Congress in 1972, Senator Perez (he was elected to the Senate on the Marcos ticket in 1965) was appointed Chairman of the Commission on Elections.

36. Some of the better known leaders of the "student left," past and present, were former editors of the Philippine Collegian or former chairmen of the UP Student Council, including Simeon Rodriguez, Angel Baking, E. Voltaire Garcia II, Benjamin N. Muego, Nelson A. Navarro, Fernando Barican, and Ericson Baculinao.

37. Jose V. Abueva, "The Prospects for Revolution in the Philippines: Conflicting Evaluations,"

paper presented at the Conference of Southeast Asian Students, University of Indiana, Bloomington, Indiana, 26 March 1970.

38. Ibid., p. 4.
39. Lipset and Wolin (eds.), The Berkeley Student Revolt: Facts and Interpretations, p. 6.
40. For an excellent discussion of the nexus between political socialization and student activism in Indonesia, see Stephen A. Douglas, Political Socialization and Student Activism in Indonesia (Urbana: The University of Illinois Press, 1970), especially pp. 153-74.
41. Tilman, "Student Unrest in the Philippines: The View From the South," pp. 900-909.
42. Ibid., p. 900.
43. Ibid., p. 908.
44. Proclamation No. 889, dated 21 August 1971, came in the wake of the critical wounding of all eight Liberal party senatorial candidates at Plaza Miranda in downtown Manila. Marcos blamed the "Maoists" for the attack. Some Liberal party and student leaders blamed the bombing on Marcos. For a graphic "blow by blow" account of the situation before and after the proclamation, see Crisostomo, Marcos the Revolutionary, pp. 128-53.
45. Senator Jose W. Diokno (Nacionalista) together with Senator Benigno S. Aquino, Jr., of the opposition Liberal Party were among those arrested on 22 September 1972. Diokno was released after more than two years of detention on "humanitarian grounds." Aquino was tried (he adamantly refused to participate in the proceedings) and convicted in absentia by a military tribunal for "subversion," "illegal possession of firearms," and "murder" on 26 November 1977. The sentence of death by musketry meted out to Aquino provoked widespread domestic and international outrage. Marcos himself ordered a retrial although this was later invalidated by the Supreme Court. Aquino was permitted to leave for the United States in 1980 where he remained in self-exile for three years. Returning to the Philippines in August 1983, Aquino was brutally assassinated evidently by government agents assigned to provide him "security."
46. The Philippine Times, 15 January 1972, p. 1.
47. The Lansang v. Garcia (G.R. No. L-33964) decision was promulgated on 11 December 1971; in this decision the Supreme Court took judicial

notice of the existence of a "state of insurrection and rebellion" in the Philippines.

48. Some of the more daring and spectacular of these bombings were those of: the Court of Industrial Relations on 23 June; the Philippine Trust Company on 24 June; the Philam-Life Building at United Nations Avenue in Manila on 3 July; the Tabacalera Cigar and Cigarette Factory Compound at Marquez de Comillas in Manila on 27 July; the Philippine Long Distance Telephone Company Exchange Office at East Avenue, Quezon City on 15 August. After a brief lull, Joe's Department Store on Carriedo Street, Quiapo, Manila was bombed on 5 September causing death to one woman bystander and injuries to thirty-eight others. The City Hall of Manila was bombed on 8 September and the water mains of San Juan, Rizal were blown up on 12 September. The "grande finale" of the bombing offensive was the dynamiting of the City Hall of Quezon City on 18 September.

49. Strategic Survey, 1972 (London: The International Institute for Strategic Studies, 1973), pp. 54-55.

50. See T.J.S. George, "How it all happened," Far Eastern Economic Review, 30 September 1972.

51. Wurfel, "Martial Law in the Philippines: The Methods of Regime Survival," p. 6.

52. Crisostomo, Marcos the Revolutionary, p. 178.

53. For a good account of how some of the arrests were made, see "Army Arrests Marcos Critics," The Philippine Times, 30 September 1972, p. 1.

54. Statement of Marcos on the proclamation of martial law in the Philippines in a nationwide radio and television broadcast. For the full text of the statement, see Vital Documents on the Declaration of Martial Law in the Philippines, Vol. I (Manila: National Media Production Center, 1973), pp. 1-12.

55. The pertinent provision reads: "The President shall be Commander-in-Chief of all the armed forces of the Philippines and whenever it becomes necessary he may call out such armed forces to prevent or suppress lawless violence, invasion, insurrection or imminent danger thereof, when the public safety requires it, he may suspend the privilege of the writ of habeas corpus, or place the Philippines or any part thereof under martial law." [Emphasis mine.] For an extended

discussion of the genesis of this particular provision in the 1935 Constitution, see Chapter I.

56. See Walter Lippmann, <u>The Public Philosophy</u> (New York: A Mentor Book, 1955), pp. 55, 57; Marcos apparently modified Lippmann's concept of "assimilation," as a means of including a great number of people in the body politic, and he renamed it "liberal revolution."

Chapter 5

1. For a more thorough explication of this concept, see Marcos, <u>Notes on the New Society of the Philippines</u>, p. 76.

2. Rolando V. del Carmen, "Constitutionalism and the Supreme Court in a Changing Philippine Polity," pp. 15-16.

3. Article VII, Section 5 of the 1935 Constitution.

4. Article VI, Section 2 of the 1935 Constitution.

5. Article VIII, Section 1 of the 1935 Constitution.

6. Tilman (ed.) <u>Man, State, and Society in Contemporary Southeast Asia</u>, pp. 12-13.

7. For an explanation of the relationship of these three factors and their significance in terms of identifying citizen interests, see Philip E. Converse, "The Nature of Belief System in Mass Publics," in David E. Apter (ed.), <u>Ideology and Discontent</u> (New York: Free Press, 1964), pp. 206-61.

8. An excellent cross-national study which found Americans generally apolitical is Gabriel Almond and Sidney Verba, <u>The Civic Culture</u> (Boston: Little, Brown and Company, 1963); Cf., Jean Grossholtz, <u>Politics in The Philippines</u>, especially her discussion of "political attitudes" and "political behavior," pp. 186-87, 239, and of "political participation," pp. 7, 74. See also Henry S. Albinski (ed.), <u>Asian Political Process</u> (Boston: Allyn and Bacon, Inc., 1971), pp. 157-69.

9. Lester W. Milbrath, <u>Political Participation</u> (Chicago: Rand McNally and Company, 1965).

10. For an excellent discussion of the factious nature of political parties in the Philippines, see Lande, <u>Leaders, Factions and</u>

      Parties, also Grossholtz, <u>Politics in The Philippines</u>, pp. 136-56.
11.   During the 1957 elections, a third party candidate, Manuel P. Manahan (Progressive Party of the Philippines or PPP) won over both Nacionalista Carlos P. Garcia and Liberal Jose A. Yulo in most of the metropolitan Manila area. Raul S. Manglapus, also running under the banner of the PPP, topped all senatorial candidates in the greater Manila area and other urban centers. Both Manahan and Manglapus, however, were overwhelmed by their Nacionalista and Liberal rivals in the provinces and lost the election.
12.   The shift to a parliamentary form of government from the presidential system patterned after that of the United States was pushed through the Constitutional Convention by Marcos loyalists. According to David F. Roth in an unpublished study entitled "The Choice of a Political Formula in a Third World Nation: The Case of the Philippines 1971-1973," the parliamentary system of government was a Marcos project from the start. For a review of other issues discussed in the convention see Jose Luna Castro, "The Promise and the Change in the 1971-1972 Constitutional Convention," in Vicente Albano Pacis, et al, <u>Founders of Freedom: The History of the Three Philippine Constitutions</u> (Quezon City: Capitol Publishing House, Inc., 1971), pp. 326-35.
13.   Article VIII of the 1973 Constitution.
14.   The ten cabinet departments in the Second Philippine republic were Foreign Affairs, Justice, National Defense, Agriculture and Natural Resources, Finance, Education, Labor, Commerce, and Public Works and Communications. For a good and thorough discussion of governmental services in the Second Philippine Republic, see Jacobini and Associates, <u>Governmental Services in the Philippines</u>.
15.   Examples are the Commission on Audit (formerly the General Auditing Office or GAO).
16.   Article XI of the 1973 Constitution.
17.   Article XI, Section 2 of the 1973 Constitution.
18.   Article XI, Section 3 of the 1973 Constitution.
19.   Article XI, Section 4 of the 1973 Constitution.
20.   See Roth,"The Choice of a Political Formula."

21. Article VII, Section 1 of the 1973 Constitution.

22. Article VII, Section 6 of the 1973 Constitution.

23. <u>Constitution of the Philippines</u> (Manila: Bureau of Printing, 1969).

24. The Progressive Party of the Philippines was founded by the "Magsaysay boys" Manuel P. Manahan, Raul S. Manglapus, Vicente A. Araneta, Cesar C. Climaco, Frisco T. San Juan, and Eleuterio M. Adevoso, among others, in the mid-1950's after the untimely death of Ramon F. Magsaysay; see also Note 11, supra.

25. The "payola" scandal which allegedly involved the First Lady, Imelda Romualdez-Marcos, and a number of Con-Con delegates was exposed on the convention floor by Delegate Eduardo Quintero. Quintero charged that he was given eighteen envelopes containing a total of P379,320.00 to bribe Con-Con delegates into voting against the "ban-Marcos movement," disqualifying Ferdinand and Imelda from serving as either prime minister or president in the proposed parliamentary government. For other details, see "Con-Con Scandal Tells on Imelda, RP Officialdom," <u>The Philippine Times</u>, 15 June 1972, p. 1; also "'Payola' Linked to Ban-Marcos Proposal," <u>The Philippine Times</u> 30 June 1972, p. 1.

26. Previous administrations--Roxas', Quirino's, Garcia's and Macapagal's--all went down in defeat because of charges of "graft and corruption;" it may be argued that the inclusion of "graft and corruption" as a ground for the impeachment of the president and members of the judiciary was a delayed reaction to those infamous years.

27. Article XIII, Section 5 of the 1973 Constitution.

28. Article XIII, Section 6 of the 1973 Constitution.

29. Ordinance Appended to the 1935 Constitution.

30. Jesus G. Barrera was a retired member of the Supreme Court and married to the widow of the great nationalist Claro Mayo Recto. Salvador Araneta was also a member of the 1935 Constitutional Convention and, as explained in Chapter I was one of those who unsuccessfully opposed the grant of the power to suspend the writ of habeas corpus to the president. Enrique Voltaire R. Garcia II was a youth

leader and activist before he was elected as a delegate to the 1971 Constitutional Convention from the province of Rizal. Garcia was arrested on 22 September 1972, released, then placed under house arrest a month later. A year later he died of a lingering illness.

31. Article XIII, Section 5 of the 1973 Constitution.
32. Article XIII, Section 9 of the 1973 Constitution.
33. Article XIII, Section 11 of the 1973 Constitution.
34. Prominent among those who voted against the "Transitory Provisions" were Rev. Pacifico A. Ortiz, S.J., Enrique Voltaire R. Garcia II, Jose Mari Velez, Raul S. Manglapus, and Heherson T. Alvarez.
35. United Press International report in the Straits Times, 4 February 1978. For an analysis of the Liberal party's official position vis-a-vis the 7 April 1978 election and its ten demands submitted to President Marcos, see "Too Normal for Comfort," in Asiaweek, 10 February 1978, pp. 18-21.
36. Del Carmen, "Constitutionalism and the Supreme Court," p. 6.
37. General Order No. 3, dated 22 September 1972.
38. See Larawan (Newsletter of the Embassy of the Philippines in the United States), p. 3.
39. Rolando V. del Carmen, "Changes in the Philippine Judiciary Under the New Constitution," a paper presented at the Midwest Conference on Asian Affairs at Lawrence, Kansas, on 1 November 1974, p. 9.
40. These five areas were (1) all cases in which the constitutionality or validity of any treaty, executive agreement, law, ordinance, or executive order or regulation was in question; (2) all cases involving the legality of any tax, impost, assessment, or toll, or any penalty imposed in relation thereto; (3) all cases in which the jurisdiction of any inferior court was in issue; (4) all criminal cases in which the penalty imposed was death or life imprisonment; and (5) all cases in which only an error or question of law was involved.
41. Article X, Section 5, paragraph 2-e.
42. Article VIII, Section 2, paragraph 5 of the 1935 Constitution.

43. The counterpart provision of the 1935 Constitution read: "All cases in which the constitutionality or validity of any treaty, law, ordinance, or executive order or regulations [was] in question." Note the absence of any qualifying clause.

44. Del Carmen, "Changes in the Philippine Judiciary," p. 3.

45. Article X, Section 5, paragraph 3 of the 1973 Constitution.

46. Article X, Section 5, paragraph 4 of the 1973 Constitution.

47. The Philippine Times, 31 January 1973, p. 1.

48. Presidential Decree No. 73 ordered the cancellation of the schedluled nationwide plebiscite on the new Constitution. For the full text of PD No. 73, see Vital Documents on the Declaration of Martial Law in the Philippines, Vol. II (Manila: National Media Production Center, 1973).

49. Proclamation No. 1102 was entitled "Announcing the Ratification by the Filipino People of the Constitution Proposed by the 1971 Constitutional Convention."

50. "Supreme Court Hears Suit on New Charter," The Philippine Times, 28 February 1973, p. 1.

51. Ibid., p. 1.

52. Ibid., p. 1.

53. The New York Times, 17 February 1973, p. C-6.

54. Rolando V. del Carmen, "Constitutionalism and the Supreme Court," p. 10.

55. The New York Times, 3 April 1973, p. L-3.

56. "New RP Constitution in Force: Justices Censure Marcos," The Philippine Times, 15 April 1973, p. 1.

57. From the joint opinion of Justices Querube Makalintal and Fred Ruiz Castro, as reproduced in The Philippine Times, 15 and 31 May 1973, pp. 6, 7, 10, and 12, respectively.

58. Editorial, The St. Louis Post Dispatch, 1 August 1973.

59. "Chief Justice Concepcion Quits: 5 Candidates for Tribunal are Listed," The Philippine Times, 30 April 1973, p. 1.

60. The Times Journal, 18 September 1974, p. 1.

61. The Philippines Daily Express, 18 September 1974, p. 1.

62. Ibid., p. 1.

63. Ibid., p. 1.

64. The Philippines Daily Express, 21 September 1974, p. 1.

65. "The Tribunal Speaks." Editorial, <u>The Times Journal</u>, 21 September 1974.
66. <u>Pahayag</u>, September 1975, p. 2.
67. Ibid., p. 2.
68. Ibid., p. 2.
69. Ibid., p. 2.
70. Finer, <u>The Man on Horseback</u>, p. 10.
71. Janowitz, <u>The Military in the Political Development of New Nations</u>, p. 28.
72. Ibid., p. 28.
73. "Building the New Society," <u>The New York Times</u>, 10 June 1973, p. 4.
74. Ibid., p. 4.
75. "Opposition Forces Still Around," article originally published in <u>Far Eastern Economic Review</u> and reproduced in <u>The Philippine Times</u>, 31 January 1973, p. 8.
76. <u>Pahayag</u>, November 1974, p. 8.
77. Ibid., p. 8.
78. The term "Ilocano" refers to persons who speak Iloko, and are usually natives of any of the northern Luzon provinces of Ilocos Norte, Ilocos Sur, Abra, La Union, Cagayan, Isabela, Nueva Vizcaya, the Mountain Province. Parts of the central Luzon provinces of Tarlac, Nueva Ecija, Pangasinan, and Zambales, are also Iloko-speaking. Since Ilocanos are known for their great mobility and industry, however, they are dispersed all over the country, from Batanes, the northernmost province, to Sulu, the southernmost. Ilocanos are also known to be a tightly-knit or even clannish lingo-ethnic group. Marcos, a native of Batac, Ilocos Norte, is an Ilocano, and so were Presidents Quirino and Magsaysay.
79. See "The Military Balance, 1977," in <u>Asian Defence Journal</u> (November/December 1977), p. 106.
80. "The Military Balance, 1977," p. 108. For comparative purposes, see "The Republic of the Philippines," in John Paxton (ed.), <u>The Statesman's Yearbook 1972-1973</u> (New York: The Macmillan Press, Ltd., 1972), p. 1242.
81. "The Military Balance, 1977," p. 106.
82. See Honesto M. Isleta, "The Role of the Military in the New Society: A New Challenge," in <u>Asian Defence Journal</u> (June 1977), pp. 21, 23, 83.
83. "The Military Balance, 1977," p. 108.
84. Ibid., p. 108.
85. Ibid., p. 108.

86. Ibid., p. 108.
87. "Philippine Constabulary: 60th Anniversary," <u>Armed Forces of the Philippines</u> (August 1961), p. 28.
88. De Borja, "Some Career Attributes and Professional Views of the Philippine Military Elite," p. 407.
89. David Wurfel in George McTurnan Kahin (ed.) <u>Governments and Politics of Southeast Asia</u>, Second Edition. (Ithaca: Cornell University Press, 1964), p. 716.
90. See Floyd Hunter, <u>Community Power Structure</u> (Chapel Hill: University of North Carolina Press, 1953). For a similar view, see Robert Presthus, <u>Men at the Top</u> (New York: Oxford University Press,1964) and Henry Kariel, <u>The Decline of American Pluralism</u> (Stanford: Stanford University Press, 1961).
91. See Robert A. Dahl, <u>Who Governs?</u> (New Haven: Yale University Press, 1961) and Aaron Wildavsky, <u>Leadership in a Small Town</u> (Totowa, N.J.: The Bedminster Press, 1964). See also Nelson W. Polsby, <u>Community Power and Political Theory</u> (New Haven: Yale University Press, 1963).
92. In a letter to the author in August 1970.
93. In a letter to the author in September 1970.
94. Gregorio Castro, et al. "The Military in the Philippines: A Study of Its Role in Socio-Economic Development and Some of the Political Implications of this Role," College of Public Administration, University of the Philippines, mimeographed, p. 23.
95. Amos Perlmutter, <u>Military and Politics in Israel</u> (London: Frank Cass, 1969), p. 134.
96. De Borja, "The Philippine Military Elite," p. 400.
97. Ibid., p. 400.
98. Ibid., p. 401.
99. Ibid., p. 401.
100. Ibid., p. 402.
101. <u>The Philippine Times</u>, 31 December 1973, p. 1.
102. "Military Personnel Receive More Presidential Benefits," <u>The Philippine Times</u>, 15 January 1974, p. 9.
103. Ibid., p. 9.
104. "Local Officials Wield Power, But Army Calls the Shots," <u>The Philippine Times</u>, 15 October 1972, p. 2.
105. Bernard Wideman, "Corruption in the Military," originally published in the <u>Far Eastern</u>

Economic Review and reproduced in the *Philippine Times,* 16-31 January 1975, p. 24.

106. *Utang na loob* ("debt of the inside") permeates almost every aspect of the Filipino's life: it regulates his relationship with the government, with his peers, and with his immediate community. An *utang na loob* relationship is created when one extends a favor or makes a sacrifice for another in a manner that the recipient cannot repay. The recipient (*may utang na loob*) of the favor becomes bound in gratitude to the giver (*may pautang na loob*). For an interesting discussion of *utang na loob* and other indigenous Philippine values such as *hiya* ("shame"), *compadrazgo* and the like, see Hollnsteiner, *The Dynamics of Power in a Philippine Municipality* and Frank Lynch (comp.), *Four Readings on Philippine Values* (Quezon City: Ateneo de Manila University Press, 1968).

Chapter 6

1. See RP National Media Production Center, *The New Society in the Philippines,* (Manila: National Media Production Center, 1973), pp. 25-30; *The Philippines and Its New Society* (Manila: National Media Production Center, 1973), pp. 9-10; and *President Ferdinand E. Marcos' Constitutional Revolution: The Philippines and the New Society,* (Manila: National Media Production Center, 1973), pp. 12-13.
2. The Philippines and Its New Society, p. 10.
3. Remarks made by Carlos P. Romulo in a dinner tendered in his honor by United States Ambassador William P. Sullivan on 26 August 1973, as reported in the *Philippine Daily Express* on 28 August 1973.
4. The *Kabatuang Makabayan* (Patriotic Youth) and the *Movement for the Advancement of Nationalism* (MAN) established in 1964 were sharply critical of what it called the "lop-sided relationship" between the Philippines and the United States and, among other things, advocated the abrogation of Parity Rights and all other Filipino-American treaties and agreements that the Parity Rights Amendment to the 1935 Philippines Constitution spawned. Kabatuang Makabayan was a student organization

primarily based at the University of the Philippines while MAN included government officials, professionals, peasants, and workers. The two organizations complemented each other and had overlapping membership rolls.

5. See Claro Mayo Recto, My Crusade (Manila: Pio C. Calica and Nicanor Carag, 1955) for the late Senator Recto's speeches on the Parity Amendment to the Constitution, the RP-US Mutual Defense Treaty, and the Military Bases Agreement; Cf., Prudente, Sa Mga Kuko Ng Limbas and George E. Taylor, The Philippines and the United States: Problems of Partnership (New York: Frederick A. Praeger, 1964).

6. Ordinance Appended to the Constitution; this superseded Article XIII, Section 1 of the 1935 Constitution which reserved the right to own lands, operate vital public utilities, and exploit and develop natural resources to citizens of the Philippines or to corporations whose capital was at least sixty percent Filipino.

7. Teodoro C. Benigno, "RP Evolving Foreign Policy of Accommodation," The Manila Chronicle, 2 March 1972.

8. Carlos P. Romulo, "Foreign Policy Under the New Society," Toward the New Society (Manila: National Media Production Center, 1974), p. 31.

9. Report to the Nation (1974), p. 57.

10. Ibid., pp. 57-58.

11. Ibid., p. 57.

12. The Philippine Times, 15 November 1974, p. 2.

13. Report to the Nation (1974), p. 33.

14. Lopez, New Directions in Philippine Foreign Policy, p. 15.

15. The New York Times, 18 April 1975.

16. The Philippine Times, 1-15 May 1975. The report emanated from Manila and was dated 27 April.

17. The New York Times, 25 April 1975.

18. Ibid.

19. See for instance, David A. Andelman, "Marcos Regime Seeks Abrogation of Bases Treaty," The New York Times, 25 April 1975; Bernardino Ronquillo, "Indochina Aftermath: Marcos Looks in New Directions," Far Eastern Economic Review, 10 June 1975; and Priscilla Bonato, "Marcos Going to Red Orbit," The Philippine Times, 1-15 May 1975.

20. The Philippine Times, 16-30 September 1975, p. 5.
21. Ibid., p. 20.
22. Ibid., p. 20.
23. New York Times, 18 April 1975.
24. Ibid.
25. For an excellent discussion of this particular point see Taylor, The Philippines and the United States, especially Chapter 11, pp. 233-49; Cf., "The Military Bases Issue: A Position Paper," issued by Protestant and Roman Catholic prelates and laymen in Manila and released in New York City by Dr. Edwin M. Luidens, Director of the East Asia Office of the National Council of Churches of Christ in the USA, on 4 July 1975.
26. Ronquillo, "Indochina Aftermath," p. 3.
27. The Philippine Times, 1-15 May 1975, p. 1; Imelda Marcos personally delivered the letter to President Soeharto who in turn endorsed the Philippine position in a statement issued through Foreign Minister Adam Malik.
28. The New York Times, 25 July 1975. The SEATO of course was formally abolished on 30 June 1977 although the decision to phase it out was reached in September 1975.
29. "Defense Fact--A Dead Letter?" The New York Times, 27 May 1975.
30. Ronquillo, "Indochina Aftermath," p. 3.
31. Ibid.
32. See President Marcos' Report to the Nation, delivered on 21 September 1974 at the Maharlika Hall of Malacanang Palace, p. 15. The President said in his Report that the "self-reliance military program is now developing a logistic system to serve the logistical needs of the armed forces, from shell casings, cartridges and basic types of weaponry to military vehicles and naval patrol craft." See also, The AFP Today (40th AFP Day Commemorative Edition), pp. 147-74.
33. World Military Expenditures and Arms Trade 1963-1973 published by the U.S. Arms Control and Disarmament Agency, especially Table III (World Arms Trade--Recipient Countries by Major Suppliers, Cumulative 1964-1973), p. 68.
34. U.S. Senate Appropriations Committee Hearings, Foreign Assistance and Related Programs FY 1973, (Washington, D.C.: Government Printing Office, 1974), p. 1602; see also U.S. Senate Appropriations Committee Hearings, Foreign

Assistance and Related Programs FY 1975
(Washington, D.C.: Government Printing Office,
1974), 1452.

35. The National Coordinating Committee of the
Anti-Martial Law (Philippines) Movement, "The
Logistics of Repression," Philippines
Information Bulletin, 3 (July 1975), p. 6.

36. In May 1974, President Marcos announced his
plan to beef up the troop strength of the
Armed Forces of the Philippines to 100,000 by
the end of 1974 and 256,000 by 1975.

37. The Philippine Times, 1-15 June 1975, p. 1.

38. Ibid., p. 2.

39. See The Philippines in the World: The Foreign
Relations of the Republic in the New Society
(Manila: Department of Public Information,
1976), p. 6.

40. Robert L. Youngblood, "Public Attitudes and
Philippine Foreign Policy," paper presented at
the Western Conference of the Association for
Asian Studies, in Boulder, Colorado, 10-11
October 1975, p. 16.

41. One of these presidential decrees was PD No.
713 which allowed Americans to own property in
the Philippines after the expiration of the
Laurel-Langely Agreement on 4 July 1974. For
an enumeration of the incentives offered to
foreign investors by the New Society see
Vicente T. Paterno, "The BOI: Its Role in
Philippine Industrial Development," The
Philippine Quarterly, (June 1973), p. 29. See
also "Haven for Foreign Investors," in an
expensive 32-page full color advertisement in
the New York Times of 10 June 1973, pp. 16-17.
PD No. 713 was an obvious attempt by Marcos to
allay the fears of many Americans, most of
them of Philippine ancestry, that properties
they had acquired during the lifetime of the
Parity Amendment would revert to Filipinos
after 1974.

42. Some of the most powerful and visible men in
the Marcos regime were technocrats, for
example, Cesar E. A. Virata, Secretary of
Finance (Wharton); Vicente T. Paterno,
Secretary of Industry and Chairman of the
Board of Investments (Harvard); Gerardo P.
Sicat, Chairman of the National Economic
Development Authority (MIT); Arturo R. Tanco,
Secretary of Agriculture (Harvard); Onofre D.
Corpuz, President of the Development Academy
of the Philippines and the University of the

Philippines (Harvard); Orlando J. Sacay, Assistant Secretary for Cooperatives (Cornell); Vicente Valdepenas, Assistant Secretary of Commerce (Cornell); Roman A. Cruz, Jr., Chairman of the Government Services Insurance System and President of the state-owned Philippine Air Lines (Harvard); and Juan Ponce Enrile, Secretary of National Defense (Harvard). For an interesting explanation of these technocrats' ascension to power, see Laquian, "Martial Law in the Philippines to Date," especially pp. 24-31. Cf., "Philippine Prospects," in The New York Times, 10 June 1973, pp. 16-17.

43. International Documentation on the Contemporary Church, The Philippines: American Corporations, Martial Law, and Underdevelopment (New York: IDCC-North America, Inc., 1973), p. 12.
44. International Documentation on the Contemporary Church, The Philippines, p. 13.
45. For a complete list of the top one hundred companies in the Philippines, see Securities and Exchange Commission report of 15 May 1975, as reproduced in The Philippine Times, 15-31 August 1975, p. 20.
46. International Documentation on the Contemporary Church, The Philippines, p. 47
47. Jovito R. Salonga, "Multi-national Firms and RP Development," Lecture delivered at the Institute of Social Work and Community Development, University of the Philippines, Diliman, Quezon City, on 20 September 1974.
48. Goodsell, American Corporations and Peruvian Politics.
49. Ibid., p. 222.
50. Ibid., p. 216.
51. Ibid., p. 216.
52. Robert B. Stauffer, "The Political Economy of a Coup: Transnational Linkages and Philippine Response," Journal of Peace Research, 11 (1974), p. 174.
53. Romulo, Toward the New Society, p. 30.
54. One of these critics was Salvador P. Lopez, former Secretary of Foreign Affairs, President of the University of the Philippines, and Ambassador to the United States. Lopez described the New Society's foreign policy as a "multilinear, omnidimensional foreign policy, the first ever devised by a Philippine president with a valid claim to a substantial

199

measure of independence of criterion." and he acknowledged that "this innovative foreign policy was one of the incontestable achievements of the Marcos administration under martial law." For the rest of Lopez' analysis, see Lopez, New Directions in Philippine Foreign Policy and "Trends in Philippine Foreign Policy," paper presented during the "Trends in the Philippines Seminar" sponsored by the Institute of Southeast Asian Studies, in Singapore, on 7 January 1978.

55. Youngblood, "Public Attitudes," pp. 16-17.
56. Some of these fringe benefits included an AFP Commissary similar to the US military's PX, increased wages, special insurance policies for servicemen and their dependents in addition to regular GSIS coverage, a special housing area for enlisted men; by decree, Marcos also raised by one grade the ranks of AFP flag-level officers and chiefs of command.
57. "Role in Society Splits Catholics," The Philippine Times, 1-15 August 1975, p. 1.
58. The Philippine Times, 1-15 December 1974, p. 20.
59. According to Corpuz (The Philippines, pp. 32-34), "the grant originally consisted in the right to collect the tributes of the natives living within the boundaries of the grant." See also Bauzon, Philippine Agrarian Reform 1880-1965, pp. 1-11.
60. For a definitive study on the extent of peasant unrest in the Philippines prior to the Huk rebellion, see Benedict J. Kerkvliet, "Peasant Society and Unrest Prior to the Huk Revolution in the Philippines," in Asian Studies, 9 (August 1971), pp. 164-213. See also James Scott and Ben Kerkvliet, "The Politics of Survival: Peasant Response to 'Progress' in Southeast Asia," in Journal of Southeast Asian Studies, IV (September 1973), pp. 262-68.
61. J. David Martin, "Philippine Land Reform in a Historical Perspective," paper presented at the Midwest Conference on Asian Affairs, Lawrence, Kansas, 31 October-2 November 1974, pp. 13-14.
62. Interview with Luis M. Taruc as quoted by Martin, "Philippine Land Reform," p. 14.
63. Luis M. Taruc was one of six Democratic Alliance candidates who won congressional seats in the national elections of 1946 but

were prevented from assuming their seats in Congress, supposedly as a result of a Roxas-landlord conspiracy. The disqualification of Taruc and his five DA colleagues was tied to the controversy over the adoption of the Parity Amendment to the 1935 Constitution. For more details, see Corpuz, The Philippines, pp. 110-11.

64. The surrender of Taruc was negotiated by Benigno S. Aquino, Jr., then a junior reporter for the Manila Times. Years later, Aquino was elected to the Philippine Senate and was one of several opposition politicians arrested by military authorities on 22 September 1972. Aquino was brutally murdered by still unknown assailants on 21 August 1983, at the Manila International Airport, on his way home from self-imposed exile in the United States. Aquino's martyrdom later served as the focal point for concerted anti-regime activity eventually culminating in the downfall of the Marcos regime in February 1986. For a good account of the Huk organization and Taruc's political ideas, see Luis M. Taruc, Born of the People (New York: International Publishers, 1953).

65. Report to the President of the United States by the Economic Survey Mission to the Philippines (Washington, D.C.: United States Government Printing Office, 9 October 1950).

66. Robert S. Hardie, Philippine Land Tenure Reform: Analysis and Recommendations (Manila: U.S. Mutual Security Agency, 1952).

67. For a good account of how Magsaysay induced the Huks to surrender in exchange for land in government resettlement projects, see Alvin Scaff, The Philippine Answer to Communism Stanford: Stanford University Press, 1956).

68. Martin, "Philippine Land Reform," p. 26.

69. From an address delivered on the occasion of the 16th Commencement Exercises of Central Luzon State University in Munoz, Nueva Ecija, on 29 April 1968 and on his conferment by Central Luzon State University of the degree of Doctor of Laws, honoris causa.

70. Marcos, Notes on the New Society of the Philippines, p. 138.

71. Isabelo T. Crisostomo, Marcos the Revolutionary (Quezon City: J. Kriz Publications, 1973), p. 190.

72. From Presidential Decree No. 2, promulgated on 26 September 1972; for the full text of the decree, see Vital Documents on the Declaration of Martial Law in the Philippines, Vol. II (Manila: The National Media Production Center, 1973), pp. 65-67.

73. From speech delivered on 20 October 1972, the signing of PD No. 27. The contents of the decree were officially released the following day, 21 October 1972.

74. "Building the New Society," The New York Times, 10 June 1973, Section 11, p. 4.

75. From Presidential Decree No. 27 issued on 21 October 1972. For the full text of the decree see Vital Documents on the Declaration of Martial Law in the Philippines, Vol. II, pp. 65-67.

76. Benedict J. Kerkvliet, "Land Reform in the Philippines Since the Marcos Coup," Pacific Affairs, 47 (Fall, 1974), p. 287.

77. Ibid., p. 287.

78. Civil Liberties Union of the Philippines, The State of the Nation After Three Years of Martial Law (Makati, Rizal, Philippines: Civil Liberties Union of the Philippines, 1975), p. 50.

79. "Rural Development Panel Seminar on Land Reform in the Philippines," in SEADAG Reports (New York: Southeast Asia Development Advisory Group of the Asia Society, 1975), p. 25.

80. Civil Liberties Union of the Philippines, The State of the Nation, pp. 51-52.

81. Ibid., pp. 51-52.

82. Ibid., pp. 51-52.

83. Ferdinand E. Marcos, Report to the Nation, 1974, (Manila: The National Media Production Center, 1975), pp. 23-24.

84. Conrado F. Estrella, Agrarian Reform in the New Society (Manila: The Marcos Foundation, Inc., 1974).

85. Wurfel, Philippine Agrarian Policy Today: Implementation and Political Impact, p. 8.

86. Ibid., p. 11.

87. Kerkvliet, "Land Reform", p. 290.

88. Wurfel, Philippine Agrarian Policy, pp. 1, 5.

Chapter 7

1. Three of the seven top generals in the Armed Forces of the Philippines during the martial

law period were Ilocanos. They were Lieuten-
ant General Fidel V. Ramos, chief of the
Philippine Constabulary; General Fabian C.
Ver, chief of the elite Presidential Guard
Regiment and later, chief of staff; and Major
General Jose L. Rancudo, chief of the
Philippine Air Force. The other four were
Tagalog, namely General Romeo C. Espino, AFP
chief of staff; Rear Admiral Hilario M. Ruiz,
chief of the Philippine Navy; and Major
General Rafael G. Zagala, chief of the Army.

2. See Report of an Amnesty International Mission
   to the Philippines, 22 November-5 December
   1975 (London: Amnesty International, 1976);
   The Decline of Democracy in the Philippines: A
   report of Mission by William J. Butler, Esq.
   (Geneva: International Commission of Jurists,
   1977); and Human Rights and U.S.Policy:
   Argentina, Haiti, Indonesia, Iran, Peru, and
   the Philippines, a report of the Department of
   State to the Committee on International
   Relations, 94th Congress, 2nd session, 31
   December 1976.

3. According to the International Commission of
   Jurists, supra, the results of the six
   referenda were not valid because (1) martial
   law was in effect, (2) free public debate was
   prohibited, (3) political opponents were in
   jail and some were tortured and maltreated,
   (4) there was no free press, radio, or
   television, (5) the public media, especially
   television and radio, were used only as
   instruments of government propaganda, (6)
   there was no freedom of assembly, (7) military
   forces dominated the nation, (8) the secrecy
   of the ballot was not preserved, with the
   inevitable effect of a substantial element of
   intimidation, (9) the counting and evaluation
   of the voting was done by government nominees,
   (10) the issues presented were framed by the
   government in a manner likely to achieve a
   certain response, and (11) there was limited
   judicial review and no legislative control.

4. For instance, Marcos issued a decree on 19
   March 1978, three weeks before the election,
   increasing the insurance and retirement
   benefits of all civil servants and their
   dependents. This was followed seven days
   later by an announcement that all civil
   servants who lived in Metro Manila for at
   least one year could vote in Metro Manila and

did not have to go home to their respective provinces. This was followed by a warning that all civil servants who could not support the New Society and its objectives might be dismissed from their jobs. See related stories in The Straits Times, 20 March 1978 and 26 March 1978, pp. 2 and 3, respectively. In addition Marcos was on television almost daily denouncing "alien interference" in the elections, and warning about the likelihood of violence in the event that the opposition LABAN candidates won.

5. Beth Day, The Philippines: Shattered Showcase of Democracy in Asia (New York: M. Evans and Company, Inc., 1974), p. 148.
6. See Francisco Nemenzo, Jr., "The Political System," a paper presented at a conference on "The Philippines Into the Twenty-First Century" held at the University of the Philippines Alumni Center on 25 February 1978.
7. For a detailed and longer analysis of the state of the opposition, five years after the proclamation of martial rule, see Muego, "Martial Law Five Years Later: The Status of the Opposition," pp. 215-26.
8. Philippine Times, 15 September 1977, p. 1.
9. See Reuter report from Manila in The Straits Times, 21 September 1977, p. 1.
10. Philippine Times, 16-30 September 1977, p. 5. The full text of the People's League for Freedom platform and Salvador P. Lopez' keynote speech were also reproduced in the same issue.
11. Asiaweek, 12 August 1977, p. 10.
12. Ibid., p. 11.
13. Ibid., p. 14.
14. International Commission of Jurists, "The Decline of Democracy in the Philippines," p. 32.
15. Asiaweek, 12 August 1977, p. 14.
16. Salvador P. Lopez, then president of the University of the Philippines, called for the "dismantling of martial law" in a Dillingham Lecture at the East-West Center of the University of Hawaii on 30 October 1974.
17. Philippine Times, 15-30 September 1977, p. 5.
18. Some of the more publicized cases involving foreign journalists and correspondents were those of Bernard Wideman of the Far Eastern Economic Review and the Washington Post (he was later acquitted) and Arnold Zeitlin, a

long-time correspondent for the Associated Press who was expelled on 2 November 1976. Marilyn Odchimar of the Japanese Kyodo Agency, Nelly Sindayen of the <u>Yomiuri Shimbun</u>, and Rey Palarca of United Press International, were all arrested but later released on 12 June 1977.

19. Salonga, "Multinational Corporations and their Participation in Philippine Development."

20. <u>Times Journal</u>, 22 August 1977, p. 1.

21. International Commission of Jurists, "The Decline of Democracy in the Philippines," p. 46.

22. Several years after Marcos' dramatic announcement in Kuala Lumpur, the Philippines' renunciation of her Sabah claim had yet to be formally implemented. A Reuter report from Manila on 22 March 1978, quoted Marcos as having told Lord Goronwy-Roberts, British Minister of State for Foreign and Commonwealth Affairs that the Constitutional amendment to formalize the dropping of the Sabah claim will be made at an "appropriate time." See <u>The Straits Times</u>, 23 March 1978, p. 32.

23. From an Agence France Presse report in <u>The Straits Times</u>, 2 April 1978, p. 3.

24. Such as Cesar E. A. Virata (Wharton), Secretary of Finance; Vicente T. Paterno (Harvard), Secretary of Industry and Chairman of the Board of Investments; Gerardo P. Sicat (MIT), Chairman of the National Economic Development Authority; Onofre D. Corpuz (Harvard), President of the Development Academy of the Philippines and the University of the Philippines; and Arturo R. Tanco (Harvard), Secretary of Agriculture. For other names see Note 43 in Chapter 5.

25. Nemenzo, "The Political System," p. 5.

26. Geoffrey R.B. Currey, "The Definition of Development," in Rex Mortimer (ed.), <u>Showcase State-Illusion of Indonesia's Accelerated Modernization</u> (Sydney: Angus & Robertson, 1973, p. 21.

27. Lopez, Dillingham Lecture, p. 5.

28. Wurfel, Martial Law in the Philippines: The Methods of Regime Survival," p. 28.

SELECTED BIBLIOGRAPHY

Official Publications and Documents

Amnesty International. Report of an Amnesty International Mission to the Philippines, 22 November-5 December 1975 (London: Amnesty International, 1976.)

International Commission of Jurists. The Decline of Democracy in the Philippines: A Report of Missions by William J. Butler, Esq.; Professor John P. Humphrey; and G.E. Bisson, Esq. (Geneva: International Commission of Jurists, 1977).

R.P. Board of Investments. "Questions and Answers on Foreign Investments in the Philippines," 1974.

R.P. Official Gazette. "Land Reform and Democracy," speech at the Joint FAO/ECAFE/ILO Seminar on the Implementation of Land Reform in Asia and the Far East, WHO building, Manila, on July 12, 1969, vol. 65, no. 29, July 21, 1969, pp. 7415-21.

_____. "Some Words of Caution and Advice to the Armed Forces," speech at the testimonial parade and review at Camp Aguinaldo on September 10, 1969, vol. 65, no. 37, September 15, 1969, pp. 9594E-9594J.

_____. "To Transform the Nation--Transform Ourselves," Second Inaugural Address, Rizal Park, December 30, 1969, vol. 66, no. 1, January 5, 1970, pp. 46A-46F.

_____. "National Discipline: The Key to our Future," Speech by President Ferdinand E. Marcos during the State of the Nation Message, January 26, 1970, vol. 66, no. 5, February 2, 1970, pp. 989-1044.

_____. President Ferdinand E. Marcos' Nationwide Address on Radio and Television on the Attempt of Subversive Elements to Destroy Malacanang Palace on January 31, 1970, vol. 66, no. 6, February 9, 1970, pp. 887-985.

_____. "Change and the Constitution," Extempor-
aneous Speech of President Ferdinand E. Marcos
at the Traditional Cocktails for surviving
delegates to the Constitutional Convention,
Malacanang Palace, vol. 66, no. 7, February
16, 1970, pp. 1550-53.

_____. "We Are Committed to Liberal Democracy,"
Speech at the Annual District Dinner, Conference of the Rotary International District
380, Manila Hilton, February 27, 1970, vol.
66, no. 10, March 9, 1970, pp. 2319-2321G.

_____. "The Scale of Reform," Speech at the
Special National Convention of the Philippine
Jaycees, Rizal Provincial Capitol, Pasig,
Rizal, March 6, 1970, vol. 66, no. 11, March
16, 1970, pp. 2570A-2570D.

_____. "Call for National Unity," Speech at the
closing dinner of the First National Credit
Congress, sponsored by the Credit Management
Association of the Philippines, Hotel Inter-
continental, April 4, 1970, vol. 66, no. 21,
May 25, 1970, pp. 5193(29)-5192(34).

_____. "Land Justice for All," Speech at the
closing ceremony of the Executive Seminar on
"Land Reform in the '70's," Magsaysay Hall,
Social Security Building on August 17, 1970,
pp. 7574-7574S.

_____. "Change and the Law," Speech by President
Ferdinand E. Marcos at the opening of the
LAWASIA Conference, Philamlife Auditorium,
January 18, 1971, vol. 67, no. 4, pp. 485-88.

_____. "On A New Philippine Constitution,"
Speech delivered by President Ferdinand E.
Marcos before the opening of the Constitutional Convention at the Manila Hotel on June
1, 1971, vol. 67, no. 3, June 7, 1971, pp.
4436-37.

_____. Executive Order No. 333, creating a
Presidential Administrative Assistance
Committee relative to the implementation of
Proclamation No. 889, dated August 21, 1971,
suspending the Privilege of the Writ of Habeas
Corpus, vol. 67, no. 35, August 30, 1971, p.
6859.

_____. Proclamation No. 889, suspending the
Privilege of the Writ of Habeas Corpus in
certain cases, vol. 67, no. 35, August 30,
1971, pp. 6864-65.

_____. Proclamation No. 889-C, further lifting
the Privilege of the Writ of Habeas Corpus in

other areas, vol. 67, no. 47, November 22, 1971, p. 9186B.

_____. Proclamation No. 889-D, further lifting the Privilege of the Writ of Habeas Corpus in other areas, vol. 67, no. 47, November 22, 1971, pp. 9186B-9187.

_____. Executive Order No. 890, lifting the Privilege of the Writ of Habeas Corpus, vol. 68, no. 3, January 17, 1972, p. 384.

_____. "Strength Through Crisis, Growth and Freedom," State of the Nation Message, vol. 68, no. 5, January 24, 1972, pp. 852-914.

_____. In the matter of the Petition for Habeas Corpus of Teodosio Lansang, et. al. vs. Brigadier General Eduardo M. Garcia; Rogelio V. Arrienda vs. Secretary of National Defense, et. al.; Luzvimindo David vs. Brigadier General Eduardo M. Garcia, et. al.; Nemesio E. Prudente, et. al. vs. Brigadier General Manuel T. Yan, et. al.; Gerardo Tomas vs. Brigadier General Eduardo M. Garcia, et. al.; Reynaldo Rimando vs. Brigadier General Eduardo M. Garcia; Sgt. Filomeno S. de Castro, et. al. vs. Brigadier General Eduardo M. Garcia; Antolin Oreta, Jr. vs. Brigadier General Eduardo M. Garcia, et. al.; Gary B. Olivar vs. Brigadier General Eduardo M. Garcia, et. al., vol. 68, no. 8, February 21, 1972, pp. 1487-1542.

R.P. Media Production Center. Martial Law Philippine Style, by Brigadier General Guillermo A. Pecache, Deputy Chief of Staff for Home Defense, Armed Forces of the Philippines.

_____. President Ferdinand E. Marcos' Constitutional Revolution: The Philippines in the New Society.

_____. The New Society.

_____. The New Society in the Philippines.

_____. The Philippines and Its New Society.

_____. Vital Documents on the Declaration of Martial Law in the Philippines. 5 volumes.

R.P. Department of Public Information. The Philippines in the New World: The Foreign Relations of the Republic in the New Society (Manila: Department of Public Information, 1976).

_____. Primer on Philippine Foreign Policy, 1975.

_____. Development for the New Society, 1974.

U.S. Congress. Senate. Subcommittee on United

States Security Agreements and Commitments Abroad of the Committee on Foreign Relations. United States Security Agreements and Commitments Abroad. S. Rpt. 1970, 91st Congress, 2nd sess., 30 Sept.; 1, 2, 3, October 1969. Senate Miscellaneous Reports on Public Bills, Vol. I, parts 1-4.

_____. Senator Alan Cranston speaking on "Repression in the Philippines," 93rd Cong., 1st sess., 12 April 1973. Congressional Record, vol. 119.

U.S. Congress. House of Representatives. Human Rights and US Policy: Argentina, Haiti, Indonesia, Iran, Peru, and the Philippines, a report of the Department of State to the Committee on International Relations, 94th Congress, 2nd sess., December 31, 1976.

_____. Hearing before the Subcommittee on International Organizations of the Committee on International Relations on Human Rights in the Philippines: Report by Amnesty International, 94th Congress, 2nd sess., September 15, 1976.

Books

Abueva, Jose V. and de Guzman, Raul P., eds., Foundations and and Dynamics of Philippine Government and Politics. Manila: Bookmark, 1969.

Agoncillo, Teodoro A. Malolos: Crisis of the Republic. Quezon City: University of the Philippines Press, 1960.

_____. Philippine History. Manila: Inang Wika Publishing Co., 1965.

_____. Revolt of the Masses. Quezon City: University of the Philippines Press, 1956.

Agoncillo, Teodoro A. and Oscar M. Alfonso. A Short History of the Filipino People. Quezon City: University of the Philippines Press, 1960.

Almond, Gabriel A. Political Development. Boston: Little, Brown and Company, 1970.

Almond, Gabriel A. and Coleman, James S., eds., The Politics of the Developing Areas. Princeton: Princeton University Press, 1960.

Almond, Gabriel A. and Powell, Jr., G. Bingham. Comparative Politics: A Developmental Approach. Boston: Little, Brown and Company, Inc. 1966.

Apter, David E. The Politics of Modernization.
     Chicago: The University of Chicago Press,
     1965.
Arendt, Hannah. On Revolution. New York: The
     Viking Press, 1965.
Aruego, Jose M. The Framing of the Philippine
     Constitution. Volume II. Manila: University
     Publishing Co., 1949.
_____. Know Your Constitution. Manila: Univer-
     sity Publishing Co., 1950.
_____. Philippine Political Law. Manila: Univer-
     sity Publishing Co., 1950.
Averch, Harvey A., Koehler, John E., and Denton,
     Frank H. The Matrix of Policy in the
     Philippines. Princeton: Princeton University
     Press, 1971.
Baclagon, Uldarico S. Military History of the
     Philippines. Manila: St. Mary's Publishing,
     1975.
Bauzon, Leslie E. Philippine Agrarian Reform 1880-
     1965. Singapore: Institute of Southeast Asian
     Studies, 1975.
Brinton, Crane. The Anatomy of a Revolution. New
     York: W.W. Norton & Company, 1938.
Caroll, John J. Changing Patterns of Social Struc-
     ture in the Philippines 1896-1963. Quezon
     City: Ateneo de Manila University Press, 1968.
Chorley, Katherine C. Armies and the Art of
     Revolution. London: Faber & Faber, 1963.
Coleman, James S., ed., Education and Political
     Development. Princeton: Princeton University
     Press, 1965.
Constantino, Renato. The Filipinos in the
     Philippines and Other Essays. Quezon City:
     Filipino Signatures, 1966.
Corpuz, Onofre D. The Philippines. Englewood
     Cliffs, N.J.: Prentice-Hall, Inc., 1965.
_____. The Bureaucracy in the Philippines.
     Manila: Institute of Public Administration,
     University of the Philippines, 1957.
Corwin, Edward S. Total War and the Constitution.
     New York: Alfred A. Knopf, 1947.
_____. The President: Office and Powers, 1787-
     1957. Fourth Revised Edition. New York: New
     York University Press, 1957.
Crisostomo, Isabelo T. Challenge of Leadership.
     Quezon City: J. Kriz Publishing Enterprises,
     1969.
_____. Marcos the Revolutionary. Quezon City:
     J. Kriz Publishing Enterprises, 1973.

De La Costa, Horacio, S.J. The Background of
    Nationalism and Other Essays. Manila:
    Solidaridad Publishing House, 1965.
Diamant, Alfred. "Bureaucracy in Developmental
    Movement Regimes," in Riggs, Fred W., ed.,
    Frontiers of Development Administration.
    Durham: Duke University Press, 1971.
Du Bois, Cora. Social Forces in Southeast Asia.
    Cambridge: Harvard University Press, 1967.
Eisenstadt, Shmuel N. Modernization, Protest and
    Change. Englewood Cliffs, N.J.: Prentice-
    Hall, Inc., 1966.
Feit, Edward. The Armed Bureaucrats. Boston:
    Houghton Miflin Company, 1973.
Fernandez, Perfecto V., et al. A Study of the
    Philippine Constitution. Quezon City: JMC
    Press, 1974.
Fernando, Enrique M. The Constitutional Government
    of the Philippines. Manila: German Fernando &
    Company, 1951.
Finer, S.E.. The Man on Horseback: The Role of the
    Military in Politics. London: Pall Mall
    Press, 1962.
Fleron, Jr., Frederic J. Communist Studies and the
    Social Sciences. Chicago: Rand McNally &
    Company, 1969.
Gamson, William A. Power and Discontent. Homewood,
    Illinois: The Dorsey Press, 1968.
Goodsell, Charles T. American Corporations and
    Peruvian Politics. Cambridge: Harvard
    University Press, 1974.
Grossholtz, Jean. Politics in the Philippines.
    Boston: Little, Brown and Company, 1964.
Grunder, Garel A. and Livezey, William E. The
    Philippines and the United States. Norman:
    University of Oklahoma Press, 1951.
Guerrero, Amado. Philippine Society and Revolution.
    Hong Kong: Ta Kung Pao, 1971.
Gutteridge, William. Military Institutions and
    Power in the New States. New York: Frederick
    A. Praeger, 1965.
Heeger, Gerald A. The Politics of Underdevelopment.
    New York: St. Martin's Press, 1974.
Hollnsteiner, Mary R. Dynamics of Power in a
    Philippine Municipality. Quezon City:
    Community Development Research Council,
    University of the Philippines, 1963.
Huntington, Samuel P. The Soldier and the State:
    The Theory and Politics of Civil-Military
    Relations. Cambridge: Harvard University
    Press, 1967.

_____. Political Order in Changing Societies.
    New Haven: Yale University Press, 1968.
_____. Changing Patterns of Military Politics.
    New Haven: Yale University Press, 1969.
Jackson, Robert J. and Stein, Michael B., eds.,
    Issues in Comparative Politics; A Text With
    Readings. New York: St. Martin's Press, 1971.
Jacobini, H.B. and Associates. Governmental Ser-
    vices in the Philippines. Manila: Institute
    of Public Administration, University of the
    Philippines, 1956.
Janowitz, Morris. The Military in the Political
    Development of New Nations: An Essay in
    Comparative Analysis. Chicago: The University
    of Chicago Press, 1964.
_____. The Professional Soldier: A Social and
    Political Portrait. Glencoe: The Free Press,
    1960.
Janowitz, Morris and Little, Roger. Sociology and
    the Military Establishment. Revised Edition.
    New York: Russell Sage Foundation, 1965.
Johnson, Chalmers, ed., Change in Communist Systems.
    Stanford: Stanford University Press, 1970.
_____. Revolutionary Change. Boston: Little,
    Brown and Company, Inc., 1966.
_____. Revolution and the Social System.
    Stanford: Hoover Institution Studies, no. 3,
    1964.
Johnson, John J., ed., The Role of the Military in
    Underdeveloped Countries. Princeton:
    Princeton University Press, 1962.
Kalaw, Maximo M. The Present Government of the
    Philippines. Manila: The McCullough Printing
    Co., 1921.
Kautsky, John H. The Political Consequences of
    Modernization. New York: John Wiley and Sons,
    1972.
Kelley, George A. and Brown, Jr., Clifford W., eds.,
    Struggles in the State: Sources and Patterns
    of World Revolution. New York: John Wiley and
    Sons, 1970.
Lachica, Eduardo. The Huks: Philippine Agrarian
    Society in Revolt. New York: Frederick A.
    Praeger, 1961.
Lande, Carl H. Leaders, Factions and Parties. New
    Haven: Yale University Press, 1965.
La Palombara, Joseph and Weiner, Myron, eds.,
    Political Parties and Political Development.
    Princeton: Princeton University Press, 1966.

Larkin, John A. The Pampangans: Colonial Society in a Philippine Province. Berkeley: University of California Press, 1972.

Lasswell, Harold D. and Lerner, Daniel, eds., The World Revolutionary Elites. Cambridge: Massachusetts Institute of Technology Press, 1966.

Lerner, Daniel. The Passing of the Traditional Society. New York: The Free Press, 1958.

Lipset, Seymour Martin and Wolin, Sheldon S., eds., The Berkeley Student Revolt: Facts and Interpretations. Garden City, New York: Doubleday & Company, 1965.

Lissak, Moshe. Center and Periphery in Developing Countries and Prototypes of Military Elites. vol. v, 1969-1970, no. 7: Studies in Comparative International Development. New Brunswick, New Jersey: Rutgers University Press, 1970.

Longaker, Richard P. The Presidency and Individual Liberties. Ithaca: Cornell University Press, 1961.

Lopez, Salvador P. New Directions in Philippine Foreign Policy. Quezon City: University of the Philippines Law Center, 1975.

Lynch, Frank, S.J., comp. and ed., Four Readings on Philippine Values. Quezon City: Ateneo de Manila University Press, 1964.

Mahajani, Usha. Philippine Nationalism. St. Lucia, Queensland: University of Queensland Press, 1971.

Majul, Cesar A. The Political and Constitutional Ideas of the Philippine Revolution. Quezon City: University of the Philippines Press, 1960.

Makil, Perla Q. Mobility by Decree: The Rise and Fall of Philippine Influentials Since Martial Law. Quezon City: Institute of Philippine Culture, Ateneo de Manila University Press, 1975.

Marcos, Ferdinand E. Today's Revolution: Democracy. Manila: Marcos Foundation, Inc., 1971.

_____. Notes on the New Society of the Philippines. Manila: Marcos Foundation, Inc., 1973.

_____. A Dialogue With My People. Manila: Department of Public Information, 1973.

Mecham, J. Lloyd. Church and State in Latin America. Revised Edition. Chapel Hill: The University of North Carolina Press, 1966.

Mendoza, Vicente V. Perspectives on the New Constitution. Quezon City: University of the Philippines Law Center, 1974.

Millikan, Max P. and Blackmer, Donald L.M., eds., The Emerging Nations: Their Growth and United States Policy. Boston: Little, Brown and Company, 1961.

Montgomery, John D. and Siffin, William J., eds., Approaches to Development: Politics, Administration and Change. New York: McGraw-Hill, 1966.

Muego, Benjamin N. "Martial Law Five Years later: The Status of the Opposition," in Southeast Asian Affairs 1978, Singapore: Heinemann Educational Books, Ltd., 1978.

_____. "The Philippines: From Martial Law to Crisis Government," in Southeast Asian Affairs 1979, Singapore: Heinemann Educational Books, Ltd., 1979.

Pacis, Vicente Albano. Philippine Government and Politics. Revised Edition. Quezon City: Bustamante Press, 1963.

Palmer, Monte. Dilemmas of Political Development: An Introduction to the Politics of Developing Areas. Itasca: F.E. Peacock Publishers, 1975.

Palmer, Monte and Stern, Larry, eds., Political Development in Changing Societies: An Analysis of Modernization. Lexington: D.C. Heath & Company, 1971.

Perlmutter, Amos. Military and Politics in Israel. London: Frank Cass & Co., 1969.

Prudente, Nemesio E. Sa Mga Kuko Ng Limbas (On the Talons of the Eagle). Quezon City: Malaya Books, 1972.

Pye, Lucian W. Cases in Comparative Politics: Asia. Boston: Little, Brown and Company, 1970.

_____. Aspects of Political Development. Boston: Little, Brown and Company, 1966.

_____. Southeast Asia: Political Systems. Englewood Cliffs, N.J.: Prentice-Hall, 1967.

Pye, Lucian W. and Verba, Sidney. Political Culture and Political Development. Princeton: Princeton University Press, 1965.

Ravenholt, Albert. The Philippines: A Young Republic on the Move. New York: D. Van Nostrand Co., 1962.

Rich, Bennett M. The Presidents and Civil Disorder. Washington, D.C.: The Brookings Institution, 1941.

Riggs, Fred W. Administration in Developing Countries: The Theory of the Prismatic

Society. Boston: Houghton Mifflin Company, 1964.

_____. ed., Frontiers of Development Administration. Durham: Duke University Press, 1971.

Roche, John P. "Executive Power and Domestic Emergency: The Quest for Prerogative," in Johnson, Donald Bruce and Walker, Jack L., eds., The Dynamics of the American Presidency. New York: John Wiley & Sons, Inc., 1964.

Romani, John H. The Philippine Presidency. Manila: Institute of Public Administration, University of the Philippines, 1956.

Rossiter, Clinton L. Constitutional Dictatorship: Crisis Government in Modern Democracies. Princeton: Princeton University Press, 1948.

_____. The Supreme Court and the Commander in Chief. New York: Da Capo Press, 1970.

Schubert, Jr., Glendon A. The Presidency in the Courts. Minneapolis: University of Minnesota Press, 1957.

Shaw, L. Earl, ed., Modern Competing Ideologies. Lexington: D.C. Heath and Company, 1973.

Shils, Edward. Political Development in the New States. The Hague: Mouton, 1968.

Spence, Hartzell. For Every Tear a Victory: The Story of Ferdinand E. Marcos. New York: McGraw-Hill, 1964.

_____. Marcos of the Philippines: A Biography. New York: The World Publishing Company, 1969.

Stene, Edwin O. and Associates. Public Administration in the Philippines. Manila: Bureau of Printing, 1955.

Story, Joseph. Commentaries on the Constitution of the United States. Two Volumes. Boston: Little, Brown and Company, 1873.

Tachau, Frank, ed., The Developing Nations: What Path to Modernization? New York: Dodd, Mead & Company, 1972.

Tilman, Robert O., ed., Man, State, and Society in Contemporary Southeast Asia. New York: Frederick A. Praeger, 1969.

Ventura, Mamerto S. United States-Philippine Cooperation and Cross-Purposes. Quezon City: Filipiniana Publications, 1974.

Waldo, Dwight. Temporal Dimension of Development Administration. Durham: Duke University Press, 1970.

Weaver, Jerry L. Political Style of the Guatemalan Military Elite, Vol. V., 1969-1970, No. 4;

216

Studies in Comparative International Development. New Brunswick: Rutgers University
Press, 1970.

Weidner, Edward. Developing Administration in Asia.
Durham: Duke University Press, 1970.

Welch, Claude E., ed., Political Modernization: A
Reader in Comparative Political Change.
Belmont: Wadsworth Publishing Company, 1971.

Wilber, Charles K., ed., The Political Economy of
Development and Underdevelopment. New York:
Random House, 1973.

Wurfel, David O. Philippine Agrarian Policy Today:
Implementation and Political Impact.
Singapore: Institute of Southeast Asian
Studies, 1977.

Journal Articles and Unpublished Materials

Abueva, Jose V. "The Philippine Political Tradition
and Change," Asian Survey, X (January, 1970),
56-64.

_____. "The Prospects for Revolution in the
Philippines: Conflicting Evaluations," paper
presented at the Conference of Southeast Asian
Students; Bloomington, Indiana; March 26,
1970.

Adkins, John H. "Philippines 1971: Events of the
Year, Trends of the Future," Asian Survey, XII
(January 1972), 78-85.

Anthony, Garner. "Martial Law in Hawaii,"
California Law Review, XXX (May, 1942),
371-96.

_____. "Martial Law, Military Government, and
the Writ of Habeas Corpus in Hawaii,"
California Law Review, XXXI (1943), 486-502.

Barrett, W. Scott and Ferenz, Walter S. "Peacetime
Martial Law in Guam," California Law Review,
48 (March, 1960), 1-30.

Butwell, Richard. "The Changing of the Guards,"
Asian Survey, VI (January, 1966), 43-48.

_____. "The Philippine Prelude to Elections,"
Asian Survey, V (January, 1965), 43-48.

_____. "The Philippines: America's Former(?)
Colony," Washington Monthly, (February, 1970),
72-82.

Campos, Maria Clara L. "Multinational Corporations
and the Philippines as Host Country," lecture
under the Benito Lopez Professorial Chair,
University of the Philippines College of Law,
delivered on January 28, 1975.

Castro, Gregorio; Gatmaitan, Armando; Train, Angeles; and de Borja, Quintin R. "Notes on the Role of the Military in Socio-Economic Development," Philippine Journal of Public Administration, XII (July, 1968), 10-16.

Cespedes, Carol H. and Gibbs, Eugene. "The New Middle Class in the Philippines: A Case Study in Culture Change," Asian Survey, XII (October, 1972), 879-86.

Chavez, Francisco I. "Martial Law: Scope, Problems and Proposals," Philippine Law Journal, XLV (July, 1970), 325-43.

Correspondent, A. "Premiere Marcos," Far Eastern Economic Review, 78 (November 4, 1972), 16-26.

Darling, Frank C. "Political Development in Thailand and the Philippines," Southeast Asia, 1 (Winter-Spring, 1971), 91-116.

De Borja, Quintin R. "Some Career Attributes and Professional Views of the Philippine Military Elite," Philippine Journal of Public Administration, XIII (October, 1969), 1-16.

Del Carmen, Rolando V. "Constitutionalism and the Supreme Court in a Changing Philippine Polity," University of Wisconsin-Oshkosh, mimeographed, 1974.

Douglas, Louis H. "Modernization in a Transitional Setting: A Philippine Case Study," Civilisations, XVIII (1968), 204-31.

Duenas, Michael. "President Marcos to the Nation," Philippines Free Press, (January 29, 1972), 5, 43.

Fairman, Charles. "The Supreme Court on Military Jurisdiction," Harvard Law Review, LIX (1946), 833-82.

_____. "The Law of Martial Rule and the National Emergency," Harvard Law Review, LV (1942), 1253-1302.

Fisher, S. G. "The Suspension of Habeas Corpus During the War of Rebellion," Political Science Quarterly, III (1888), 454-88.

George, T. J. S. "Marcos Interview: Kicking Old Habits," Far Eastern Economic Review, 78 (December 23, 1972), 11-12.

_____. "The Party's Over," Far Eastern Economic Review, 78 (November 18, 1972), 14.

_____. "The Siblings' Tales," Far Eastern Economic Review, (November 4, 1972), 26-28.

_____. "Mr. Marcos Shapes the New Society," Far Eastern Economic Review, 76 (October 10, 1972), 13-15.

_____. "Rainy-day Guns," _Far Eastern Economic Review_, 77 (July 1, 1972), 14.

_____. "A Quiet Consensus of Dissent," _Far Eastern Economic Review_, 76 (June 17, 1972), 11-12.

_____. "The Philippines Under Martial Law: The Road Ahead," _Pacific Community_, 4 (July, 1973).

Goodman, Grant K. "The Problem of Philippine Independence and Japan: The First Three Decades of American Colonial Rule," _Southeast Asia_, 1 (Summer, 1971), 165-92.

Gorospe, Vitaliano R., S.J. "Some Basic Values in the 1971 Constitutional Convention: A Christian Perspective," _Philippine Studies_, 20 (First Quarter, 1972), 166-175.

Grossholtz, Jean. "The Philippines: Midterm Doldrums for Marcos," _Asian Survey_, VIII (January, 1968), 52-57.

_____. "The Philippines: New Adventures with Old Problems," _Asian Survey_, IX (January, 1969), 50-57.

Hopkins, Keith. "Civil-Military Relations in Developing Countries," _The British Journal of Sociology_, XVII (June, 1969), 165-182.

Isleta, Honesto M. "The Role of the Military in the New Society: A New Challenge," _Asian Defence Journal_ (June, 1977), 21, 23, 83.

Kelly, George A. "The Global Civil-Military Dilemma," _The Review of Politics_ (July, 1963), 291-308.

King, Archibald. "The Legality of Martial Law in Hawaii," _California Law Review_, XXX (September, 1942), 599-633.

Kiunisala, Edward R. "Party in Crisis," _Philippines Free Press_ (January 8, 1972), 5, 42, 44.

_____. "The Presidential System: Why Change It?" _Philippines Free Press_ (January 15, 1972), 5, 44, 45.

_____. "Delegates Go Home!" _Philippines Free Press_ (January 29, 1972), 4, 46.

_____. "Why is President Marcos so Afraid of His Own People?" _Philippines Free Press_ (February 5, 1972), 4, 46.

_____. "The Constitutional Convention: Nakakahiya: Part I," _Philippines Free Press_ (February 12, 1972), 2, 32-A.

_____. "The Constitutional Convention: Nakakahiya: Part II," _Philippines Free Press_ (February 19, 1972), 4, 18-B.

Lande, Asuncion Nobleza. "Multilingualism, Politics and 'Filipinism'," _Asian Survey_, XI (July, 1971), 677-92.

Lande, Carl H. "Parties and Politics in the Philippines," _Asian Survey_, VII (September, 1968), 725-47.

Laquian, Aprodicio A. "Martial Law in the Philippines to Date," paper presented at the Twenty-Sixth Annual Meeting of the Association for Asian Studies; Boston, Massachusetts, April 1-3, 1974.

Littaua, Ferdinand Z. "Some Insights Into the Student Movement in the Philippines," _Asia Quarterly_ (1972-1973), 203-16.

Locsin, Teodoro M. "The Supreme Court and Our Liberties," _Philippines Free Press_ (January 1, 1972), 2, 46.

_____. "No Thanks," _Philippines Free Press_ (January 8, 1972), 3, 46.

Locsin, Jr., Teodoro M. "In 1973?" _Philippines Free Press_ (January 8, 1972), 2, 46.

Machado, Kit G. "Changing Aspects of Factionalism in Philippine Local Politics," _Asian Survey_, XI (December, 1971), 1182-99.

Meadows, Martin. "Recent Developments in Philippine-American Relations: A Case Study in Emergent Nationalism," _Asian Survey_, V (June, 1965), 305-18.

_____. "Colonialism, Social Structure and Nationalism: The Philippines Case," _Pacific Affairs_, XLIV (Fall, 1971), 337-53.

Muego, Benjamin N. "The Political Elite in Philippine Society," _Trends: A Journal of Ideas of the Philippine College of Commerce_, I (November, 1967-February, 1968), 1-25.

_____. "The Politicization of the Filipino-American: A Pilot Study in Immigrant Political Socialization," unpublished M.A. thesis; Kansas State University, Manhattan, Kansas, 1971.

_____. "The Philippine Student Movement of the 1970s and the 'New society'," paper presented at the Midwest Conference on Asian Affairs; University of Kansas, Lawrence, Kansas, November 1-3, 1974.

_____. "The Politics of Accommodation: Foreign Policy Under the 'New Society'," paper presented at the Midwest Conference on Asian Affairs; Ohio University, Athens, Ohio, October 24-25, 1975.

_____. "The 'New Society' of the Philippines: A Case Study of a Developmental Movement Regime," unpublished Ph.D. dissertation; Southern Illinois University, Carbondale, Illinois, 1976.

_____. "The Executive Committee in the Philippines: Successors, Power Brokers, and Dark Horses," Asian Survey, XXIII (November, 1983), 1159-70.

Nussbaum, Bruce. "Defending Malacanang," Far Eastern Economic Review, 76 (May 13, 1972), 26-27.

Overholt, William H. "Martial Law, Revolution and Democracy in the Philippines," Southeast Asia, II (Spring, 1973), 159-92.

Paterno, Vicente T. "Manila: Asia's New Financial Center," The Philippines Quarterly, 5 (June, 1973), 18-30.

Radin, Max. "Martial Law and the State of Siege," California Law Review, XXX (September, 1942), 634-47.

Rama, Napoleon G. "For a Senate of the Filipino People," Philippines Free Press (February 19, 1972), 3, 46.

_____. "The House Expensive: The Latest Break-down of Congressional Allowances," Philippines Free Press (February 12, 1972), 5, 45.

_____. "The Senate Power Struggle," Philippines Free Press (February 5, 1972), 6, 44.

_____. "The Lame-Duck President Gimmick," Philippines Free Press (January 15, 1972), 7, 42.

_____. "Imelda Marcos: Will She Run?" Philippines Free Press (January 8, 1972), 6, 42.

_____. "The Uses of the Supreme Court Decision: How President Marcos Had Been Exploiting It," Philippines Free Press (January 1, 1972), 3, 47.

Ronquillo, Bernardino. "The Supreme Court: Whose 'Last Bulwark'?" Far Eastern Economic Review, 75 (January 8, 1972), 14.

_____. "Marcos Faces His Options," Far Eastern Economic Review, 75 (January 15, 1972), 17.

_____. "Con Con Can't," Far Eastern Economic Review, 75 (February 26, 1972), 13-14.

_____. "Credibility and Mrs. Marcos," Far Eastern Economic Review, 76 (April 29, 1972), 14.

_____. "Nacional Interest," Far Eastern Economic Review, 76 (May 27, 1972), 15.

_____. "Week of Change," Far Eastern Economic Review, 78 (October 10, 1972), 15.

_____. "Managed Media," Far Eastern Economic Review, (November 11, 1972), 15.

Roth, David F. "The Choice of a Political Formula in a Third World Nation: The Case of the Philippines, 1972-1973," Lafayette, Indiana: Department of Political Science, Purdue University, mimeographed, 1974.

Salonga, Jovito R. "Multinational Corporations and their Participation in Philippine Development," St. Thomas More lecture, delivered at the University of Santo Tomas, Manila, on February 12, 1975.

Starner, Frances. "The Philippines: Politics of the 'New Era'," Asian Survey, III (January, 1963), 41-47.

_____. "Instant Revolution," Far Eastern Economic Review, 75 (January 15, 1972), 18-20.

Stoodley, Bartlett H. "Normative Attitudes of Filipino Youth Compared With German and American Youth," American Sociological Review, 22 (October, 1957), 550-61.

Tilman, Robert O. "The Philippines in 1970: A Difficult Decade Begins," Asian Survey, IX (February, 1971), 139-48.

_____. "Student Unrest in the Philippines: The View From the South," Asian Survey, X (October, 1970), 900-909.

_____. "The Impact of American Education on the Philippines," Asia, 21 (Spring, 1971), 66-80.

Tucker, Robert C. "Towards a Comparative Politics of Movement Regimes," American Political Science Review, LV (June, 1961), 281-93.

Wurfel, David O. "The Philippines: Intensified Dialogue," Asian Survey, VII (January, 1967), 46-52.

_____. "Martial Law in the Philippines: The Methods of Regime Survival," Pacific Affairs, 50 (Spring, 1977), 5-30.

222

ISBN Prefix 0-89680-
Africa Series

25. Kircherr, Eugene C. ABBYSSINIA TO ZIMBABWE: A
    Guide to the Political Units of Africa in the
    Period 1947-1978. 1979. 3rd ed. 80pp.
    100-4 $ 8.00*

27. Fadiman, Jeffrey A. MOUNTAIN WARRIORS: The
    Pre-Colonial Meru of Mt. Kenya. 1976. 82pp.
    060-1 $ 4.75*

36. Fadiman, Jeffrey A. THE MOMENT OF CONQUEST:
    Meru, Kenya, 1907. 1979. 70pp.
    081-4 $ 5.50*

37. Wright, Donald R. ORAL TRADITIONS FROM THE
    GAMBIA: Volume I, Mandinka Griots. 1979.
    176pp.
    083-0 $12.00*

38. Wright, Donald R. ORAL TRADITIONS FROM THE
    GAMBIA: Volume II, Family Elders. 1980.
    200pp.
    084-9 $15.00*

39. Reining, Priscilla. CHALLENGING DESERTIFICA-
    TION IN WEST AFRICA: Insights from Landsat into
    Carrying Capacity, Cultivation and Settlement
    Site Identification in Upper Volta and
    Niger. 1979. 180pp., illus.
    102-0 $12.00*

41. Lindfors, Bernth. MAZUNGUMZO: Interviews with
    East African Writers, Publishers, Editors, and
    Scholars. 1981. 179pp.
    108-X $13.00*

42. Spear, Thomas J. TRADITIONS OF ORIGIN AND
    THEIR INTERPRETATION: The Mijikenda of Kenya.
    1982. xii, 163pp.
    109-8 $13.50*

43. Harik, Elsa M. and Donald G. Schilling. THE
    POLITICS OF EDUCATION IN COLONIAL ALGERIA AND
    KENYA. 1984. 102pp.
    117-9 $11.50*

44. Smith, Daniel R. THE INFLUENCE OF THE FABIAN
    COLONIAL BUREAU ON THE INDEPENDENCE MOVEMENT IN
    TANGANYIKA. 1985. x, 98pp.
    125-X $ 9.00*

45. Keto, C. Tsehloane. AMERICAN-SOUTH AFRICAN RELATIONS 1784-1980: Review and Select Bibliography. 1985. 159pp.
128-4 $11.00*

46. Burness, Don, and Mary-Lou Burness, ed. WANASEMA: Conversations with African Writers. 1985. 95pp.
129-2 $ 9.00*

47. Switzer, Les. MEDIA AND DEPENDENCY IN SOUTH AFRICA: A Case Study of the Press and the Ciskei "Homeland". 1985. 80pp.
130-6   9.00*

48. Heggoy, Alf Andrew. THE FRENCH CONQUEST OF ALGIERS, 1830: An Algerian Oral Tradition. 1986. 101pp.
131-4 $ 9.00*

49. Hart, Ursula Kingsmill. TWO LADIES OF COLONIAL ALGERIA: The Lives and Times of Aurelie Picard and Isabelle Eberhardt. 1987. 156pp.
143-8 $9.00*

50. Voeltz, Richard A. GERMAN COLONIALISM AND THE SOUTH WEST AFRICA COMPANY, 1894-1914. 1988. 143pp.
146-2 $10.00*

52. Northrup, David. BEYOND THE BEND IN THE RIVER: African Labor in Eastern Zaire, 1865-1940. 1988. 195pp.
151-9 $12.00*

53. Makinde, M. Akin. AFRICAN PHILOSOPHY, CULTURE, AND TRADITIONAL MEDICINE. 1988. 175pp.
152-7 $11.00*

Latin America Series

1. Frei, Eduardo M. THE MANDATE OF HISTORY AND CHILE'S FUTURE. Tr. by Miguel d'Escoto. Intro. by Thomas Walker. 1977. 79pp.
066-0 $ 8.00*

4. Martz, Mary Jeanne Reid. THE CENTRAL AMERICAN SOCCER WAR: Historical Patterns and Internal Dynamics of OAS Settlement Procedures. 1979. 118pp.
077-6 $ 8.00*

5. Wiarda, Howard J. CRITICAL ELECTIONS AND CRITICAL COUPS: State, Society, and the Military in the Processes of Latin American Development. 1979. 83pp.
    082-2 $ 7.00*

6. Dietz, Henry A., and Richard Moore. POLITICAL PARTICIPATION IN A NON-ELECTORAL SETTING: The Urban Poor in Lima, Peru. 1979. viii, 102pp.
    085-7 $ 9.00*

7. Hopgood, James F. SETTLERS OF BAJAVISTA: Social and Economic Adaptation in a Mexican Squatter Settlement. 1979. xii, 145pp.
    101-2 $11.00*

8. Clayton, Lawrence A. CAULKERS AND CARPENTERS IN A NEW WORLD: The Shipyards of Colonial Guayaquil. 1980. 189pp., illus.
    103-9 $15.00*

9. Tata, Robert J. STRUCTURAL CHANGES IN PUERTO RICO'S ECONOMY: 1947-1976. 1981. xiv, 104pp.
    107-1 $11.75*

10. McCreery, David. DEVELOPMENT AND THE STATE IN REFORMA GUATEMALA, 1871-1885. 1983. viii, 120pp.
    113-6 $ 8.50*

11. O'Shaughnessy, Laura N., and Louis H. Serra. CHURCH AND REVOLUTION IN NICARAGUA. 1986. 118pp.
    126-8 $11.00*

12. Wallace, Brian. OWNERSHIP AND DEVELOPMENT: A Comparison of Domestic and Foreign Investment in Columbian Manufacturing. 1987. 186pp.
    145-4 $12.00*

13. Henderson, James D. CONSERVATIVE THOUGHT IN LATIN AMERICA: The Ideas of Laureano Gomez. 1988. 150pp.
    148-9 $11.00*

14. Summ, G. Harvey, and Tom Kelly. THE GOOD NEIGHBORS: America, Panama, and the 1977 Canal Treaties. 1988. 135pp.
    149-7 $11.00*

31. Nash, Manning. PEASANT CITIZENS: Politics, Religion, and Modernization in Kelantan, Malaysia. 1974. 181pp.
018-0 $12.00*

38. Bailey, Conner. BROKER, MEDIATOR, PATRON, AND KINSMAN: An Historical Analysis of Key Leadership Roles in a Rural Malaysian District. 1976. 79pp.
024-5 $7.00*

40. Van der Veur, Paul W. FREEMASONRY IN INDONESIA FROM RADERMACHER TO SOEKANTO, 1762-1961. 1976. 37pp.
026-1 $4.00*

43. Marlay, Ross. POLLUTION AND POLITICS IN THE PHILIPPINES. 1977. 121pp.
029-6 $7.00*

44. Collier, William L., et al. INCOME, EMPLOYMENT AND FOOD SYSTEMS IN JAVANESE COASTAL VILLAGES. 1977. 160pp.
031-8 $10.00*

45. Chew, Sock Foon and MacDougall, John A. FOREVER PLURAL: The Perception and Practice of Inter-Communal Marriage in Singapore. 1977. 61pp.
030-X $6.00*

47. Wessing, Robert. COSMOLOGY AND SOCIAL BEHAVIOR IN A WEST JAVANESE SETTLEMENT. 1978. 200pp.
072-5 $12.00*

48. Willer, Thomas F., ed. SOUTHEAST ASIAN REFERENCES IN THE BRITISH PARLIAMENTARY PAPERS, 1801-1972/73: An Index. 1978. 110pp.
033-4 $ 8.50*

49. Durrenberger, E. Paul. AGRICULTURAL PRODUCTION AND HOUSEHOLD BUDGETS IN A SHAN PEASANT VILLAGE IN NORTHWESTERN THAILAND: A Quantitative Description. 1978. 142pp.
071-7 $9.50*

50. Echauz, Robustiano. SKETCHES OF THE ISLAND OF NEGROS. 1978. 174pp.
070-9 $10.00*

51. Krannich, Ronald L. MAYORS AND MANAGERS IN THAILAND: The Struggle for Political Life in Administrative Settings. 1978. 139pp.
073-3 $ 9.00*

54. Ayal, Eliezar B., ed. THE STUDY OF THAILAND: Analyses of Knowledge, Approaches, and Prospects in Anthropology, Art History, Economics, History and Political Science. 1979. 257pp.
079-2 $13.50*

56. Duiker, William J. VIETNAM SINCE THE FALL OF SAIGON. Second edition, revised and enlarged. 1986. 281pp.
133-0 $12.00*

57. Siregar, Susan Rodgers. ADAT, ISLAM, AND CHRISTIANITY IN A BATAK HOMELAND. 1981. 108pp.
110-1 $10.00*

58. Van Esterik, Penny. COGNITION AND DESIGN PRODUCTION IN BAN CHIANG POTTERY. 1981. 90pp.
078-4 $12.00*

59. Foster, Brian L. COMMERCE AND ETHNIC DIFFERENCES: The Case of the Mons in Thailand. 1982. x, 93pp.
112-8 $10.00*

60. Frederick, William H., and John H. McGlynn. REFLECTIONS ON REBELLION: Stories from the Indonesian Upheavals of 1948 and 1965. 1983. vi, 168pp.
111-X $ 9.00*

61. Cady, John F. CONTACTS WITH BURMA, 1935-1949: A Personal Account. 1983. x, 117pp.
114-4 $ 9.00*

62. Kipp, Rita Smith, and Richard D. Kipp, eds. BEYOND SAMOSIR: Recent Studies of the Batak Peoples of Sumatra. 1983. viii, 155pp.
115-2 $ 9.00*

63. Carstens, Sharon, ed. CULTURAL IDENTITY IN NORTHERN PENINSULAR MALAYSIA. 1986. 91pp.
116-0 $ 9.00*

64. Dardjowidjojo, Soenjono. VOCABULARY BUILDING IN INDONESIAN: An Advanced Reader. 1984. xviii, 256pp.
118-7 $26.00*

65. Errington, J. Joseph. LANGUAGE AND SOCIAL
    CHANGE IN JAVA: Linguistic Reflexes of Moderni-
    zation in a Traditional Royal Polity. 1985.
    xiv, 198pp.
    120-9 $12.00*

66. Binh, Tran Tu. THE RED EARTH: A Vietnamese
    Memoir of Life on a Colonial Rubber Plantation.
    Tr. by John Spragens. Ed. by David Marr.
    1985. xii, 98pp.
    119-5 $ 9.00*

67. Pane, Armijn. SHACKLES. Tr. by John McGlynn.
    Intro. by William H. Frederick. 1985. xvi,
    108pp.
    122-5 $ 9.00*

68. Syukri, Ibrahim. HISTORY OF THE MALAY KINGDOM
    OF PATANI. Tr. by Conner Bailey and John N.
    Miksic. 1985. xx, 98pp.
    123-3 $10.50*

69. Keeler, Ward. JAVANESE: A Cultural Approach.
    1984. xxxvi, 523pp.
    121-7 $18.00*

70. Wilson, Constance M., and Lucien M. Hanks.
    BURMA-THAILAND FRONTIER OVERSIXTEEN DECADES:
    Three Descriptive Documents. 1985. x, 128pp.
    124-1 $10.50*

71. Thomas, Lynn L., and Franz von Benda-Beckmann,
    eds. CHANGE AND CONTINUITY IN MINANGKABAU:
    Local, Regional, and Historical Perspectives on
    West Sumatra. 1986. 363pp.
    127-6 $14.00*

72. Reid, Anthony, and Oki Akira, eds. THE
    JAPANESE EXPERIENCE IN INDONESIA: Selected
    Memoirs of 1942-1945. 1986. 411pp., 20 illus.
    132-2 $18.00*

73. Smirenskaia, Zhanna D. PEASANTS IN ASIA:
    Social Consciousness and Social Struggle. Tr.
    by Michael J. Buckley. 1987. 248pp.
    134-9 $12.50

74. McArthur, M.S.H. REPORT ON BRUNEI IN 1904. Ed.
    by A.V.M. Horton. 1987. 304pp.
    135-7 $13.50

75. Lockard, Craig Alan. FROM KAMPUNG TO CITY. A Social History of Kuching Malaysia 1820-1970. 1987. 311pp.
    136-5 $14.00*

76. McGinn, Richard. STUDIES IN AUSTRONESIAN LINGUISTICS. 1988. 492pp.
    137-3 $18.50*

77. Muego, Benjamin N. SPECTATOR SOCIETY: The Philippines Under Martial Rule. 1988. 232pp.
    138-1 $12.50*

78. Chew, Sock Foon. ETHNICITY AND NATIONALITY IN SINGAPORE. 1987. 229pp.
    139-X $12.50*

79. Walton, Susan Pratt. MODE IN JAVANESE MUSIC. 1987. 279pp.
    144-6 $12.00*

80. Nguyen Anh Tuan. SOUTH VIETNAM TRIAL AND EXPERIENCE: A Challenge for Development. 1987. 482pp.
    141-1 $15.00*

81. Van der Veur, Paul W., ed. TOWARD A GLORIOUS INDONESIA: Reminiscences and Observations of Dr. Soetomo. 1987. 367pp.
    142-X $13.50*

82. Spores, John C. RUNNING AMOK: An Historical Inquiry. 1988. 190pp.
    140-3 $13.00*

ORDERING INFORMATION

Orders for titles in the Monographs in International Studies series should be placed through the Ohio University Press/Scott Quadrangle/Athens, Ohio 45701-2979. Individuals must remit pre-payment via check, VISA, MasterCard, CHOICE, or American Express. Individuals ordering from the United Kingdom, Continental Europe, Middle East, and Africa should order through Academic and University Publishers Group, 1 Gower Street, London WC1E 6HA, England. Other individuals ordering from outside of the U.S., please remit in U.S. funds by either International Money Order or check drawn on a U.S. bank. Postage and handling is $2.00 for the first book and $.50 for each additional book. Prices and availability are subject to change without notice.